W9-DES-025

DISCARDED

How Racism and Sexism Killed Traditional Media

Recent Titles in
Racism in American Institutions
Brian D. Behnken, Series Editor

The Color of Politics: Racism in the American Political Arena Today
Chris Danielson

How Do Hurricane Katrina's Winds Blow?: Racism in 21st-Century
New Orleans
Liza Lugo, JD

Out of Bounds: Racism and the Black Athlete
Lori Latrice Martin, Editor

Color behind Bars: Racism in the U.S. Prison System
Volume 1: Historical and Contemporary Issues of Race and Ethnicity in
the American Prison System
Volume 2: Public Policy Influence(s) toward a Racial/Ethnic American
Prison System
Scott Wm. Bowman, Editor

White Sports/Black Sports: Racial Disparities in Athletic Programs
Lori Latrice Martin

Racism in American Popular Media: From Aunt Jemima to the
Frito Bandito
Brian D. Behnken and Gregory D. Smithers

Voting Rights under Fire: The Continuing Struggle for People of Color
Donathan L. Brown and Michael Clemons

The Race Controversy in American Education
Lillian Dowdell Drakeford, PhD, Editor

How Racism and Sexism Killed Traditional Media

Why the Future of Journalism Depends on Women and People of Color

JOSHUNDA SANDERS

Racism in American Institutions
Brian D. Behnken, Series Editor

 PRAEGER™

An Imprint of ABC-CLIO, LLC
Santa Barbara, California • Denver, Colorado

Copyright © 2015 by Joshunda Sanders

All rights reserved. No part of this publication may be reproduced, stored in a retrieval system, or transmitted, in any form or by any means, electronic, mechanical, photocopying, recording, or otherwise, except for the inclusion of brief quotations in a review, without prior permission in writing from the publisher.

Library of Congress Cataloging-in-Publication Data

Sanders, Joshunda V.

  How racism and sexism killed traditional media : why the future of journalism depends on women and people of color / Joshunda Sanders.

     pages cm. — (Racism in American Institutions)

  Includes bibliographical references and index.

  ISBN 978-1-4408-3081-5 (hardback) — ISBN 978-1-4408-3082-2 (electronic)

1. Mass media and race relations—United States.   2. Sexism in mass media—United States.   3. Racism in mass media—United States.   4. Mass media and minorities—United States.   I. Title.

  P94.5.M552U665 2015

  305.8—dc23   2015013427

ISBN: 978-1-4408-3081-5
EISBN: 978-1-4408-3082-2

19 18 17 16 15   1 2 3 4 5

This book is also available on the World Wide Web as an eBook.
Visit www.abc-clio.com for details.

Praeger
An Imprint of ABC-CLIO, LLC

ABC-CLIO, LLC
130 Cremona Drive, P.O. Box 1911
Santa Barbara, California 93116-1911

This book is printed on acid-free paper ∞

Manufactured in the United States of America

Previously published articles in *Bitch* magazine and at the Maynard Institute for Journalism Education are included here with permission.

Contents

Series Foreword

How Racism and Sexism Killed Traditional Media is the second monograph that explores institutional racism in the media to be published in the Praeger series, Racism in American Institutions (RAI). With ongoing examples of racism in a variety of media outlets, especially journalism, racism as an institutional factor in American newsrooms is a pressing topic. The RAI series examines the ways in which racism has become a part of the fabric of many American institutions. For example, while the United States may have done away with overtly racist policies such as Jim Crow segregation, racism still affects many of America's established institutions from public schools to corporate offices. Similarly, schools may not be legally segregated, and yet many districts are not integrated. While much has changed, people of color often discover that finding jobs in journalism is difficult, and if jobs are found black people tend to be pigeonholed in positions whereby they report on "minority issues." This open-ended series of one-volume works examines the problem of racism in established American institutions. Each book traces the prevalence of racism within that institution throughout the history of the United States and explores the problem in that institution today, looking at ways in which the institution has attempted to rectify racism, but also the ways in which it has not.

How Racism and Sexism Killed Traditional Media explores racism and sexism in journalism from a historical, social, and personal point of view. Joshunda Sanders has much experience in this regard, having worked for many years as a reporter in a variety of news outlets. She notes that for generations segregated newsrooms attempted to block people of color's access to mass market media. Instead, African Americans and other ethnic groups developed their own media outlets, especially newspapers in the nineteenth and twentieth centuries. When newsrooms began to take proactive steps to bring about a measure of desegregation in the 1970s and 1980s, they often did so in stereotypical ways. Black reporters could report on "black issues" or issues the editors and managers deemed salient to minority communities. In some ways, skin color gave reporters of color access to jobs, but only jobs that in the eyes of their bosses pertained to communities of color. This has not only resulted in a stereotypical and jaundiced view of black journalists; it has also made it difficult for news organizations to retain reporters who come from ethno-racial communities. The result is the perpetuation of media racism, and not its eradication.

Joshunda Sanders is well positioned to write this book. Her many years of experience in the news industry, as well as a broad variety of journalism jobs, make her an expert on this subject. *How Racism and Sexism Killed Traditional Media* touches on a myriad of topics, from media bias and discrimination to integration and its failures in the media, from race and social media today to the historic evolution of African American and female journalists. The wide variety of topics explored in this book makes it an important contribution to our understanding of institutionalized racism.

Brian D. Behnken
Iowa State University
Ames, Iowa

Acknowledgments

The idea for this book emerged while I was doing grant-funded media critiques for Dori J. Maynard at the Maynard Institute for Journalism Education. I have a depth of gratitude that is unmatched in most areas of my life for the Maynard Institute, Dori, Elizabeth Pinio, Evelyn Hsu, Bill Elsen, and Michael Frisby, with whom I worked from 2012 into 2013 when I was a freelance writer in Austin. The feedback, ideas, and editing from this group of people kept me afloat emotionally and financially during a particularly difficult time in my development as a journalist, writer, and scholar, and I honestly have no idea how I would have made it through that really difficult time without them.

The librarians at the Library of Congress were gracious, attentive, and endlessly helpful and patient. Thank you. I should know my way around the place, but there is something so special about your library that it made my brain stop working as soon as I walked in.

Speaking of special libraries and librarians, thank you to Jenna Freedman, Shannon O'Neill, and Martha Tenney at the Barnard College Archives for the generous research award, which lent a valuable component to this work that I would have not been able to include without your gracious enthusiasm, support, and encouragement.

During the writing of this book, two of my most influential mentors in newspaper journalism, Kenneth Bunting and Dori Maynard died suddenly. Ken Bunting was a tremendously generous man, and he offered me hope for ascendance in work—not as a woman or a woman of color, but as a person with heart and integrity. I hope he would have been proud of this work, like my many other great mentors including Tommy Miller, Dori J. Maynard, Celina Ottaway, David Steele, Evelyn C. White, Alice Walker, Mary Ann Roser, Susan Sward, La Tricia Ransom, Paul Wilner, Marianne Constantinou, Ellen Sweets, and Andy Alford.

A special thanks to Marcia Z. Nelson, Andi Zeisler, Lynn Garrett, and Clay Smith for helping me keep myself fed as I embarked on writing this book before I found a day job.

I am thankful to my students at the University of Texas Austin and the Bay Area Multicultural Media Academy at San Francisco State University for keeping me up to speed on new technology and the color of our future, as well as the Center for the Integration of Journalism, the Journalism and Women's Symposium, and Richard Prince for offering me connection early on in my life as a former Texas resident living in D.C.

To my many sisters, especially Rita Scarborough, Shequila Purnell-Saunders, Kristen Mack, Kalisse Anderson, Vicki McClure, Elizebeth Chavez, Helena Brantley, and Laura Donnelly, thank you for reminding me that I am loved and that I should be writing. I am endlessly grateful to my writing teacher and great friend Frank Bergon, as well as the lovely Holly, for so many years of encouragement.

Introduction

When I fell in love with telling stories, the traditional media world was very different than it is today. There were only singular ways for audiences to receive news. In the 1980s and 1990s, there were just a handful of television channels and radio stations and limited programming. There were a few well-known national magazines and dozens of well-known national newspapers.

Broadcast news was confined to mornings and evenings. Newspapers were delivered to doorsteps in mornings and afternoons. Radio was for easy listening instead of constant background noise. Compared to our current media landscape, information moved slowly through the world in a way that makes the past feel far more distant.

We are now in an information age that exposes us to so much more information and news. There are many thousands of satellite radio stations and hundreds of cable television channels from which to choose. The Internet delivers a constant stream of information to our laptops and smartphones via social networks or apps. Television is something consumers choose to consume whenever and however they want, instead of on the timing of industry executives.

Despite being exposed to more information, accelerating changes in the news industry that have led to large-scale restructuring of newsrooms have actually led to less actual news reporting than in years past, so we are also increasingly subjected to entertainment masquerading as news, or infotainment. This is evident in the rise of reality TV and brand-based journalism that relies on the celebrity-centered delivery of news instead of reporter-based media.

Our current journalism landscape or media ecosystem is one I could never have imagined when I first became enamored of the written word. My affection for journalism began at a kitchen table in Chester, Pennsylvania, where I learned to read by staring down the pages of the *Philadelphia Inquirer* at the age of four or five. I had no idea what I was taking in, only that the weight of the broadsheet in my small hands made me feel powerful and grown up. I loved the faint smell of ink as I flipped through the pages and the idea that this one document contained so much information about the world and that it could be delivered right to my house.

I am the youngest of five children, but a busy single mother raised me as an only child. Marguerite Sandoval was a woman nearing the end of her childbearing years and had borne four children in rapid succession a decade before I was born. Toward the end of her life, she was diagnosed with bipolar and borderline personality disorders. Aspects of her mental illness shaped me, which is perhaps the unavoidable result of growing up in the shadow of it.

Bipolar people, for instance, have a tendency to write manically—reams of paper at a time, whether or not these pages convey anything of import. In Marguerite's case, this took the form of letters she wrote to me almost daily as soon as I could read. Because these letters were often not very clear, I learned that my mother was not the most reliable narrator of the world and that I would have to find one, or many others, on my own. So at the beginning of my life, I was hungry for clear writing, for information that introduced to me how I was supposed to be, operate, and move in the world.

This may understandably seem like it is outside of the scope of a book about how racism and sexism have decimated traditional media, but the point of explaining my first experiences with narrative, stories, and journalism is to describe the framework from which I write. My working frame for consuming news and narratives about black women was built largely outside of my mother's influence. In other words, my mother often left me to my own devices. Like most Generation Xers, I spent my childhood watching a lot of television and consuming a lot of popular culture by way of music and print media. The lens of traditional media was the one that I took as the authoritative version of normalcy.

Even when we scored hand-me-down color televisions, the world of traditional media seemed literally and figuratively black and white. I learned that there were other ethnicities, gender expressions, and sexualities only when we left Philadelphia for New York City in 1984. It was there I discovered that the world was so much larger than I'd imagined, so much more diverse than the white, male world that was transmitted to me as a foundational worldview via television news and newspapers. This seemed to be the natural order of the world, and it wasn't anything I ever thought much about or questioned until I was older.

Growing up with a mentally ill parent does not provide a child with many routines, but on Saturday morning, I had mine. With a bowl of Frosted Flakes, I plopped down on our sofa and could not be moved until *Soul Train* and *American Bandstand* were over. This era would bring the *Jackson 5ive* cartoon, *Fat Albert, Looney Tunes, The Cosby Show,* and the occasional Michael Jackson music video. On television news, I rarely saw black people featured unless the stories were about crime, tragedy, or entertainment. Throughout the course of my life, that reality would be the rule rather than the exception.

From newspapers, I learned that important people were often on the front page. Few of those people, unless they were victims, were women or people of color. The fact that I never saw people who looked like me on the front page of the *Philadelphia Inquirer* served to reinforce my belief that women weren't that important and that black people weren't of significance. From television, I saw that black people were good entertainment and good at sports, but they were rarely bestowed with the great responsibility of delivering the news. As the natural order of news, and the world that informed it, I didn't question how or why this was the case until I became a working journalist. I could only imagine that the same dearth of diversity applied to AM and FM news, since I stuck to the black radio stations on the FM dial where I heard songs I could relate to and disc jockeys that sounded like they could be from my neighborhood.

As I grew older and we settled in the Bronx, I tapped into hip hop, the burgeoning music and culture that would define my generation, both as part of my immediate milieu but also by listening to the radio and watching public access television. Hip hop informed the pulsing zeitgeist of my generation but more important, it was a catalyst for discovering my own storytelling abilities. It was also my first exposure to a different kind of media; one that had a more global, diverse reach than I'd ever imagined.

This was a powerful lens since, like so many latchkey kids, I was fundamentally shaped by overt and subtle popular culture narratives, but I didn't grow up believing that I could participate as a creator or editor of those narratives. Until the advent of what came to be called hip hop journalism, I knew of no black woman writers from the Bronx, or journalists/creators of color writing stories, that revealed the humanity of women and people of color instead of simplistic stereotypes. Like most serious writers I would come to know, I shirked the hip hop journalist label as a descriptor of others and eventually myself because it became a kind of elitist code for a journalistic imposter in mainstream shorthand. While I was proud of coming from the birthplace of hip hop and I considered hip hop to be an essential part of my identity, when it became a global phenomenon and badge of street credibility for suburban acolytes, it became important to detach that label from the creative lives of women and people of color.

When I became a newspaper reporter in 2000, I was the only one of my college classmates to do so and the only one of my peer group from New York City to enter mainstream media. There were so few women in the business that I could count the ones I knew on both hands, and the same was true of people of color. Because it was my first adult job outside of internships at Goldman Sachs and Simon and Schuster, I didn't know enough to find it strange. This seemed to only be a minor inconvenience by the time I graduated, not a systemic issue that mirrored the racist and sexist apathy of other sectors like the science, technology, engineering and mathematics workforce.

The problem then, unlike now, wasn't that there weren't any jobs that paid something close to a decent wage. Journalism has always been a low-paying profession and for women and people of color, who have historically always made less than white males, equal pay has always been a particularly hard sell. The difficulty of recruiting and retaining a diverse cadre of journalists has come from the limited trajectory of journalists of color and women in media. When women and people of color are hired in traditional media, they are infrequently promoted to positions that carry influence and prestige. The bias and prejudice that women and people of color experience outside of newsrooms has also been part of a larger pattern of exposure to microaggressions and hostile working environments within newsrooms. The result over the years has been the frequent departure of women and people of color from newsrooms into other industries where they can find better-paying, less antagonistic work.

I had been an English major determined to write books and teach writing at a college some day, so journalism as a career hadn't occurred to me as something that was even possible until I had been producing reporting as a hobby. I figured the complaints and concerns that I'd heard from other black women about working in journalism were simply about their dispositions, not about the industry. I needed to find out for myself whether I could hack it as a reporter.

From the start of my journalism career, I only cared about three things: I wanted to write for a living, I wanted to tell the stories of people like me, and I never wanted to be homeless—the way I had frequently been with my mother in New York City—again. I gave no consideration to the institution of journalism or the invisibility of women and people of color as power brokers in media, with few exceptions.

It took 11 years as a newspaper reporter and almost 15 years as a freelancer working in several different news markets to understand the longstanding and persistent disconnect between newsrooms and the increasingly diverse audiences they claim to serve or to want to serve. My career as a journalist was similar to how James Baldwin has described love: A growing up. All my life, I had prepared myself to follow another Baldwin edict: That my crown had been bought and paid for and all I needed to do was wear it. But in newsrooms, I was not only *not* treated like royalty, but I was generally regarded as a charity case, an affirmative action hire who didn't really know how to be a good 'ol boy and could never truly live up to the credo required to be a bona fide reporter because of my gender and my race.

As with everything, of course, there were exceptions. My first mentors were white male veteran journalists. Their guidance and feedback helped keep me from making terrible mistakes, including assuming that all white men would be my natural enemies in corporate America. Tommy Miller, an editor at the *Houston Chronicle*, was especially helpful by sending me books to read, binders to study and Edna Buchanan's classic, *The Corpse Had a Familiar Face*. Without the patronizing, overbearing demeanor of a white savior, Tommy guided me with kindness and consideration through peculiar office politics specific to newspapers, the bumps and bruises of corrections, and sad story assignments (like covering the least compelling aspects of the rodeo) that marked the life of a rookie.

Tommy was from the South, and he knew the long history of discrimination against black people within and outside of newsrooms because he had lived through it. His colleague in the Hearst Newspapers Corporation and a rather intimidating and formidable editor in his own right at the *Beaumont Enterprise*, Tim Kelly, made sure that I thought strategically about writing for publication at a level appropriate for my skill set. Paul Wilner, Jon Carroll, Susan Sward, and Carolyn White at the *San Francisco Chronicle* are all names that come to mind when I think of the sheer number of white journalists who helped me become a better reporter and writer.

But while they were each skilled and practiced in the many technical aspects of journalism—how to be a more assertive reporter, develop leads, and become a stronger writer—navigating racism and sexism in legacy media was something they could not help me with. In ways that were both helpful and invalidating, they urged me to disregard bias as a hurdle and power through beyond any underestimation. They did not help me avoid the assumption that I would have white allies throughout my career and that those allies would be powerful enough to overcome the systemic challenges that made traditional media permanently hostile to the diversity it would need to remain relevant for audiences for years to come.

Traditional media were borne in America as a system of propaganda—a way of spreading information to those who could afford to purchase those narratives and consume them as well as those who could afford to operate printing presses and news operations. In their 1988 book, *Manufacturing Consent: The Political Economy of Mass Media*, Edward S. Herman and Noam Chomsky articulate what they refer to as a propaganda model. The authors describe mass media as an organ that "serves to mobilize support for the special interests that dominate the state and private activity," as well as a system that allows the powerful to "fix the premises of discourse."[1] By laying the foundation for legacy media in America as a model for how to tell and share stories that would influence business, policy, and more, white men shaping American stories naturally excluded racial and ethnic minorities and women.

In the absence of a way to communicate within their respective communities, people of color made their own media. This took the form of alternative daily and weekly newspapers, radio and television shows, and later on, entire networks and media companies. This would later be true for women, too, who were regarded at the time the press was born and developed as property akin to children. With the natural progress of time, they would come to assert their voices and identity in media in myriad, powerful ways.

Every people and nation needs a narrative. In America, ours could easily be summed up as *E Pluribus Unum*—Out of Many, One. But as the United States has become increasingly diverse, women and people of color have not been able to tap equally into the potential to synthesize the nation's many voices, to tell one singular story. For centuries now, traditional media, like other American institutions, have refused the part of America's narrative defined by the growing autonomy and independence of women as well as the ubiquity of racial and ethnic diversity. This has been clear both in how selected stories are framed and in the omission of stories altogether, though the latter has been remedied in many ways by social media. It is a stubborn systemic refusal that begins with the resistance to diversity in academic institutions that teach journalism and communications and the economic inequality that impacts who is selected for and able to participate in journalism-pipeline internships and continues with the problems of proper integration of women and people of color into legacy media newsrooms where racist and sexist behavior often drive them into other professions.

For decades, traditional mass media outlets have failed to properly reflect the demographic realities of the United States. While some of the financial challenges of print media are related to a lack of contingency planning for a present and future dependent on digital advertising, a core part of the demise of traditional media has been a passive and slow-moving response to a diversity imperative as a key aspect of what makes media relevant to its many audiences. Failure to develop content that reflects women and people of color in ways that are not condescending or tone-deaf is, in part, related to a dearth of diverse journalists to create and influence that kind of content.

As advertisers have moved dollars away from legacy media into the digital and mobile spheres, and traditional media have scrambled to keep up, diversity has flat-lined in traditional news media across the country. The justification for a monolithic workforce with just a few women and racial minorities has almost always fallen along two lines: There aren't enough qualified applicants for the jobs that are available and that money is too tight to hire or promote. But studies show that industries that diversify are worth more than those that don't, so the cost of refusing this quintessential American narrative has been an increasingly omnipresent death knell for the news business.[2]

Women have fared decently well in broadcast television and have also made inroads as management in some high-profile cases—notably, former *New York Times* executive editor Jill Abramson and *New York Times Book Review* editor Pamela Paul were two of the highest-ranking women in the newspaper business; now Pamela Paul is on her own after Abramson was fired. Still, the fact that in 2015 there were not more women at the helm of traditional media that weren't dedicated to ethnic or women's niches is disheartening and curious. The same is true for the success of people of color.

As often as media leaders like to speak with nostalgia and pride about the many accomplishments of traditional media as guardians of truth and organs for the cultivation of equality and justice, our dying media system has not lent itself to democratization when it comes to racial and gender diversity. It is a strange irony for a profession that proclaims to afflict the comfortable and comfort the afflicted that more people of color have not been hired to write those first rough drafts of history or to comfort the afflicted that usually do not look anything like them. Independent, family, and alternative press options continue to fill in the gaps where traditional media were lacking, but there are still few sustainable models for keeping those businesses around for decades to come. Now, since most traditional media companies are owned by just a handful of corporate behemoths, even without knowing it, readers, listeners and viewers are often listening to the same corporate line across radio and television stations or in print magazines.

On Racism and Sexism in Traditional Media

In the 1980s, like most American institutions, affirmative action was still a new concept within journalism. For an industry focused on being a force for ethical, democratic ideals and delivering useful information to loyal audiences in exchange for fiscal sustainability and bragging rights, it was another irony that accepting that women and people of color offered a broader perspective and cadre of sources that could only improve news products seemed challenging for decision-making media leaders. Throughout my adolescence, however, popular culture proved ready for multiculturalism even if news operations weren't quite sure how to adjust. The scope of traditional media that began to reflect the diversity of women and people of color was heartening and, it appeared, effective for connecting with audiences.

For several reasons, the tragic cultural pivot point for my generation, September 11, changed traditional media in the way that it changed everything else. It exacerbated financial problems for the media while also calling into question their credibility and ability to serve as necessary watchdogs for democracy and fairness. I had joined the ranks of the battered industry only a year before, before I understood that journalism increasingly needed to make money to reinforce its own historical sense of smug importance and despite the fact that traditional media had failed to respond to the gradual progress of women and people of color in every arena of American and global life in a way that might have ensured its permanent relevance for generations to come.

Discussions about racism and sexism in newsrooms are often marginalized when they should be central to exploring the demise of print, broadcast, and nonprofit journalism media models. Like hiring and promotion practices, this is an aspect of American life that is not confined only to media. Throughout American society, delving into racist constructs, behavior, and practices proves to be a volatile activity.

Racism, like sexism, is a hard word to write and an even more difficult claim to prove, particularly when lobbing the word against a fact-centered industry. They are uncomfortable, subjective words. At the same time, patterns of differential treatment based on race and gender are in evidence daily as they have been for many years—they are usually simply discussed without using specific language. It has become standard practice to refer, for instance, to "racially insensitive" remarks instead of calling them racist, or say something was "racially offensive" or "racially tinged."

A retired white male journalist and editor I interviewed for this book (and the only one who agreed to be interviewed on the record) said it would be challenging to make the case that racism has been the main reason for news diversity failures, or one of the main causes of the collapse of the journalism infrastructure—and I certainly (mostly) agree. He remembered a time when recruiters were actively trying to bring more minorities and women into the fold and he was one of the white men on the frontlines of that effort. But in the words of author and professor David J. Leonard, "Talking about institutional racism is seen as someone bringing up issues of racism unnecessarily. In some people's minds, the arguments are what lead to divisiveness and not the inequalities always present . . . [and] that basically reaffirms the privilege of whiteness."[3] The same is true for gender bias. So while I understood my colleague's point, I only agree partially with it.

In the politically correct United States, racism is the least uttered word in mixed company, but that doesn't mean that it doesn't add an important lens to a necessary discussion. Not discussing racism does not make the reality or fact of it an inaccuracy, and yet, racism is arguably the most polarizing word to use in any context, and the word most likely to draw complaints of overreaction and unfairness from whites. Social scientists who study and write about bias note that most of us, after all, are generally more biased than we'd like to think we are.[4] The discrimination at the heart of white superiority, referred to by feminist scholar bell hooks as "patriarchal white supremacy," is omnipresent. Moreover, racism as connected to the legacy of black-white relationships in America directly correlates to how other people of color have been treated in the past, are treated in the present, and will be continued to be treated unless or until the forecasted majority-minority population begins to force our overarching racial conversation to change.

A common definition of racism is prejudice plus power, and that's one reason it is easy to equate the financial and social decline of journalism's reach, particularly before the advent of the Internet, with institutionalized racism. Still, outside of off-the-record conversations, there is little public acknowledgment of the role of racism or sexism in the lack of diversity that remains a defining aspect of traditional media. This book is a modest attempt to look at the impact of those forces on media.

I know from personal experience that one of the reasons traditional media have failed to retain women and people of color has been that they are often considered to be the de facto torch bearers on these issues, despite the fact that they have not been hired or promoted to positions that would allow them to make long-term systemic changes to the traditional media infrastructure. In newsrooms where management has been taken to task for offensive or exclusive coverage, it has typically been a result of the work of minority coalitions and committees. Unfortunately, as much as women and people of color have to contribute to the future of the profession as it expands online, the hierarchy that has persistently ignored women and people of color in traditional media is currently being replicated online in digital news startups that are largely as segregated as their analog counterparts.

This is particularly interesting because the election of President Barack Obama and the subsequent media-driven narrative of a post-racial society have not equated to racial parity in other areas of American life, especially media, which are considered the organs of democracy. While the president is considered a symbol of U.S. progress on matters of race, his presidency has also revealed the extent to which the country still has an uneasy relationship with minorities. Coverage of President Obama and the First Lady Michelle Obama, alone, shows the long reach of racist and sexist tropes—whether Fox News is referring to the married first lady as Obama's "baby mama" or we look at the outsize reaction to her clothing, which at times revealed chiseled arms and a little too much leg for some, or even characterizing President Obama as a Muslim—as if, to paraphrase Colin Powell, that would be a bad thing.

The coded and overt racist and sexist tropes that are in evidence in some traditional media that are leveled against the president and the first lady also extend to other groups. Black boys and men are still disproportionately profiled by police as evidenced by the high-profile fatal shootings of Michael Brown in Ferguson, Missouri, 12-year-old Tamir Rice in Cleveland, Ohio, and Trayvon Martin in Sanford, Florida. The failure of grand juries to indict police officers in the death of Eric Garner in New York City or in Michael Brown's death displays a pattern of racial inequity that is difficult to accept, witness, or dismiss. A key component of how the American public contemplates and either validates or invalidates racist patterns is traditional media coverage, which still have the power—albeit greatly diminished—to reach many millions of people and inform their level of agency in reaction to tragic events.

Generally, traditional media offer response to these racial inequities in the form of opinion pieces from minority spokesmen or utilize the few people of color still in their employ to become interpreter-reporters instead of investing considerable reporting and journalism resources in investigative pieces, produced by interracial teams, which could go a long way toward influencing real political and social change.

Similarly, as the status of women has changed, and there is the widespread social impression that women are ever closer to financial parity with men, the social progress of women has not translated into equal pay for equal work. The average American woman makes between 58 cents and 78 cents for every dollar the average American man earns. Depending on a woman's ethnicity, she makes even less. Women are still portrayed as if they are less important to humanity if they are unmarried, childless, or both; female political leaders like Hillary Clinton are covered in traditional media according to how close to far from the notion of ideal womanhood they fall. In Clinton's case, media stories have described her sartorial decisions and her financial status with more energy than the details of her opinions on policy matters.

The United States has changed a great deal since the inception of legacy media, but only incrementally and, in some ways, superficially. Americans are not colorblind or post-racial as much as they are reluctant to disagree about how they should handle difference and how they can collectively move beyond their long-held fears and biases to move their country toward its better nature. Against this backdrop, it makes sense that there has been no significant change in the number of people of color or women in newspapers, radio, or television in several decades. What is surprising is the extent to which digital news—the only hope for the sustainability of old media in a different form—looks a lot like legacy news.

As journalists scramble to figure out how to make digital news lucrative, a spate of startups like *Vox* and *FiveThirtyEight* have garnered enough capital to launch often without a single person of color on their virtual mastheads and usually without many women in the mix. Since integration gains for women and minorities in journalism occurred early on only by federal mandates, lawsuits and, in the case of minorities, the duress that resulted from violent turmoil, it makes sense that the absence of these elements has created a dearth of interest and energy for true diversity online.

Social media have made a huge difference for new media inclusion, or at least their potential. The responsive Internet works as a mostly free tool for women and minorities to utilize their collective and individual voices in order to operate in the place of expensive litigation—and often with direct access to the outlets or brands that are spreading harmful stereotypes or lackluster coverage. In media spaces where there are no producers, editors, or decision makers who are people of color or women, racist and sexist content thrives; it is disseminated until waves of people of color and their white allies protest, then an apology is issued, and the news cycle about the perpetuation of historically racist writers, editors, and producers dies down before the next outrage begins.

Those of us who care deeply about journalism and its importance in a democracy have talked very often to one another about online anonymous comments and trolls. I believe an entire book could be written about that—I cannot address it fully here. But I believe it is worth noting that online commenters very rarely add respectful, enlightening or engaging content to what is already presented by journalists. Instead, comment threads on stories often augment stories about race or gender with virulent racist and sexist screeds that make the jobs of reporters even more difficult for having to sift through them and manage them on a daily basis. As a journalist who has covered a range of high-profile murders, crime sprees, and stories replete with opportunities for racial and sexual commentary, I found myself traumatized by the racist, condescending commentary that I was ultimately responsible for navigating and addressing respectfully, usually through erasure. I believe the same kind of trauma is another valid reason women and people of color have little incentive to help traditional media navigate their lack of diversity.

Throughout history, a spate of commission reports, studies, and individual pleas calling for journalists, the gatekeepers of American history, to air or print stories that include a fuller range of voices have been published and discussed, but ultimately those calls have been all but forgotten. Diversity has not become an important part of the American story because of the nation's complicated relationship with racial and ethnic difference as well as ambivalence about the progress of women beyond the scope of their domestic duties and as authoritative arbiters of information in a traditionally male field. Much of what has kept traditional media irrelevant has been the stubbornness of old narratives which portray people of color as inferior to whites and women as inferior to men.

Part of America's narrative at the advent of journalism was defining the identity of distinguished and powerful white settlers with dominion over African American slaves and Native American indigenous people in the United States. Upon the creation of printed materials, supported by the wealthy with the means to afford the costly apparatuses required to create a mainstream press, people of color had to pioneer their own separate drafts of history to reflect a more inclusive narrative of America. This has led to alternative sources of media created by Native Americans, African Americans, Latinos, and Asians for as long as media have been in existence. Women have created their own media, too, since when they have entered traditional media spaces they have often been pigeonholed, their stories sent to the "pink ghetto," as the Features sections of most papers are colloquially known, or their talents diverted to issues of domesticity, children, food, and relationships instead of hard news.

This book argues that the continued marginalization and alienation of people of color and women as the country becomes a minority-majority nation is at the heart of why mainstream media continue to lose profits, shutter or consolidate operations, fail a growing proportion of their audience (thus losing subscribers and attention), and founder as they continue to resist telling new narratives about significant social, gender, racial, and economic shifts in America. While the Internet has allowed for a democratized system of delivering information to more diverse audiences, the diversity problems that have kept newsgathering staffs stalled in a heterogeneous zone remain a multimedia plague. Still, there have been some changes that suggest that the future of journalism will be dependent on diverse audiences, who will be the primary consumers of content as the country's majority.

This book attempts to reckon with the treatment of race within newsrooms before and after the 1968 Kerner Commission Report that lambasted majority white newsrooms for their failure to integrate people of color into media organizations. I also address the glacial gains of women in journalism, many of whom were subjected to the same kind of condescending and disrespectful treatment as minority journalists. Pioneers in broadcast television, radio, print, and online media from Belva Davis and Raul Ramirez to Ed Bradley and Markos Moulitsas who have been on the frontlines of one of America's most trenchant narratives—the narrative of inclusion in a melting pot of ethnicity, in spite of economic, geographic, or political adversity—are featured here, though not every trailblazer in every arena of journalism is featured.

How Racism and Sexism Killed Traditional Media is as much about the financial ramifications of bias as it is a book about the disruption of traditional media by the Internet and social media. As the number of news organizations considered legacy or traditional media has plummeted with increasing frequency, the number of people of color who create, aggregate, and follow news online has continued to grow.

At the same time, news organizations have inexplicably failed to hire more than 12 or 13 percent of people of color in their newsrooms since the inception of the ASNE Newsroom Census in 1997, despite the fact that Asian Americans, Latinos, Native Americans, and African Americans are now more than 30 percent of the American population. While women have fared somewhat better, they are still too often left out of fair and equal promotion practices—a fact that is true from news media to the movie industry and beyond.

I left the newspaper industry in 2011 after working at dailies in Austin, San Francisco, Seattle, Beaumont, and Houston. The decade I'd spent in newspapers had been fulfilling and exhausting because the business seemed to be in a constant state of flux, though each year things only got worse instead of better. Publishers and editors held staff meetings that were never celebratory, so the convening of them always interrupted reporters' newsgathering with a dreaded stop in our workflow to hear our collective fate: A new round of buyouts or vague explanations of how layoffs in other parts of the print chain might impact staff positions. Sometimes, the entire copy desk was being outsourced to other cities, or a managing editor quit because of the interference of consultants who wanted to dictate what type of local news should be on a front page even though they knew very little about the historical context that informed front-page story selection.

Job instability aside, I left newspaper journalism only after I was provoked by the culmination of personal and professional losses. Though I knew when I left the newsroom that I would never find another job quite like the one I had grown to love as a reporter, I also had finally accepted that the newspaper industry would never provide me with the camaraderie or affirmation it had offered so many of my white male colleagues. Being a part of the newspaper industry was like being marginally accepted into a fraternity that had suddenly fallen out of social favor with the masses—women and people of color still had their colleagues, even if they didn't have universally recognized status among anyone but themselves. For a young woman who had grown up with a lot of instability and beyond the reach of anyone in my family aside from my mother, most of the newsrooms I worked in offered me at least the guise of solace and community for a while. They were places where I could channel my restlessness and harness the gifts resilience bestows on those of us who have the blessing and curse of growing to love reporting.

So, while I loved being part of what many of us considered a noble profession with some of the smartest colleagues I'd ever known, a copy editor friend once described working in journalism as akin to working with an abusive partner. Reporters—especially women and people of color—were rarely praised for their contributions, and the women among us certainly weren't compensated accordingly. Newspaper journalists did, however, regularly receive criticism from editors, colleagues, and readers, and it was expected that every staff member respond to such criticism as if it were a normal part of doing business. No matter how hard one worked, it was difficult to know what the value of remaining a reporter in this day and age was on a daily basis. The journalists I was proud to work with for more than a decade all appreciated the purpose and mission behind the work—but the blows to morale begged the question of what the long-term personal costs would be.

Staff photographers, for example, produced beautiful, quality work quickly and efficiently around the clock, day after day. Yet, increasingly their work was placed side by side with audience-produced photos on Flickr and Instagram, as if amateur photography on a smartphone could truly compete with professional equipment and tailored news photography expertise. The sad thing was that during the tectonic shift from a slow-responding, old world media to a scrambling, 24/7 news cycle, the work of polished, Pulitzer Prize–winning photographers became increasingly judged alongside the work of anyone with good timing, luck, and a device that took passable photos or video.

Writers shared the same sorry lot. Blogs hardly have the same cachet they once held for readers, but they signaled the beginning of a kind of end for print media reporters. We continued to take the time to do original reporting: Calling and vetting sources, going to scenes and knocking on doors to conduct interviews, and combining that work with extensive research—only to find within hours of our work being posted online that some blogger had taken the same details, recast and paraphrased our work, then posted it on a national platform to give the story more prominence in his or her voice. Once, there had been a kind of insider's code among reporters to give credit where credit was due and to honor the work that went into reporting along the way. In the new media world, that code was utterly ignored.

In the meantime, the business of reporting news became like trying to sip water from a fire hose. The incessant stream of news along with a growing number of ways to consume it at all hours of the day and night, combined with the slow but certain collapse of the business model that led to massive staff restructuring, left more work for the people in the newsroom who remained after shifts, layoffs, and early retirements. In addition to those challenges, attempts at diversifying coverage as a reporter either left me pigeonholed at the newspapers where I worked, bitter, or both.

As a black woman reporter, I carried a triple burden of being African American, female, and young. At the intersection of these "other" identities, largely absent from traditional media spaces unless they were a part of sensationalized crime reports, tragedy, or comic entertainment, I felt a hyper-visible invisibility. On one hand, I often stood out as an anomaly within newsrooms. Visitors and sometimes sources more readily and incorrectly identified me as a secretary or an assistant before I was recognized as a reporter just like the majority of my mainly white male colleagues. As one of many ways that everyday racism manifested in newsrooms, I was also often mistaken for the few other black women who worked for the companies I did, even when we looked nothing alike. In Austin, a white male manager took note of me and the only other black women in the newsroom on our way to lunch and asked if the three of us were planning a riot. While these kinds of microaggressions weren't a daily occurrence, the ongoing threat of them in newsrooms lingered daily over my work and quality of life in a way that made me feel helpless and vulnerable to dismissal for trying to bring all of my identities to work in the same ways that my white colleagues did.

Outside of the newsroom, particularly when I covered communities of color and women for mainstream newspapers, I was presumed to be some kind of spy. It was assumed, particularly among an older generation of black folks, that I had been sent to do the bidding of powerful white men and I was not to be trusted. In the few cases where I was given the benefit of the doubt, lack of media savvy sometimes led to unfortunate misunderstandings. When I went out of my way to quote an African American woman during a festival one weekend in Austin and I asked her age—standard reporting procedure—she chafed, called me rude, and walked away. While I had experienced worse in the course of reporting, it struck me that even so-called insiders to a culture were not exempt from having to navigate the nuances of difference effectively.

This book was mostly developed and written while I was trying to make a living as a full-time freelancer in Texas. When I left newspapers, I started to immediately work on a blog that I would later develop into an e-book while also continuing to teach and search for paid writing fellowships and gigs. I learned a lot working for myself in an era during which reporters are required to think about themselves as brands and position themselves in the niche that is the Internet. One of the most important observations for me was not just that the digital space has killed much of the content domination for traditional media, but that the incredible diversity of the blogosphere meant that those who traditionally had to rely on mainstream media as their sole source of information posed a larger threat than immediate analog versus digital woes.

While there was good journalism being produced increasingly by women and people of color, the attention span of the viewing and reading public seemed to be growing ever shorter. Unfortunately, it seemed impossible to find steady journalism work that offered both a reasonable wage and reasonable expectations.

The good old boy network that defines the masthead at most print publications that are geared toward "serious news consumers" (read: other white men) is still present in online iterations of print publications, but the many silos and apps that people now use to get their news do not segregate by audience because they can't. Instead, they leave it up to millions of readers and users to self-segregate, if they can. That means social media have become the great equalizers of information, for better or worse, and with the diversity of the user bases for Instagram, Facebook, and Twitter, this has serious implications for how people of color and women can and will drive news usage in the future.

While the question of creating a sustainable news model into the future is still largely an unanswered one, there is no question that the journalism of the present and the future is very different from the one with which the nation began centuries ago. By examining our journey from the inception of the press and news organizations of the past, I hope to frame the significant impact of racism and sexism throughout American history on the journalism being produced in the United States today.

Chapter 1

Traditional Media, Race, and Gender before the 1970s

The media write and report from the standpoint of a white man's world.
—Kerner Commission Report 1968

Fifty years since racial integration became law, it is easy to dismiss the racial- and gender-stratified origins of American journalism because people in America have little context for how hostile their nation was just five decades ago. But from their inception, traditional media were organized around white male patriotism and as ways for government to spread propaganda quickly and cheaply. Racism and sexism are ugly stitches in American society's fabric and in media, so the story of the slanted lens through which people of color and women have long been viewed in legacy media is also at the heart of the story of racism and sexism in America.

Because of the social and economic gains people of color and women have made, we have long regarded inclusive coverage as a natural byproduct of that success. But the men and whites who control the frame of popular cultural narratives have not. Even as a nation comprised of immigrants, marginalizing the other has become a key part of widely circulating narratives about people of color and women. Many of the stereotypes and caricatures that haunt news coverage and media have their origins in an exclusive frame that ignores racial and ethnic progress in favor of old ideas.

If widely circulated and exclusive narratives are a reflection of the society in which we live, what they depict is not a true picture of American democracy. From the outset of the development of the press in America, if the purpose of journalism was to seek common ground and tell universal truths, each segment of America had its own individual truth. The lens of traditional media, beginning with print, specifically transmitted the truth of white men and conveyed it as though it were universally applicable.

At the inception of America's national identity, when the Penny Press was created in the 1830s, the main paying audience was white and male, solidifying the connection of producing and consuming journalism to power, money, and privilege. Though journalists and historians have perpetuated the notion of traditional media as the Fourth Estate and an organ of public service, traditional news was actually created with the interests of big business, advertising, and politics in mind. The creation of print newspapers was inextricably tied to American government by way of contracts with the U.S. Post Office.

Later the Federal Communications Commission (FCC) and its regulation of radio and television stations would also be tied to business motives and interests. And the creation of newswires via a partnership between the Associated Press and Western Union later in the century only exacerbated what journalism historians Joseph Torres and Juan L. González refer to as the white racial narrative. Torres and González go on to describe federal policies that helped perpetuate a white supremacist narrative when the Post Office bowed to slaveholders and refused to deliver abolitionist papers to Southern readers.[1]

This extraordinary concentration of power would later reemerge for the media industry time and again, but with the pinnacle of its reach beginning in the late 1990s through the 2000s, when monopolies would become common from Clear Channel Communications (radio) to cable television (a 2014 merger between Comcast and Time Warner was universally greeted with apathy.) The Associated Press was important particularly in early journalism and when traditionally print organizations would start to lose staff and slash budgets because it offered a central clearinghouse for objective reporting. Small-town newspapers or big-city ones that had lost big reporting staffs to layoffs, buyouts, and corporate downsizing could always rely on filling their papers with Associated Press copy.

But there was a time when the reporting of wire services like the Associated Press reflected a more sinister tone related to people of color, which made its ubiquity especially troubling. Stories that would add fuel to the white imagination regarding the lynchings of hundreds of blacks and Latinos in the South were sometimes spread to smaller towns where the flames of racial hatred were fanned by a sense that the acts of sanctioned murder were widespread and justified. In the absence of local narratives that humanized people of color and women in local publications, ignorance and racial terror reigned, and that remained the case in small print markets for years.

In media, the main historical and present power brokers have been white men. This is significant because as the gatekeepers for money and political power, white publishers, editors, and businessmen utilized newspapers, radio, and television media to perpetuate stereotypes, incite racial violence, and leave true stories about people of color and women languishing at the margins. As González and Torres put it, "At the birth of American democracy, people of color possessed no press of their own."[2] In some ways, centuries later, the lack of full press ownership by racial and ethnic minorities is astounding, even if the press people of color own is not a money-making press.

That there are media produced and disseminated by people of color and women is in and of itself a success given the history of bias in mainstream media channels. The victories of women and people of color in journalism, however, are rarely recognized in context with mainstream journalism histories. By telling the stories of the challenges these groups have faced in modern history, this book attempts to trace the impact of racism and sexism on traditional media from its early days into the present.

"White Follows Black"

Stanford law professor Ralph Richard Banks notes in his 2011 book, *Is Marriage for White People? How the African American Marriage Decline Affects Everyone*, that "white follows Black," meaning that whatever impacts African Americans will eventually affect broader society (I will use black and African American interchangeably referring to black American members of the African Diaspora). More to the point: Whatever impacts black people will also eventually impact whites. This is relevant to media coverage of racial, ethnic, and gender minorities because they are eventually poised to become majorities, begging the question of whether the narratives of white Americans will be disproportionately marginalized as a result.

African Americans serve as appropriate litmus tests for gauging bias against others who also face racial or gender bias in America as one of the nation's least economically and socially powerful groups. This is true for a number of reasons, including that for much of American history, racial difference was discussed solely in black and white terms. That certainly doesn't mean that racism against blacks is the only prejudice that matters in traditional or new media, but merely that there are valuable indicators about how anti-black frames and journalism coverage easily trickle over into harmful portrayals of other groups.

As one of the largest and most visible ethnic groups in America, and one that was targeted with racist press most voraciously in the 1800s, it is appropriate to tell the story of the origins of racism in traditional media by starting with African American journalists and the African American narrative in the United States. Blacks, along with Native Americans, were the main victims of publishers who instigated "horrific acts of racial violence," González and Torres wrote. "The centralization of news delivery in late nineteenth century America represented a huge setback for the portrayal of race relations."[3] This was particularly true in small-town newspapers, where editors could edit the content from the Associated Press as they saw fit to perpetuate or ignite racial violence and stereotypes.[4] Press historian Mark Wahgren Summers has documented repeated examples of vicious stereotyping of black politicians and voters by Reconstruction-era reporters.[5]

The real-life consequences of this stereotyping are not hard to measure. Between 1889 and 1918, more than 3,200 people were lynched; 78 percent of them were black.[6] The unique history of African Americans as American citizens first introduced in the American narrative as slaves, then granted freedom without reconciling how they would overcome the psychological, social, and economic challenges of the powerful belief that they were not fully human, let alone truly American, is a challenge that all ethnicities encounter in the face of assimilation. There is no other ethnic group, though, that bears the unique challenges of defying or overcoming stereotypes after being property in the land that both enslaved and freed it as part of developing a greater national identity.

While the specific circumstances of arrival in America and treatment by whites may differ among racial minority (soon-to-be-majority) groups, the fact that everyone who has to hyphenate, in the words of author Toni Morrison, is considered inferior to white people is our common designation. This is important to stress in a conversation about race and racism in traditional media because racist ideology informs the hiring practices, story development, placement, and emphasis within legacy media whether it is acknowledged or unacknowledged.

What blacks have in common is that they are marginalized and othered because of perceived gulfs between their experience and that of white Americans. All bias leveled against blacks in America does not cover the myriad ways racism is used against other ethnic groups. But African Americans have a longer, more visible history of experiencing racism in America, so their story within and as a result of traditional media narratives extrapolates to the ways other people of color and women have been treated in journalism.

True assimilation that has been accessible to some Jewish, Italian, or Irish immigrants in American society has never been possible for blacks. That inability to blend in has worked against them in a journalism environment that rewards people of color for making white people (mainly white men) comfortable enough to hire them or, at the very least, consistently tell the stories of their lives.

Like Japanese Americans, who would face internment and detention in American camps and Chinese and Mexican Americans who were murdered in violent riots or lynched in attacks covered gleefully by the mainstream press, African Americans have experienced the gamut of racial terrorism. Women and ethnic groups have responded throughout history to the resistance and apathy of the mainstream by creating alternative means of controlling and disseminating their stories.

This is even true for groups that have historically had to overcome significant barriers to media literacy. That African Americans were property before they were even allowed to read and write, for example, often is a significant contextual point omitted from discussions related to African American literacy, especially when it comes to news. The historical memory of being a people who relied on oral history and other means of expression cannot be dismissed as a strong deterrent for participating in activities that were once punishable by the lash.

Despite that, before the Civil War, people of color published more than 100 newspapers in America, more than a century after the publication of the first colonial American newspaper, *Publick Occurences*, in 1690. Between 1824 and 1828, three of America's pioneer publications by people of color were born: *El Habanero*, the *Cherokee Phoenix*, and the first-black owned newspaper in America, the *Freedom's Journal*, first published in 1827 by John Russwurm and Samuel Cornish.[7] At least 80 Spanish-language publications were started before 1860 in the United States. Only community-based outlets initiated by racial and ethnic minorities provided in-depth coverage of anything other than white males until the middle of the century.

Early Pioneers in the Minority Press

What would become an emblematic American narrative about people of color was framed early and without their consent or input. In *News for All the People: The Epic Story of Race and the American Media*, Juan González and Joseph Torres write that media played a significant role in perpetuating racist views among the general population for hundreds of years. "The news media thus assumed primary authorship of a deeply flawed national narrative: the creation myth of heroic European settlers battling an array of backward and violent non-white peoples to forge the world's greatest democratic Republic."[8]

At the inception of the press in America, people of color started their own newspapers to counter narratives that Native Americans were warrior heathens, Asian Americans were dirty communists, Latinos were lazy interlopers, and African Americans were the embodiment of all three.

According to the *Encyclopedia of Journalism*, the bilingual *El Misisipi*, a publication for Spanish exiles in 1808, and *La Prensa* in New York were among the first examples of minority press and narrative ownership.[9] The former, founded in New Orleans and the first Latino newspaper in the United States that was named for the river that runs by the city, was written primarily in Spanish with some English editorial copy and all of the advertising translated to English.[10]

Attempts at targeting minority audiences in the press that weren't pioneered by people of color had mixed results. In the 1850s, for instance, when Americans tried to create Chinese-language newspapers in the United States, they did so while perpetuating a white narrative since the publications were started and managed by Americans who considered the Chinese inferior.[11] (Unfortunately, the first Chinese-owned daily newspaper launched in 1856 by Ze Too Yune had a circulation of 200 and survived less than two years.[12]) But there were other early templates of success in the ethnic press.

While gender equality wouldn't be a media focus for decades to come, in the minority press, women of color played pivotal roles in journalism. One excellent example is that of Ida Wells-Barnett, who was born into slavery but freed after the Emancipation Proclamation in 1863. Wells-Barnett became a journalist by way of what was then considered a traditionally women's profession: Teaching. Through writing about inequities she both faced and witnessed in segregated schools, Wells-Barnett was offered a position for the Memphis, Tennessee-based *Free Speech and Headlight*, and she negotiated with editors J.L. Fleming and Rev. Taylor Nightingale to become an editor. Eventually, Wells-Barnett bought Rev. Nightingale's shares of the newspaper and became a co-owner. Wells-Barnett would become best known for her role as a leading anti-lynching crusader, following in the tradition of Frederick Douglass and Sojourner Truth for elevating the challenges faced by African Americans in the black press.

The nation's best-known African American newspaper, the *Chicago Defender*, and the *China Times* were also early minority media startups, along with the *Amsterdam News* in New York, which was first published in 1909 with a $10 investment at a time when only 50 other black newspapers in the country were in existence.[13]

In the meantime, across decades and centuries, half-hearted industry efforts and government reports calling for the integration of people of color into the news industry, mainstream media—also known as traditional or legacy mass media (other terms used interchangeably throughout the book)—would remain predominately white and male, even as social and demographic changes diversified audiences. Throughout American history, only a handful of mainstream newspapers, magazines, television, and radio stations have been owned by women or people of color, probably due in large part to the history of news production as an exclusive one for far too long.

Women worked in largely invisible roles as publishers and editors early on because the societal mores attached to their domestic duties made it difficult to assume more visible ones. Elizabeth Timothy, who became America's first female newspaper publisher in 1738 following the death of her husband, encountered the social restrictions associated with patriarchy to keep women from taking on leadership roles absent the death of a male relative or spouse.[14] Timothy operated the *South Carolina Gazette* in partnership with Benjamin Franklin under the name of her 13-year-old son.[15]

Either writing under pseudonyms as some of their male counterparts did to avoid controversy or submitting to the social constrictions that defined women's limited roles to publications that emerged after the American Revolution, women found an early voice in America's traditional media landscape, albeit one with restrictions placed on its range. Dozens of women's publications were in circulation by the time the Civil War was underway, for example, and their general focus on fashion, recipes, marriage, childbearing advice, and poetry would shape the limited imagination of publishers seeking to market content to women for years to come.[16]

From the end of the Civil War and beyond, there were dozens of pioneering journalists of color who were given marginal assignments in traditional media. There were only a handful of women and people of color who were hired as writers in the early mainstream press. Among them was Thomas Morris Chester, who became the first black war correspondent for the *Philadelphia Press*, writing about black Union troops for the big-city American daily in 1864.[17]

Thousands of miles away and decades later, an Oakland maid, therapist, author, and columnist named Delilah Beasley was hired as an *Oakland Tribune* news correspondent in 1915. Her hire made her the first African American woman to write for a mainstream or predominately white newspaper in the country, and she did so while working on a book about prominent African Americans in the state, *Negro Trailblazers of California*.

Beasley's columns "chronicled a range of activities among the black elite," San Francisco State University professor Venise Wagner writes. "From the quotidian to the exceptional, (Beasley) provided white readers with positive portrayals of African Americans that were not commonly available to white audiences."[18]

Such portrayals of people of color were rare in traditional media because the ethnic press continued to mushroom even after the advent of the telegraph, which transformed America's system of mass communication. The telegraph also spawned what González and Torres called "the first communications cartel" between the Western Union company and the Associated Press, which was abusive in its pricing policies in part because the partnership allowed it to rapidly emerge as "the main gatekeeper of the nation's supply of information."[19]

The monopoly and subsequent ubiquity of Associated Press material, combined with the new speed of the telegraph, would have a profound impact on journalism. It also transformed the impact of the racial narrative in America in a way that would foreshadow the digital future of news. "The new technology's instant speed and its monopoly pricing structure demanded shorter and simpler news items, action over reflection, screaming headlines over nuanced analysis," González and Torres observe.[20]

By 1930, there were 2,000 daily newspapers with a circulation of 40 million, and they were all wedded—like other legacy media—to the white racial narrative.[21] Sally Lehrman, in an entry about race and ethnicity for the *Encyclopedia of Journalism*, chronicled early traditional media hires of African American journalists: "In 1948, Carl T. Rowan took a job as a copy editor at the formerly all-white *Minneapolis Tribune*; in 1950, Marvel Cooke began reporting for the *Daily Compass* in New York; and in 1952, Simeon Booker became the first black reporter at a major newspaper, *The Washington Post*. The desegregation battles did not, however, inspire news outlets to integrate their own pages in any comprehensive way."

Because integration was so slow in traditional media, in addition to publishing newspapers, people of color began attempting to make forays into other media. For almost a decade, Latinos had been purchasing unpopular radio time slots early in the morning or late at night when radio licenses they sought from the federal government were largely denied. In 1946, the first U.S. radio station licensed to a Latino was granted to Spanish-language radio broker Raoul Cortez. Later a radio license was issued to Denver broadcaster Paco Sánchez, although the majority of stations were white-owned with programming geared toward Latinos.

Coincidentally, the year after Cortez received his license, the Hutchins Commission report, "A Free and Responsible Press," was published. Spearheaded by Time-Life owner Henry Luce, the report called for more diversity in a broad sense in all mass communications agencies. The report called on the press to diversify at least as it related to audience-specific content, even if it wouldn't be particularly lucrative at the beginning: "Discriminating serious minorities are prisoners of the estimate of mass taste made by the industry. Motion pictures, radio programs, newspapers and magazines aimed at these minorities may not make money at the beginning. They require a considerable investment. . . . The responsibility of the industry for diversity and quality means that it should finance ventures of this kind from its other business."[22]

There was slow progress diversifying traditional media in myriad ways until a business case was clear for doing so. In *News for All the People*, González and Torres wrote: "In their search for untapped markets, an increasing number of white owners changed the format of their stations to serve communities of color. For most, the decision was purely economic. African-American purchasing power had grown to $15 billion by 1953 and advertisers were suddenly intent on reaching black consumers."[23] In the mid-to-late 1940s, KCOR in San Antonio and WERD in Atlanta became the first commercial radio stations owned by people of color; the latter was the first truly integrated station in the country.[24] In a July 2011 FCC report, "The Information Needs of Communities," Steven Waldman along with an FCC working group described other programming of interest on the National Negro Network (NNN), which was launched by Leonard Evans, a black advertising executive, in 1954. NNN was a group of 40 stations that programmed news summaries, wire-copy, and music.[25]

In the meantime, Latinos also sought television licenses when that technology expanded in the early 1950s. In 1954, Puerto Rico's *El Mundo* newspaper opened San Juan station WKAQ-TV, the first station in what is now the national Telemundo television network. The next year, San Antonio's Cortez also was granted the first UHF television license in the country. In 1961, Cortez sold the television station to a group of investors that included his son-in-law, Emilio Nicolás, Mexican broadcast mogul Emilio Azcárraga Viduarreta, and others to become KWEX-TV, the first station in the Spanish International Network (SIN), now known as Univision.[26]

There would be more calls, commissions, and reports for years to come, but one of the strongest and most pointed calls for a moratorium on bias in media emerged from the 1967 National Advisory Commission on Civil Disorders formed by President Lyndon Johnson after years of riots in predominantly black urban centers.

The 1960s, Unrest, and the Kerner Commission Report

In the 1960s, the world of most traditional media creators and consumers was very white and segregated. In this sense, mainstream media reflected the America of the time. Because mass media were concentrated then, news anchors and reporters were public figures and household names. Many of the best-known reporters of this volatile era were white men—Walter Cronkite, Edward Murrow, David Halberstam, and Tom Wolfe, to name a few. White women, too, were making names for themselves, among them: Barbara Walters, Helen Thomas, and Helen Gurley Brown. In the minority press, women like Ethel Payne and Alice Dunnigan, as well as others, were nationally known, too, but nothing matched the scale of their white peers in traditional media.

Payne became a White House correspondent for the *Chicago Defender*, and over time, the newspaper's most recognized scribe; Dunnigan was her peer as the first female African American correspondent to receive White House credentials. As a legendary and aggressive member of the White House Press Corps, Payne landed on the front page of newspapers around the country after asking President Dwight Eisenhower why the administration failed to support a ban on segregated interstate bus travel.[27] She also epitomized the way the advancement of equal civil rights accelerated the demise of the black press, as mainstream media began poaching black reporters for their staffs during the civil rights era and advertisers followed.

Lehrman noted, "Latinos, Asians, and American Indians remained absent in coverage, except at times as criminals and threats. For the most part, it was white reporters that covered the civil rights movement for the civil rights press. The American Society of Newspaper Editors (ASNE) had no nonwhite members at all until 1965, when it allowed the membership of John H. Sengstacke, the editor of the famed black newspaper, the *Chicago Defender*. Some news outlets relegated coverage of black people to one or two special pages. For the general public, to paraphrase a common sentiment, it was as if African Americans, American Indians, and people of Hispanic and Asian descent never gave birth, married, achieved in their lives, or died."[28]

This separate and unequal division in journalism made the significance of unfolding events of the civil rights movement all the more evident. One example is the coverage of the 1961 Freedom Rides. A group of interracial activists including members of the Congress of Racial Equality (CORE) rode buses on May 14, 1961, from Washington, D.C., to New Orleans, Louisiana, to test the Interstate Commerce Commission's ban on segregated buses and facilities. Reporters and photographers from the black press had covered these activists with empathy and in context compared with initial mainstream news coverage. The framework of coverage in the ethnic press laid the groundwork for white journalists to follow up on a story that mollified the nation and changed the tenor of civil rights coverage.

According to PBS, when the activists survived the bombing of a bus in Anniston, Alabama, and vicious beatings in Birmingham, among other hostilities,

> the images and eyewitness accounts changed the country's consciousness. Footage of a burning bus shocked the nation, as did photographs of the beatings inflicted during the riot at the Birmingham Trailways Bus Station and of the bandaged face of Freedom Rider James Peck lying in a hospital bed. . . . Images drove home the brutality of the white segregationist regime in a way that words alone could not convey. Klan members attacked *Birmingham Post-Herald* photographer Tommy Langston along with other members of the media and attempted to destroy their film; miraculously, the roll of film inside Langston's smashed camera survived intact.[29]

In one instance, it wouldn't be until decades later that the *Birmingham News* would apologize for the short-sighted and error-riddled reporting conducted to by its staff in the 1960s. Hank Klibanoff, who coauthored *The Race Beat*, described on National Public Radio the Birmingham newspapers as "either afraid of the civil rights story or paralyzed by it," but overall, responsible for dismissing one of American history's most pivotal stories while national papers across the country gave civil rights front-page treatment.[30]

The paper also reported in 2006, according to Barbara Friedman and John Richardson, that a photo intern had found a cardboard box of 5,000 images taken at the height of the civil rights struggle but never published.

Another southern newspaper, the Lexington (Ky.) *Herald-Leader*, marked the fortieth anniversary of the Civil Rights Act of 1964 with a front-page article acknowledging that it, too, had failed to adequately cover the civil rights movement. *Herald-Leader* editors said the paper failed to meet journalism's most basic obligations. Negligent coverage had "irreparably damaged the historical record and caused the newspapers' readers to miss out on one of the most important stories of the 20th century." Civil rights leader Dr. Martin Luther King, Jr., even noted how difficult it was to move forward without "the moral support of the national press to counteract the hostility of local editors."[31]

Julian Williams, writing about the *Mississippi Free Press*—a newspaper developed by slain civil rights leader Medgar Evers—wrote that "the mainstream press in Jackson, Mississippi, presented a perspective which reflected the segregationist attitudes of the power structure."[32] Although there was some evidence that television news in Virginia was more balanced in its civil rights coverage,[33] African Americans in search of news that included them and didn't portray them as lawless marauders turned to the black press. In some cases, as in Mississippi, neither the civil rights movement nor its activists were an editorial priority. Instead, at the *Jackson Advocate*, editor Percy Greene encouraged patience and cooperation with whites. Other papers focused on social, church, and educational activities.[34]

In the North, things were only slightly different. In Chicago, editors knew what they didn't know. Ellis Cose, a columnist, writer, and speaker, is a pioneering black journalist who has worked as a columnist and contributing editor for *Newsweek* magazine and is also the author of several books. Cose began his journalism career as a weekly columnist for the *Chicago Sun-Times*. At age 19, he was the youngest editorial page columnist ever employed by a major Chicago daily.

"This was 1969, 1970, and I was in college at the time. I wrote a letter to the *Sun-Times*, telling them they needed to hire me." Cose said.[35] He was editing a publication at the University of Illinois. The editor who hired him told him that he was bright and talented, but "we don't hire 18-year-olds to be columnists."

Still, they hired Cose to write a column aimed at young readers. It was an opportunity Cose believes might have been available to him solely because of his race. "If I had been a young talented white guy, would they have made the same space for me? It's not a question that I can answer, but clearly they were aware that there was something lacking and one of the things lacking was any representation at all of people of color," Cose said. "I appeared out of nowhere and helped solve that problem for them. Race was such a huge story and the fact was that they didn't have anybody—in Chicago there were four mainstream white newspapers, *Chicago Sun Times, Tribune, Daily News*, the *American*—the *Daily News* had hired Lou Palmer, also owned by Marshall Fields. I'm sure the *Tribune* didn't have anyone. When Vernon Jarrett came on, he came on after I did and he was twenty years old. I'm sure that race was part of their thinking."

That the stories of these pioneers and countless others are footnotes in American history is one example of how the mainstream press operates as a microcosm of broader societal examples that indicate how some of the nation's most powerful white men have failed to allow diversity to become a parallel narrative to the country's prosperity for at least two centuries. This consistent lack of recognition is part of what led to the widespread unrest between 1964 and 1971 that decimated black urban neighborhoods after more than 750 riots left 228 people dead and injured more than 12,000.[36] The challenges that would continue to plague the news industry into the millennium, however, came down to a bad business model informed by the arrogance of white supremacy and a refusal to grant people of color's narratives the same print space or air time as the stories of white men.

Cose, for example, remembers the coverage during the periods of urban unrest as subpar. "The lack of African American journalists when those riots hit was something that was reflected in the horrible coverage," he said. "It was akin to if you dropped a foreign correspondent into Nicaragua who couldn't speak Spanish. I was a kid when the riots took off in Chicago, I remember reading the coverage of the riots. I remember thinking that what I'm reading here has no resemblance to reality. It was basically from the perspective of people who looked at urban areas as jungles teeming with dangerous people who needed to be contained. That was the attitude of the coverage. Not only was it a hands-off, removed kind of coverage, it was in many cases, just bad coverage."

At the time, there was still hope that the presence of at least one black reporter reporting for a traditional media outlet could help with improving the tone and quality of journalism that had historically been tone-deaf, classist, racist, or a blend of all three. But in the decades to come, it would be clear that hiring a representative from impacted communities wasn't nearly enough. In order for the news to accurately reflect the full reality of the changing world, white male editors and producers—our nation's staunch information gatekeepers—would need to declare such stories important and significant. In order to do so, they would need to examine and interrogate their own prejudice and belief about the extent to which race was a newsworthy story.

In a nation that was still described and still living in separate and unequal black and white worlds, while white America was shocked, black America was outraged. In the sweltering summers in cities across the nation, unrest in reaction to the racial and economic conditions facing African Americans unequally led President Lyndon B. Johnson to request an investigation into the causes and solutions by the National Advisory Committee on Civil Disorders. The Kerner Commission, named after the committee chair, Governor Otto Kerner, Jr., of Illinois, produced a report that offered the most enduring indictment of the press's racial uniformity that American history has to offer. The report noted that part of what fueled unrest in cities across the country was a media system that had not reflected the full lives of African Americans, in part, because black reporters had not been hired with any real consistency or promoted within news organizations.   Specifically, the report said, "The news media have failed to analyze and report adequately on racial problems. They report and write from the standpoint of a white man's world," and that the press "contributed to a black-white schism."[37] Other key quotes from the report are equally as direct: "White society is deeply implicated in the ghetto. White institutions created it and maintain it and white society condones it," and "the press has too long basked in a white world looking out of it, if at all, with white men's eyes and white perspective."[38]

Belva Davis, a pioneering television journalist in San Francisco, described the report this way in her memoir, *Never in My Wildest Dreams*: "Noting that key segments of the media failed to report on the causes and consequences of racial disorder, the commission said, 'They have not communicated to the majority of their audience—which is white—a sense of the degradation, misery and hopelessness of life in the ghetto.'"[39]

There was by no means a massive influx of minorities into traditional and legacy media—there would be one reporter let in at a time, in a practice many regarded as tokenism. Dori J. Maynard, president of the Robert C. Maynard Institute for Journalism Education (named for her father who went on to own the *Oakland Tribune* with Nancy Maynard for 10 years between 1982 and 1992), noted that when Bob Maynard applied for a job in the late 1950s and early 1960s, "they either weren't hiring Negroes, or they already had their Negro." She said in a phone interview: "It took more than three years before he got his first job in the early 1960s. He was one of the first African Americans working in white-owned media. The civil rights movement morphed into the Black Panther movement, you had people like Malcolm X saying, 'No white reporters allowed' and editors looked up and realized that they did not have journalists on staff competent to report on the biggest stories of their time."

Kerner Report recommendations were specifically directed at hiring more black reporters and telling the stories of more black families in general. That specificity would make black reporters among the most visible growing diverse segments of legacy media in an era before diversity initiatives would stall, when news organizations would ultimately and perilously decide that diversity as a priority was in direct conflict with diversity as a financial imperative. But pressure to hire minorities eventually extended beyond African Americans to Native Americans, Latinos, and Asian Americans who were also targeted for early diversity efforts.

In the eras before the civil rights movement, affirmative action, and the Civil Rights Act, white male editors in American newsrooms had a number of convenient arguments for ignoring communities of color. Instead of saying outright that they had no interest in or knowledge of such communities, they said that there were not enough trained journalists of color, that if such journalists existed, they couldn't find them. This would also be the excuse for editors at print publications like *Newsweek* and the *New York Times* who would not promote qualified women from researchers to writers.

In traditional media, institutionalized sexism took the form of relegating women to the balcony of the National Press Club, away from male reporters, as Nan Robertson documents in her important book, *The Girls in the Balcony*. But Robertson also points out that there were exceptions, including two of the most admired and powerful women at the *New York Times* in the 1960s and 1970s, Charlotte Curtis and Ada Louise Huxtable.

The latter was hired in 1963, two years after Curtis had arrived to cover society, and was the first full-time architecture critic at an American newspaper.[40] In Lynn Povich's revealing book, *The Good Girls Revolt: How the Women of Newsweek Sued Their Bosses and Changed the Workplace*, it is clear that even college-educated women were expected to be nurses, teachers, or secretaries even after historic lawsuits at both the *New York Times* and *Newsweek* led women to fight for inclusion.

Largely, stories about racism and sexism in media became the de facto responsibility of women and people of color who took it upon themselves to publish, air, and maintain alternative narratives that would augment history books. The fight to do so within mainstream media would be long, difficult, and slow. As late as 1964, the Newspaper Guild of America found just 45 blacks among more than 50,000 employees at daily newspapers.[41] In 1971, 22 percent of daily newspaper journalists were women.[42]

The mainstream media before the late 1960s and throughout the 1970s was a cornucopia of outlets that had been conditioned to shape the news for and almost entirely about whites and men. Other institutions that produced traditional media—book publishers and movie producers—either incorporated or responded to a monolithic news culture and offered audiences narratives fraught with the same problems of omission. "The more popular and influential television became, the more efficiently women were swept off the screen," Gail Collins wrote in her 2009 book, *When Everything Changed: The Amazing Journey of American Women from 1960 to the Present.* "TV created the impression that once married, a woman literally never left her house. Even if viewers knew that this really wasn't true, many did accept the message that when matrimony began, working outside the home ended."[43] There were few visible exceptions like Marlene Sanders, who was one of the few women to do on-air network television reporting before 1960. The civil rights movement was the first major news event that showed traditional media the impact of missing significant stories by remaining male and monochromatic. But because of a persistent resistance to change in legacy media culture, it would take protests, riots, and lawsuits for real change in newsrooms and magazines for women and people of color.

One example of the resistance to diversity in newsroom culture is one of the nation's oldest traditional media organizations, the American Society of News Editors (ASNE), which was known as the American Society of Newspaper Editors until 2009. ASNE has come a long way, but for years, it had numerous opportunities to confront race and racial bias in its ranks at its conventions before the Kerner Report. Instead, the organization's refusal to accept broader social changes beyond media was impressively obstinate. It ranged from active participation in a North-South tennis tournament that served as a kind of Civil War enactment and assertion of Confederate identity to its insinuated support of sentiments expressed by Mississippi senator James Eastland in 1948 who when he addressed segregation within the organization applied a very different lens to the nation of civil rights, saying: "You are guilty of racial discrimination in the newspaper business. . . . You are not to be condemned. It is your civil right to associate with, employ and work with whomever you please."[44]

Several years later, in the wake of *Brown v. Board of Education,* ASNE finally started to note the limitations of remaining an exclusive and elitist club of white men. The organization initially restricted membership to editors of daily newspapers—most black newspapers were weeklies—and were able to resist the inclusion of people of color into the fold for decades with the excuse that there were no qualified people of color who met membership requirements instead of owning up to racist exclusion. The slow integration of women and people of color into news organizations and mass media also implicitly required white men in powerful positions to interrogate their own biases and ignorance. For instance, instead of saying explicitly that they believed black editors and journalists to be inferior, ASNE leadership invoked the organization's rule that only editors from daily newspapers could join. Most black editors at the time, however, worked for weekly newspapers, which automatically disqualified them from membership.

The world continued to advance beyond the nucleus of ASNE. Freedom Riders, key civil rights activists who were both white and black, composed of women and men, were fighting for desegregation in 1961 when future congressman John Lewis was beaten unconscious, like others, in a melee that resulted from an angry racist mob attacked the riders.[45] In Selma and elsewhere in the South, the movement, groups such as the Student Nonviolent Coordinating Committee, and history were coinciding to change how society responded (or failed to respond) to racial injustice. News was getting away from journalists involved with organizations like ASNE and others who were under the influence of groups like it.

Were ASNE the only organization to blame for such resistance, current-day discussions about the demise and death of traditional media might be fewer and farther between. A singular institution's resistance would have been easier to change, but a systemic resistance to progress was harder to circumvent and it always has been. Whether or not news media cared about telling stories about racial minorities that reflected their true participation in the American narrative, the combined effect of victories from the civil rights movement in the form of the Civil Rights and the Voting Rights acts of 1964 and 1965, respectively, along with other developments, required smart editors to find black reporters to help them tell stories in spaces that would otherwise be closed to them. Unfortunately, the ASNE wouldn't make a formal connection between widespread social integration and newsroom integration until 1978.[46]

By the end of the 1970s, less than 4 percent of journalists in newsrooms were nonwhite, compared to 17 percent of the U.S. population, according to ASNE data. While that was certainly not an impressive number, it was a start. Still, *Washington Post* deputy managing editor Ben Bradlee wrote that

from the mid-1960s into the early 1970s, "The newsroom was racist. . . .
This racism would slowly and painfully subside, if not vanish, over the next
ten years. But at the time, such racism at the *Post* (and other papers) stood
in the way of excellence."[47]

This resistance to racial inclusion was a microcosm of a broader societal
ill. Radio that appealed to black listeners had violent detractors; Ku Klux
Klan members who tore down station towers or threatened DJs on-air. It
took the FCC until 1978 to promote minority-owned networks, when people of color comprised less than 1 percent of all station owners.[48]

Then, there was journalism education, which has been historically
ignored as an essential pipeline for journalists in legacy newsrooms. Educational disparities for women and people of color, generally, have impacted
the number of minorities who choose to major in journalism or mass communications for many years. The result of those general disparities is a generally low number of graduates trained in mass communications and an
even lower number of potential journalism professors who are women or
people of color to prioritize educating future journalists in academia.

But even when schools attempted to make journalism a priority at Historically Black Colleges and Universities, for instance, they encountered larger
systemic barriers. For example, González and Torres wrote: "Despite early
adoption of radio classes by Howard University and other historically black
colleges, FM radio was in operation for 20 years before the FCC granted its
first non-commercial license to a black college."[49] This was an example of
how the FCC "handed America's white youth a ten-to-twenty-year training
advantage over black youth for careers in broadcasting—in what was arguably the most influential industry of modern society," the authors added.[50]
Only boycotts and protests began to change this unfair approach to leveling
the journalism-training playing field.

The historic social and journalistic strides made by people of color and
women in the 1960s and 1970s were borne of the hard work and commitment of journalists like those Belva Davis wrote about who were "beginning to bring the stories of black Americans out of the shadows . . . in vivid
detail the public could no longer ignore."[51]

Like civil rights legislation, affirmative action laws would serve to bring
employment inequity out of the shadows for women and people of color in
traditional media, but the promise of a more diverse, integrated media—like
that of a more diverse, integrated country—would not be without cost or
challenges.

Chapter 2

The Early Failures of Racial and Gender Integration in Traditional Media

The combination of rioting in America's cities, the Kerner Commission Report's clarion call for greater media diversity, and the legacy of the civil rights movement created a three-pronged foundation for the pioneering wave of integration in America's television, radio, and print newsrooms in the late 1960s and 1970s. The Civil Rights Act of 1964 also played a significant role in legislating equal opportunity for all in the workplace.

In the 1960s, the Kerner Report was a reflection of President Lyndon B. Johnson's impatience with civil unrest in America's cities particularly in black neighborhoods. Writer James Baldwin warned that there was anger about the perpetual oppression of the black underclass and the systemic impediments to their success on all fronts. Martin Luther King, Jr., Malcolm X, and the Black Panther Party began making headlines, as Freedom Riders and other luminaries of the civil rights movement continued to do. The black press had a rich tradition of appropriately elevating these stories, but traditional media often attempted to ignore those stories entirely or bury them deep inside print media.

As a reflection of the institutional racism permeating society, traditional media continued to miss its opportunity to be comprehensive and thorough because of the absence of black reporters. When newsrooms finally started to integrate, they did so sparingly—one person of color or woman at a time. The result was that reporters found within news organizations the same hostility and bias toward racial difference those reporters faced in everyday life.

The national conversation around race in those days still described American demographics in a binary that was either black or white. The early legacy of Martin Luther King, Jr., the civil rights movement in the

South, and the civil unrest he helped lead required editors and producers to sit up and take notice. Whatever white male editors felt about Bull Connor or civil rights for blacks in America, they understood as early as *Brown v. Board of Education* that they would need to grapple with integration under their auspices, even if they still harbored personal biases that could not be legislated away.

The institutions that comprise legacy media have almost always responded slowly to racial changes and power changes in America. White male power and patriarchy—in the words of bell hooks, white supremacist patriarchy—have resisted and continue to resist demographic changes which will require that power, privilege, and storytelling be more equitably distributed. For instance, one of the oldest and most respected organizations of traditional media power in America, the American Society of Newspaper Editors (ASNE) acted as a microcosm of how racism has functioned within traditional media for centuries—and not only in its social activities.

While there was no explicit exclusion of minorities from ASNE membership, despite never citing whiteness as a membership criterion, the organization regulated its membership and declined to admit a black editor to membership until 1965.[1] As Gwyneth Mellinger writes, "Whiteness usually accumulates power through tacit means and often without the conscious recognition of those who subscribe to it. This deniability perpetuates asymmetrical social and institutional relations while insulating the beneficiaries of whiteness from charges of racism."

For people of color in journalism, particularly in the early days of integration, that meant journeying into mainstays of racial and gendered privilege. Being pioneers, as Ellis Cose described, required not only doing their jobs, but also performing them perfectly, lest their example be used to explain why African Americans or any other minorities were unfit to produce news. It also required them to endure the micro-aggressions of white male editors, the beneficiaries of racial exclusion and the purported protectors of journalistic ethics.

Newsroom and news coverage sexism required women to make similar sacrifices as their colleagues from racial and ethnic minority backgrounds or start their own publications. Pioneering women journalists have myriad stories about rude and threatening male bosses who subjected them to objectification, harassment, condescension, or managed to achieve all three in the days before such behavior had severe legal consequences. Perhaps as a demonstration of how desperately women needed an outlet of their own, when Gloria Steinem famously spearheaded a group that founded *Ms.*, the glossy magazine generated more than 20,000 letters, 26,000 subscription orders and its first issue sold out in eight days.[2] Groups of women in traditional media, inspired by the consciousness-raising that marked the dawn of the feminist movement, also began confronting male editors, publishers, and producers about the way women were both treated and portrayed in media.

In March 1970, about 100 women at *Ladies' Home Journal* took over the office of the publisher and editor to demand, among other things, that the content of the magazine shift away from its sexist mores, advertising, and all. It was a protest that *New York Times* columnist and author Gail Collins said was serious because of the powerful lens of mass media through which Americans saw virtually everything, "and the newspapers, magazines and television stations that did the communicating hired very few women, promoted even fewer, and broadcast a vision of what the American woman out to be that was both trivial and stultifying."[3]

Perhaps taking a page from civil rights figures and certainly spurred on by the societal shift the women's movement prompted, women began to advocate for themselves en masse and to the great resistance of men in media. Since the heralded days of journalism pioneers Ida B. Wells, Nellie Bly, and Ethel Payne, women had been making names for themselves as journalists. But the same glacial, incremental resistance to change that led editors and producers to continue to practice de facto racial segregation kept women from making equal pay, moving themselves out of the "pink ghetto" of women's pages and generally competing at the same level as their male counterparts until they took legal action on their own behalf.

ASNE Calls for Parity

In 1978, a decade after the Kerner Report, the ASNE made a commitment to parity reflecting the national minority population by 2000 because, according to its website, "ASNE believes that diverse newsrooms better cover America's communities."[4] The organization's goal responded proactively—albeit many years later—to the insights reported by the Kerner Commission as well as the 1947 Commission on Freedom of the Press, or the Hutchins Commission.[5] Mercedes Lynn de Uriarte, a professor at the University of Texas Austin, writes that the call from ASNE was "perhaps the single most effective social force for newsroom change in U.S. Press history. But for the past quarter century, minority participation averaged an increase of only one-half of 1% per year." During that time, she continues, newsrooms did not evolve on how they determined newsworthiness. The result of the kind of tokenism that Dori Maynard described led to a kind of self-congratulatory sentiment that would not make a notable difference in how journalism included or continued to exclude people of color. What needed to change significantly were the powerbrokers in newsrooms and at television stations. With the first minorities hired, it was assumed that the work of integration was mostly completed. De Uriarte added: "Integration was assumed to assure diversity. . . . As a result, newsroom culture changed little during these years."[6]

In its first annual print newsroom census in 1979, ASNE found that minorities made up just 4 percent of all journalists. Over the years, various professional organizations and institutions worked to cultivate a burgeoning diversity industry that offered organized workshops, seminars, and exercises. Combined with scholarships, fellowships, and internships, Uriarte reports that roughly $100 million was spent on these activities and programs, led by ASNE.[7]

It was the Year 2000 Plan, part of the vision of Robert C. Maynard, that worked as an early leading model for journalism desegregation. (ASNE has published some aspects of its Time Out for Diversity efforts online.)[8] Maynard gained prominence as a correspondent and ombudsman for the *Washington Post*, but he also began in 1972 to establish himself as an industry newsroom diversity leader. In 1978, Maynard and a multiracial group of journalists created the Institute for Journalism Education (IJE) in Berkeley. Over the next 30 years, the Institute became one of the most prolific instruments of journalism diversity in the industry and trained hundreds of journalists of color.[9]

Now the Robert C. Maynard Institute for Journalism Education, IJE held a summer workshop at Columbia University to condense years of journalism experience into the summer months. In this way, it served as a model for diversity programs replicated by traditional media corporations that sought to train journalists of color quickly. IJE was responsible for training a pioneering wave of minority reporters before its funding was left in the hands of the news organizations that stood to gain the most from training a more diverse cadre of reporters but would ultimately invest the least. At that point, the summer program halted, despite having the support of a champion in Fred Friendly, a white male news executive and one of the most visible white allies for minority journalists in history.

Ellis Cose said in a 2013 interview, "I was running the Institute of Journalism Education and I think all that stuff was stuff that came along together. The summer program came out of the Michelle Clark programs, the Kerner Commission on riots . . . it all ties together. The industry got the message, starting with the riots during the 1960s, that something was wrong."

Representations of People of Color in Mainstream Media

Part of what was wrong with the industry had to do with access and accuracy of representation of people of color. IJE connected journalists of color to a network that did not quite replicate the same networks that were available to white male reporters, but it still helped. Even so, women and people of color pioneers in traditional media who joined from diversity programs or transitioned to legacy news from the ethnic press found a very different environment in the television, radio, and print outlets they integrated. So it helped to have been around other women and people of color who would be sharing the same experience.

Tanna Beebe, a Native American reporter of the Cowlitz and Quinault tribes, became a pioneering American Indian woman in television news in Seattle after completing the IJE program. Another Native American woman, Hattie Kauffman, wouldn't appear on television news until 1989.[10] The fact of these firsts, however, does not completely convey the challenges women and people of color faced socially and emotionally during the early days of gender and racial integration in traditional media. Beebe said that even though assigning editors gave her lackluster assignments in order to try and get her to quit, she covered the top stories of the day as a rookie and became a household name as a result. That was true for other reporters, like Connie Chung, the first Asian American and second woman to anchor one of America's major network news programs. Chung was hired immediately after she earned her journalism degree in 1969 at WTTG-TV in Washington, D.C.

But the indignities reporters of color and women faced while integrating newsrooms had an unfortunately long, vivid history. When Simeon S. Booker became the first black full-time reporter for the *Washington Post* in 1952, "he was instructed not to use certain restrooms out of deference to white colleagues who didn't want to share facilities with a black man."[11] Booker left the *Post* a year and a half later and joined Johnson Publications, the most successful African American publishing empire in history with publications including *Ebony*, *Jet*, and *Black World*.[12] As integration and desegregation marched on, the black talent drain from black publications left many black newspapers as only "a shell of their former selves" by 1970, according to journalism historian and New York University professor Pamela Newkirk.

Belva Davis, the first black woman television reporter hired west of the Mississippi in 1967, was working in the black press after the death of Emmett Till, a 14-year-old who was brutally murdered in Mississippi in 1955 for reportedly flirting with a white woman.[13] Davis recalled that back then, *Jet* magazine was the only publication to feature the young man's disfigured body to display racism's innate hatred. While the ethnic and minority press elevated stories that displayed the full complex humanity of people of color in America, traditional media were still not convinced.

Working for broadcast television, Davis wrote that she faced the hostility and discomfort of cameramen who didn't want to work with her because she was both a woman and an African American. At the 1964 Republican National Convention with her cameraman, delegates spat at her. Both she and her Colleague were assaulted with questions like, "What the hell are you niggers doing in here?"

It was a time when television, like other legacy media, was not at all representative of the population. "But TV stations began hiring women and minorities for three reasons," Davis wrote. "A few realized broadening their viewer demographics was smart journalism and smart business."[14] But the majority of outlets struggled with welcoming or reconciling difference.

After the unrest that prompted the ebb of diversity-focusing hiring in the 1970s, employees began pushing for structural and employment changes in traditional newsrooms and in broadcast television. A federal policy in broadcasting adopted in 1969 initially stated that operating licenses wouldn't be granted to stations practicing deliberate employment discrimination; it was amended a year later to require stations to file annual reports outlining their minority recruitment efforts. Stations with 5 to 10 employees were expected to hire women and minorities at a rate of at least 50 percent of the workforce.[15]

But just because people of color and women were hired doesn't mean that they were instantly part of the news organization where they were employed. Instead, they largely remained outsiders. Melba Tolliver, who became a reporter for WABC in New York in 1971, is a good example. She was assigned that year to cover the wedding of President Richard Nixon's daughter. The day she was scheduled to produce footage covering the wedding, Tolliver also decided to go natural, which prompted her white boss to complain that she no longer looked feminine and that she should change her hairstyle. Unfortunately, it was the kind of situation that black women broadcasters would be confronted with for decades to come.[16]

By 1970, Federal Communications Commission statistics showed that the number of minorities in broadcasting increased to 9.1 percent despite the resistance of white broadcasters to government-sanctioned racial inclusion.[17] Without a similar federal policy in place, progress in print traditional media was far slower. Newkirk writes, "Between 1968 and 1978, the percentage of minorities—who, prior to Kerner, were primarily black—increased fourfold, from less than one percent to 3.9 percent. Many of these minority hires were graduates of the handful of programs that were aimed at minority training, a response to the still common refrain that qualified minority journalists could not be found."[18]

Among those who benefited from intentional diversity efforts was Preston Davis, who joined ABC as an engineer in 1976 in Washington, D.C. Davis went on to become the first African American president of any Capital Cities/ABC division in the history of the company in 1993. There would be many more firsts as integration became part of the fabric of American life, but they came in more rapid succession after legal action on behalf of reporters who knew the true costs of integrating news organizations where they were treated as sympathy hires instead of professionals.

Physical and cultural differences aside, the same racial and gender biases that impacted people of color and women in other areas of life spilled over into news organizations. Since people of color and women were largely considered less intelligent, less competent, and less connected politically, socially, and economically than their white counterparts, it made sense that an early argument that arose about integrating traditional media had to do with whether these minorities were competent enough to do real journalism. An early and persistent critique of minority reporters was that they could not be objective, presumably given their limited social trajectory and mental agility compared to their white counterparts. As a result, minority journalists were often regarded as advocacy journalists, dedicated to writing about the pathology of the inner city, the most surface aspects of their culture or their respective communities to the exclusion of more desirable stories and generally as marginalized in their work as they were in their lives.

This marginalization occurred even as newsrooms without significant numbers of women or people of color in their ranks would consistently run afoul of good ethical standards in journalism with racist, problematic coverage. In 1981, for example, a three-part series on the black community in Los Angeles, written and edited solely by white men, criminalized blacks in poor neighborhoods and used the word "marauders" 20 times. It led to internal and external protests, and black reporters followed up with a series that was fairer in 1982; Latinos produced a similar series, the Pulitzer Prize–winning *Southern California's Latino Communities*.[19]

Landmark Lawsuits

Despite the obvious wisdom of hiring more people of color, some of the most significant gains for minorities in traditional media have come as a result of legal action. In 1972, several black reporters at the *Washington Post*, dubbed the Metro Seven, filed a landmark Equal Employment Opportunity Commission complaint against the newspaper. It is believed to have been the first of its kind in the nation.[20] Those staff members, including Richard Prince and Leon Dash, were also among the pioneering members of the National Association of Black Journalists (NABJ).

NABJ was one of several organizations for otherwise marginalized journalists that would advocate for inclusion of people of color and women in traditional media while also championing the efforts of the black press. Other organizations, like the National Association for Hispanic Journalists (NAHJ), the Native American Journalists Association (NAJA), and a coalition of these groups, UNITY, would follow in subsequent years. The goal was to create a safe space for journalists of color in mainstream journalism. (Recognizing their common missions, leaders of NABJ, NAHJ, AAJA, and NAJA held the inaugural UNITY Convention in Atlanta in 1984, which drew a reported 6,000 journalists.)[21]

The *Post* later reported that EEOC commissioners gave plaintiffs in the *Metro Seven* case a letter that entitled them to sue in federal court, but financial barriers kept them from pursuing a lawsuit. A group of female staffers, however, filed a discrimination suit, which the paper settled in 1980, the same year the *New York Times* settled a discrimination suit by black staffers and two years after the *Times* settled a suit by women in 1978.[22]

Pioneering efforts in journalism for people of color who were trying to integrate newsrooms also had some well-known white male allies who helped make forays into journalism possible for a few people of color. Among them was Fred Friendly, who in 1979 began the IJE summer program for journalists at Columbia University that would become the Robert

C. Maynard Institute for Journalism Education, the most enduring and visible organization dedicated to journalism diversity that also offers training, content analysis, and invaluable historical memory of diversity gains and failures in the news industry. The same was true for Bill Elsen, who with others worked on RezNet for Native American journalists and did other advocacy work in participation with the Maynard Institute. Belva Davis forged an alliance with Bill Hillman at her first television station before he went on to become president of the American Federation of Television and Radio Artists union, and eventually he would help her agitate for more diversity within the ranks of television stations, on-air talent, and news photographers.

While individual relationships bridging racial and gender divides were powerful, there were few long-term structural changes in traditional media that didn't require lawsuits. That was the case for women in newsrooms from *Reader's Digest* to *Newsweek*, and it was the case for black journalists into the 1980s.

In 1987, four black journalists reached an out-of-court settlement totaling more than $3.1 million and an agreement that the *New York Daily News* would start an affirmative action program after a case that took several years to make it through New York City's legal system. A federal jury determined that the newspaper had discriminated against the journalists, who, because of their race, were given less important assignments, lower salaries, and fewer promotions than their white counterparts.[23] "For the first time in history, racial attitudes in the American newsroom were put on trial, and no one was spared intense public scrutiny as charges of racism, sexual harassment, ethical breaches, and incompetence were hurled across the aisle," Newkirk writes.

Newkirk notes that there had been other cases, including a 1979 settlement between the *New York Times* and its black reporters and a joint complaint in 1978 from the women and blacks at the Associated Press that was joined in 1979 by the EEOC. The AP case was the first to enjoin the issues of race and sex discrimination, Newkirk writes, and "was, like other lawsuits at other news organizations, including ABC and *Newsweek*, settled out of court in the early 1980s."[24]

One of the ironies of these lawsuits and responses to them is that the mass media position themselves as an organs of responsive truths, meant to be essential to a more informed, active democracy. That traditional media structures would have difficulty responding to the equal and fair treatment of people of color and women in their ranks shows the limits of journalistic imagination and inclusion for people of color and women in the journalism industry, but it also underscores how complicated it is to hold the prevailing, prominent authors of the first draft of history accountable for living the ideals they profess to adhere to—among them, truly telling a range of stories that cover the full community—and who are able to deftly tell the stories of underserved and undercovered communities alongside the well-mined stories of white male citizens.

Dori Maynard of the Maynard Institute says the contributions of pioneers of color and women in journalism go unnoticed because "he that has the power to tell his own story can control his own narrative. You have to tell your own story. A lot of those institutions have gone back to being primarily white. So a lot of history is being lost, not out of ill intent, but they don't understand those contributions."

The unfortunate legacy of racism within and outside of newsrooms has always been the inability of newsrooms to reconcile internal biases against certain groups with objective news value and news judgment. No one knows this better than communities of color who have generally resisted traditional media portrayals and reports as sporadic, inaccurate, sensational, and damaging.

Chapter 3

Communities of Color and Media Bias

"The Greatest Burden and the Greatest Triumph"

Describing the core challenge of being a journalist of color in a traditional media organization, pioneering Native American reporter Tanna Beebe described succinctly the paradoxical nature of being both a representative and perceived advocate of one's community and an objective journalist. One of the legacies of racist and sexist hiring, promotion, and retention practices in mainstream media organizations is that the few people of color and women sent into their respective communities as journalists are sometimes treated as heroes or saviors. When Beebe would go to cover a community, "People I did not know would come up to me and want to talk or hold my hand or sit with me at a powwow," Beebe told veteran journalist Mark Trahant for his 1995 book about Native American journalists, *Pictures of Our Nobler Selves*. "The humbling was so great, I wondered if I could keep it up. I still don't know how to describe it, because it was the greatest burden and the greatest triumph at the same time."[1]

Journalists of color know the full weight of Beebe's sentiment firsthand. On one hand, within ethnic communities, reporters from racial and ethnic minority communities are considered to be advocates who can lend a sympathetic ear. Journalists of color are such a rarity, and the job carries with it a rare power among minorities—therein lies the sense of triumph. The burden, though, comes from the myriad challenges of telling stories about communities who are traditionally not covered by editors and producers who do not understand them.

Among the most famous accounts that detail this dichotomy in the modern era is former *Washington Post* magazine writer Jill Nelson's journalism memoir, *Volunteer Slavery*. Nelson was hired to write for the newly launched *Washington Post* magazine in 1986. She was paid in advance, even before she got to the paper—an anomaly she suspected was borne of the fact that the *Post* had a quota to fill and was looking to hire more women. It helped, too, that she was black, at least in theory.

The premiere issue of the *Post* magazine featured a stereotypical, fear-inducing photo of a menacing rapper that Nelson equated with a picture that evoked the murderous black boogeyman of Richard Wright's *Native Son*, Bigger Thomas.[2] Such racist and sexist coverage would continue across the decades, at the *Post* and elsewhere with little variation, widening the gap between a growing diverse audience and what Nelson refers to as the "effete, liberal media."

The traditional media's piecemeal coverage of communities of color generally has offered fewer reasons for journalists from racial and ethnic minority backgrounds to stay in the profession than for them to leave it. This is true for women as well, who are frequently relegated to features and soft news instead of high-profile beats and segments related to politics, international coverage, or business news. Reporters from underappreciated communities encounter a complicated Catch-22—they are asked to write what they know, but as general assignment and rookie reporters, the best way to earn their mettle is to constantly reach beyond what they know or what they think they know. Editors and producers should be doing the same, though stories have too often been framed by what and who *they* know—their golfing buddies, neighbors, and friends. When the news gatekeepers operate in a social milieu that is completely separate and apart from the worlds that reporters write and air stories from, the result is coverage that meets somewhere in the middle, a kind of compromise in both content and integrity.

The double standard is that failure to prove objectivity—a subjectively arbitrary condition—usually leads to limited success for women and people of color in newsrooms. This was my first lesson as a newspaper reporter when I went from working as an intern on the *Houston Chronicle*'s metro desk in 2000 to writing for the features department for the remaining few months of my rotation.

Early Experiences in Journalism

I began my career in newspaper journalism as part of the Hearst Newspapers Corporation Fellowship in 2000. Fellowships and special initiatives may have fallen out of favor over time, but when I began reporting, it seemed to be the only way media executives knew how to try to diversify newsrooms. A handful of young journalists were hired as part of the program every year at Hearst to augment ethnic and age diversity in newsrooms. Like the Tribune company's Metpro program and similar initiatives at other media companies, the fellowship was considered a rare opportunity for Hearst newspapers to make diversity gains while giving nontraditional rookies a shot at a newspaper career.

The fellowship's inaugural class was comprised entirely of women; I was part of the second cohort. Two of the other people in my class were white, one male, one female. The other woman of color was Asian American. We were all so excited to be writing for a living, but I was especially excited and humbled by the opportunity. I didn't consider that the same racial and social isolation I felt as one of a few women of color at boarding school and Vassar College would now be a part of my professional reality. I assumed that journalists were more savvy, committed to fairness and therefore not as inclined to racial or gender prejudice.

I was wrong. My view of journalism was influenced by the fact that I'd started writing and reporting about my community first by telling the story of my community and those communities that I encountered which were like mine. My first published pieces were about growing up poor and homeless in New York City, prisoners that I volunteered with in Upstate New York, and other narratives that are too often missing from legacy media. It was not immediately clear to me how I could be a bridge between the predominately white narratives that I consumed weekly in traditional media and communities of color until I tried to do so as part of the Hearst Fellowship.

Hearst fellows moved to a different-sized market every six months for two years. We received training about the company and the industry. We were fast-tracked into classes about libel, ethics, and best journalistic practices. Once we were assigned desks in newsrooms, we became glorified interns in the eyes of veteran staffers, though in most cases Hearst executives went above and beyond to make us feel welcome. The idea was that we would be hired during the last of multiple rotations.

I got a crash course in objectivity versus subjectivity during my nine-month stint at the *Houston Chronicle*. Objectively speaking, my skills as a writer were viewed as limited to telling the stories of African Americans. I learned this because my white editors seemed to prefer to assign me stories about African Americans. One of the first stories I covered was the funeral of Gary Graham, a black man, who was executed like many black men in Texas, guilty or not. Jesse Jackson, Sr., who I'd grown up seeing on television, stood only a few feet away from me at protests against Graham's death outside his funeral proceedings. As I would occasionally for years to come, I hid my notebook in my purse, acting on instinct. I knew that I was there to be an interpreter, not simply a reporter, and that I would be offering the details of black pain to mostly white audiences through the eyes of mostly white editors.

My job was to deliver my notes and observations to another, more senior reporter. When the stakes were lower, I was assigned other stories about blackness that fit neatly into the contours of traditional media, including a mysterious hit and run that had been unsolved for years in a part of town where most *Chronicle* reporters never ventured, stories about black photographers, artists, and—a personal favorite of every black writer you know—Black History Month because my editors presumed I could not possibly tell other stories.

When I was a rookie, I took pride in the fact that these stories were chosen for me. It made me feel like I had a specialty to draw on, even if I didn't have shoe leather reporting skills just yet. But in retrospect, that pride probably lasted for too long because it meant that most of my clips revealed a young reporter who had been pigeonholed.

I have never considered it to be anything but an honor and privilege to tell the stories of people who looked like me, but I realized over time that the price of telling the untold stories of African Americans in newspapers was the understanding that I would rarely make it to the front page, if ever. The greatest burden, as Beebe had put it, was also my greatest triumph. Feeling so grateful to be chosen in a newsroom with so few black women also meant that I would have written whatever was assigned to me. I had learned the culture of newsrooms required that rookies forgot how to utter the word "no" until they had been in the business for a while.

The price of that permissiveness was subtle, but a high one nonetheless. During the whole time I was in Houston, for instance, I had a single front-page byline with four other writers for a weather-related story. My main contribution had been following an air-conditioning repairman up into stifling attics on the hottest day of the year.

When I moved to East Texas to write for the *Beaumont Enterprise* for six months, there were so few reporters of any color that we all had to write about everything and race was not a priority. I wrote one weekend story about a race riot that my editors essentially shrugged and scratched their heads at as I reported it. This was probably because of the lingering shame and sentiment that hung in the air after the June 1998 killing of James Byrd Jr. Byrd was killed by three men, two of whom had ties to the

Ku Klux Klan. They tied Byrd to a chain and dragged him to his death from the back of a pickup truck. It was a mar on the whole of Southeast Texas and a grisly reminder of how pervasive racism remains in many small-town communities.

But working on my historical riot piece, which was not as polished in the end as I would have preferred, taught me another lesson about the coverage of communities of color. The measure of effective coverage of racial and ethnic communities was selecting stories and sources of interest to white audiences in part because most editors and producers are white. To get stories to pass muster with white men, those stories have to be considered relevant to them. But how could they be, when the social, political, and economic worlds of white male editors and their audiences rarely converged? In order for such stories to be edited, vetted, and placed in their appropriate contexts, white men have to climb incredible hurdles and it appears that the investment is not one they are generally willing to make.

In *Within the Veil*, Pamela Newkirk tells the story of Sylvester Monroe, who wrote a cover story about Nation of Islam leader Louis Farrakhan at *Time* magazine in 1994 to illustrate the difficulty of presenting a subject that has universal relevance but has to be positioned or pitched in a way that is palatable to white people. "To succeed, black journalists must continually devise strategies to present the world of black people in a way that white people can or care to process them," Newkirk writes. "Stories they propose on black people must conform to the interests, desires and tastes of a white audience."[3] So I learned, years later, why editors chafed at non-episodic, everyday coverage of African Americans or other people of color. They seemed like non-stories.

There were sometimes exceptions, usually when it came to entertainers. The death of R&B star Aaliyah Haughton in the summer of 2001 is one that stands out in my career because it was so unusual. I was sent to write a local story about the singer's tragic death in a plane crash in East Texas, but even the *New York Times* considered her a minor musician, so it afforded her death marginal coverage. The main disconnect for traditional media and their audiences was that Aaliyah was of significant import, especially to blacks and Latinos in cities throughout the country, as a rising talent at age 22.

Former *Times* editor Howell Raines pointed to this mistake as an example of the *Times* failing to be indispensable for a growing demographic in its potential readership. Raines, writing for the *Atlantic*, could have been talking about any number of outlets when he wrote: "If the *Times*' journalism continues to show contempt for the vernacular of those worlds, the paper will continue to lose subscribers. To explore every aspect of American and global experience does not mean pandering," Raines wrote.[4]

As I gained more experience, I learned that the higher visibility of working in traditional and predominantly white media as opposed to the alternative press requires that reporters of color move from "informer to informant and interpreter."[5] My experiences with white colleagues asking me to explain something "black," from black hair to music, before Google gained dominance as a verb are too numerous to count. I also had a number of encounters with African American sources who were downright hostile to me for being a representative of a mainstream media organization, particularly when I moved from Seattle, where I worked at the now out-of-print *Seattle Post-Intelligencer*, to the *San Francisco Chronicle*, in 2002.

I could understand the hostility. I worked with colleagues who had lived in the Bay Area for more than two decades, who, with a strange mixture of pride and apathy, declared that they had never crossed the Bay Bridge to visit Oakland. It made sense, then, that activists from a myriad of racial and ethnic backgrounds that I interviewed for stories were often distant and treated me coolly. Only later would I understand that from Florida to Washington, D.C., African American journalists have historically been subjected to vitriol from the black community for writing objectively about other blacks, which puts them in a psychologically vulnerable position as much as any other person of color might be when singled out for ridicule by people of their own race or ethnicity.

In 1993, Dorothy Gaiter was called "Nigger of the Year" by the local chapter director of the National Urban League in Miami after she wrote an unflattering story about an African American. Other journalists have been subjected to death threats when telling the truth about everything from the Nation of Islam to Jesse Jackson. Even Ethel Payne, the famous *Chicago Defender* reporter, was hostile to black reporters who dared to write negative investigative stories about civil rights leaders like Jackson. These kinds of dangers and the prospect of alienation from a race that is already arguably vulnerable to social and economic marginalization are implicitly understood to be an "unavoidable consequence of working in the mainstream news media, which African Americans have historically viewed as tools of oppression and degradation."[6]

It is no wonder, then, that these factors, combined with the pressure for journalists of color to produce subjectively newsworthy work competitive with white peers—peers, by the way, who are often promoted to coveted, prestigious positions at rates that far outpace the promotion of people of color and women—are considered by many to be too much to endure for the long stretch of time it would take to make a real difference in traditional media. Within the newsroom, people of color are often regarded as hostile, angry, or both when they point out to white editors and producers that biased coverage that aligns with overlapping white sentiments and stereotypes is not the definition of objectivity by any stretch of the imagination. If you have one African American reporter, for instance, who is responsible for "diversity coverage," it is likely that his or her stories fall in the purview of three subjects: Crime, sports, or entertainment. True objectivity would allow for reporters from all racial and ethnic and gender backgrounds to report on and be reflected in stories that cover the gamut in the journalistic beat system.

Stories with the potential to humanize people of color and women by centralizing them in news narratives that are about innocuous everyday stories about policy, the environment, urban planning or economics often completely obscure communities of color by omitting them as sources. The notion that people of color are not able to be authorities on instead of advocates for their communities in journalism has led to some truly damaging reporting that only reinforced the notion that diversity makes good business sense.

In 2008, esteemed journalist Chuck Philips wrote an article for the *Los Angeles Times* on Tupac Shakur based on false FBI documents. Any hip hop fan reading the article, "An Attack on Tupac Shakur Launched a Hip Hop War," with dismay, as I did, could have told Philips that his sources were bogus, but apparently none were consulted before the *Times* had to publish a rare, front-page retraction.

It would be disingenuous and inaccurate to suggest that journalists of color are the only ones who have made successful or sustained efforts to tell the stories of their communities. There have been a number of white journalists in the history of the profession who have made it a priority to tell the stories of people of color, too. At the *Clarion-Ledger* in Mississippi, Jerry Mitchell began in 1989 investigating civil rights killings that had gone overlooked and unpunished, inspired by the fictional *Mississippi Burning*. His reporting inspired others and led to 23 convictions in dozens of cases.[7] In their fascinating 2006 book, *The Race Beat*, Gene Roberts and Hank Klibanoff document many more instances of groundbreaking and courageous writing by white male reporters during the civil rights era. Taylor Branch is another example of someone who has written lengthy works that elevate the humanity of African Americans instead of condescending to them. In 2014, *New York Times* columnist Nicholas Kristof began writing a series, "When Whites Just Don't Get It," prompted by racial tension that unfolded in Ferguson, Missouri after the fatal police-involved shooting of Michael Brown, which I will discuss in greater detail in Chapter 4.

Traditional Media Coverage of Communities of Color

One of the unintended consequences of rapid and costly changes in news organizations as the economy has fluctuated and journalists have left traditional media through layoffs, buyouts, and attrition has been the change in coverage of communities of color in pivotal ways. While some old stereotypes have remained the same, the consistent need in news organizations for representation on news items of the day has in some ways sent coverage of communities of color back into the hands of those communities, their experts, think tanks, and organizations. This is true for organizations like *Huffington Post* verticals Black Voices and Latino Voices, the alternative, online-only sites like *Colorlines* and New America media, and for-profit sites like *The Root*.

For Latinos, the best example of this is an organization like Univision, which during international events such as the 2014 FIFA World Cup, drew record ratings but regularly maintains its brand through community and business-to-business partnerships. In a 1994 ASNE report, UCLA professor David Hayes Bautista put it this way: "In the mainstream media, almost the only time you see a minority is a crime or welfare story, something negative. In the Spanish-language media, you also get the human interest, the arts and sports stories. . . . Latinos are reduced to only one slice in the Anglo media, while in the Spanish media, a whole community is presented." Félix F. Gutiérrez, writing about Latino media, wrote that a common theme is a narrative and "coverage of an active, engaged and ambitious people looking to make a better life for themselves and others in the U.S., first in print and later in other media. . . . Such representation and documentation is important in countering prevailing images of Latinos as passive, unambitious, and uncultured additions to the nation."[8]

Gutiérrez pointed to alternative newspapers that since 1970 have been used deliberately for organizing and advocacy, including *El Malcriado*, *Palante*, and *El Gallo*, which were papers for the United Farm Workers Union in Delano, California, the Young Lords Party in New York City, and the Crusade for Justice in Denver, Colorado, respectively. "As the social movements grew, so did the range of media voices," he wrote, "including feminist publications, campus newspapers, organization newsletters, and journals commenting on the status of Latinos in the U.S."

Organizations like these provide the public with much-needed context and follow up coverage of people of color. They are vital for counterbalancing and often correcting negative or stereotypical portrayals of people of color. For women, magazines like *Bitch, Bust,* and *Ms.* continue to allow for stories impacting women that rarely get the space or attention they should in traditional media. Online and in print, these organizations are winning growing brand loyalty in areas where traditional media have faltered.

This has become evident in many cases for a myriad of communities, although it is difficult to know the extent of its truth in a world where social networking can have an outsized influence on how we view a story's worth. While the state and cohesiveness of journalism is still in flux, by and large traditional media still set a universal news agenda. This is clear for most minority communities and here I've provided some examples.

Flawed Coverage of Parents of Color

Dori Maynard, president of the Maynard Institute for Journalism Education since 2001, says that the absence of a conscious, coordinated, and consistent effort to hire minorities has impacted coverage and rendered traditional media an afterthought to most communities. Pointing to a 2013 *Time* magazine cover story for Father's Day featuring letters from prominent fathers to their children, Maynard said in an interview that she immediately noted that no African American or Asian fathers were represented, "reinforcing the idea that those fathers don't engage with their children," she said. When she attended the Blogging While Brown conference, Maynard said there was no reaction among attendees to the story because "*Time* doesn't have relevance in that community. When you continue to distort or ignore communities, you become irrelevant."

One might say the same is true for networks like Oxygen Media, which announced in 2013 that it had developed *All My Babies' Mamas* an hour-long special featuring Carlos Walker (better known as the rapper Shawty Lo). Before its subsequent cancellation, the show was intended to feature Walker and the 10 women with whom he has fathered 11 children. But the creation of *All My Babies' Mamas* underscored Maynard's point about a dearth of realistic portrayals of people of color that are also parents and, in this case, black mothers and fathers in mainstream media.

As the 15-minute trailer for the Oxygen cable network show spread, reaction to it as a pathological and sensationalized portrait of promiscuous and irresponsible black parents gathered support. CNN reported that a Change.org petition to cancel the show received more than 37,200 supporters, and a ColorOfChange.org petition garnered more than 40,000 signatures.

Sabrina Lamb, author and creator of the Change.org petition, considered the cancellation a triumph for the representation of healthy, complete, and positive portrayals of African American families. "The term 'Baby Mama' is a slur," Lamb said in a CNN interview. "We're saying that children don't deserve to witness your chaos. They deserve to have a mother and a father."

But the show also highlighted dissent in the African American community about who can decide what constitutes a respectable family, with or without sufficient balanced portrayals of black parents. As NPR's Gene Demby wrote, "Isn't it possible that *Babies' Mamas* could have also granted some humanity to real baby's mamas and complicated some simplistic, ugly stereotypes about them?"

Data about black families in America does not corroborate portrayals of a community teeming with fertile, promiscuous single parents. In 2010, multiple mainstream media reports about a government finding that 72 percent of black children were born to unmarried women failed to mention that fertility rates among all women are at an all-time low while births to blacks and Latinos approach fertility rates of their white and Asian counterparts, according to the Population Reference Bureau.

Citing the U.S. economic downturn, the Associated Press reported in 2012 that while half of children born in the United States are of color, the black population has grown at an annual rate of about 1 percent. Generally, mainstream media accounts assume the same negatives about black mothers that are voiced in the African American community, says Stacia L. Brown, who founded beyondbabymamas.com, which operates as a support and advocacy group for single mothers of color and works to correct shaming stereotypes perpetuated about them.

Brown says she started the site to combat stigma and shame often associated with single mothers. "*All My Babies' Mamas* is not a reflection of every black family," she says. "The reason the media pick up stories in negative ways is that we help. We say it's embarrassing to us, and mainstream culture senses that we feel a certain way about single parenthood."

"That 72 percent statistic was just picked up without any consideration of that fact that African-Americans have different family structures and [that] multigenerational living is popular in our culture as well as other cultures."

Reality television shows and parenting blogs such as MyBrownBaby.com and beyondbabymamas.com work to dispel misleading narratives about black parenting. A variety of black mothers are featured on Bravo's *The Real Housewives of Atlanta*, and VH1's *T.I. & Tiny: The Family Hustle* portrays a semblance of realistic black parenting models and blended families.

However, most mainstream media images of black motherhood are negative or completely absent. Writing in June 2012 about the release of the movie *What to Expect When You're Expecting* at the *Motherlode: Adventures in Parenting* blog for the *New York Times*, Kimberly Seals Allers noted:

> Because the "pictures in our heads" of black mothers depict them as crack heads, single mothers with deadbeat-dad issues, welfare queens, violent, uneducated or as neck-rolling sassy maids and smart-talking fishwives. . . . We are rarely seen as nurturing mothers or (gasp!) intentional parents with committed husbands, let alone successful women who don trendy shoes, fabulous handbags and have some of the same romantic-comedy-worthy struggles as any other parent or would-be parent.[9]

The media often still cover single black mothers and female-led households as the source of black America's failure to fully gain access to the American Dream, says Brittney Cooper, assistant professor of Women's and Gender Studies and Africana Studies at Rutgers University. Cooper is a regular columnist for *Salon* and the cofounder of the popular Crunk Feminist Collective blog.

Cooper cites coverage of Kelley Williams-Bolar of Akron, Ohio, who in January 2011 was convicted of two felonies and jailed for nine days for using her father's home address to enroll her two daughters in a nearby school district. Eight months later, Governor John R. Kasich reduced the convictions to misdemeanors. Cooper said the case was part of a larger, more common "national narrative that black women are deceiving the system and taking things that don't belong to them."

"The primary media conversation about black families is about the proliferation of female-headed families," Cooper said. "There's a real investment in the nuclear family, the two and a half kids and a dog, which is part of a larger conversation about African-Americans' fitness for the American dream, and it gets remixed every generation."

"We're always talking about the black family and the state of it, even when we use other terms like getting people to go to work, cutting welfare entitlements and so on." This has been true in modern journalism since release in 1965 of *The Negro Family: The Case for National Action*, a U.S. Department of Labor report, also known as the Moynihan Report after its principal author, Daniel Moynihan, then assistant secretary of labor and a future U.S. senator.

The report famously referred to black families as caught in a "tangle of pathology." Damning and bleak, it laid the foundation for decades of mainstream media reporting that would portray African Americans as incapable of being loving, whole parents while largely dismissing societal, economic, and political factors that led to the fracture of the black family.

Denene Millner, author and founder and editor of MyBrownBaby.com, said the absence of healthy, normal examples of black parents in media is part of what made the Shawty Lo program problematic.

"All too often when we're invited into the discussion, it's to talk about pathology," she says. "If you want to talk about teen parenting or how far behind black kids are in education, call a black mom. If we're talking about the hard part of being a working mother, the challenges of breast-feeding or the challenges of balancing a husband and kids, black thought is never included in the conversation. What that leaves is this very stereotypical view of single black moms and single black dads." Shows like *All My Babies' Mamas*, Millner continued, "feed into this stereotype of the black father as a wanton sexual and sexually active black guy who spreads his seed to anyone who will spread her legs and charlatan women who lay around and have babies with guys they think they can juice for their money."

Millner, who worked as an editor and columnist at *Parenting* magazine, said her experience as the magazine's sole black writer provided evidence not of racism in mainstream media but a less malignant state of oblivion.

"I can honestly tell you that the people there were not racist, they were not anti-black people," she says. "They just didn't think about it. It wasn't their reality. They didn't have, as far as I could tell, any black children or any kids with black friends. It wasn't something they thought of. And when they would run stories on black parents they would get negative responses from the readership."

As a result, stories about black nuclear families are rare, with notable exceptions in *Essence* magazine and in the black press and occasionally on reality TV. "Most of my posts had to do with being a black mom," Millner said. "But unfortunately, it wasn't the reality of people who read the site. If you're not open minded or you don't have someone in your general sphere dealing with those issues, you're either not going to care about the issues that the black mother is writing about or you're going to be offended because you don't understand it. That's the beauty of white privilege. You get to ignore someone else's plight and experience. You get to ignore someone else's plight or thoughts on the matter because it's not something you deal with on a regular basis."

Like some of *All My Babies' Mamas* defenders, Cooper, Brown, and Demby make the case that while Shawty Lo may not be a positive example, his story is still a facet of the African American parenting experience that shouldn't be ignored.

"I am concerned about negative representations of black families in the media," Cooper says, "but you can't achieve the thing you want by subtraction. Some negative portrayals exist, but I also think we have to get away from the narrative of positivity and negativity. Other people don't get to define the legitimacy of our family structures."

As for mainstream coverage of black parents, the Obama family has become the latest representation of the black family in America, for better or worse.

In 2013, the *Washington Post* published an article about feminists' reaction to First Lady Michelle Obama's 2008 announcement that she intended to be "mom-in-chief." The article discussed the stir that the highly educated Obama has caused among white and black feminists for downplaying her credentials in order to put being a mother first.

Again, the fictive ideal of the right kind of black mother was at work, Cooper says. "There's a real problem with saying that this is the way that black people should be in a family because we won't talk about economic policy, the school-to-prison pipeline or the prison-industrial complex and how they have kept us from having families in that kind of way."

The Invisible Asian American Electorate and Linsanity

The same kind of missing context that informs journalism about black parenthood and families is often omitted from stories about other people of color and women. When it comes to communities of color and legacy media coverage, contextual narratives about communities are largely disregarded in favor of outsized individual sensationalist stories. One example of this is in the Asian American community, where a more significant story about one of the nation's fastest-growing demographics and its political power has been trumped by individual stories like problematic coverage in response to the success of Asian basketball player Jeremy Lin.

When Election Day arrived in 2012, Asian Americans were largely disregarded, "sending the message that the community is neither significant in size nor an important part of the electorate."[10] There are a number of reasons why Asian Americans were omitted as a group to watch, including the small number of Asian American journalists working in traditional media positions that allow for them to make space for such stories. Many of the stories that we are allowed to see about Asian Americans focus on them as model minorities who excel academically and thrive where most other immigrant populations have failed. In traditional media there is limited discussion about the linguistic and ethnic diversity within Asian American groups or how their growing geographic diversity continues to change the United States.

Mee Moua, president and executive director of the Asian American Justice Center in Washington, D.C., noted that 31 percent of the nation's Asian American population surveyed said they were undecided in the 2012 election. Moua believed that the stealth population in battleground and tipping states could be Asian American voters because of significant growth in places like Nevada and Virginia. But mainstream media, like political parties, largely ignored the story of a growing Asian American electorate and its potential impact. "They don't know how to do outreach to our population," Moua said. "They look at how ethnically and linguistically different we are, and they throw up their hands and say, 'It's too much.'"[11]

Some of this can be attributed to what author Frank Wu calls the Connie Chung syndrome, named after the former CBS News anchor. In his book, *Yellow: Race in America beyond Black and White*, Wu describes a dearth of Asian American male reporters and journalists, particularly in visible roles on television. He writes that the ubiquity of Asian American women on television "suggests another form of racial prejudice fused with gender prejudice. Asian American women are eye candy on the six o'clock news."[12]

Helen Zia, author of *Asian American Dreams: The Emergence of an American People*, said that the virtual invisibility of Asian Americans has been magnified especially by Asian American politicians who rarely discuss their ethnicity. In their speeches at the Republican and Democratic conventions, Zia noted, South Carolina governor Nikki Haley, daughter of Indian immigrants, and California attorney general Kamala D. Harris, who is of African American and South Asian descent, did not discuss ethnicity and journalists did not ask about it.

"I find this particular election cycle to be a step backward," Zia said. "My fellow journalists are really falling down on the job on this. Some 70 percent of Asian Americans come from immigrant families, higher than Latinos that are under 50 percent immigrant. Jobs, housing, discrimination . . . they are all huge issues for Asian Americans."

But Zia regarded the absence of real coverage on Asian Americans as "a carryover from the idea that we're negligible, that we're a small minority, that we're not Americans," Zia said. "Or for many people who see an Asian-American, they assume we're not American, let alone that we have any concerns about the body politic. It's like, 'Who are they? They don't matter. They're not voters.'"

When Asian Americans achieve visibility in mainstream media outlets outside of the model minority stereotype, missteps are bound to surface, as was the case at the beginning of 2012 when Jeremy Lin's popularity made him America's highest-profile Asian American basketball player and the *New York Post* published the banner headline, "Amasian!" That was probably the least offensive of media missteps, which included an editor from ESPN writing an offensive "Chink in the Armor" cutline that appeared online for 35 minutes and led to the firing of its author, Anthony Federico, who had been with the company since 2006. "This had nothing to do with me being cute or punny . . . I am so sorry that I offended people. I am so sorry if I offended Jeremy."[13] There were a few other problematic moments, including the MSG Network's airing of a fortune cookie with Lin's image, referring to "The Knicks' good fortune," which prompted the Asian American Journalists Association to release guidelines to media about appropriate coverage of the basketball star.[14]

In his book, Wu mentions that several publications have deemed Asian Americans the model minority since at least the 1970s, but a consultant in *Advertising Age* went further, declaring Asian Americans "the Donald Trumps of the 1990s" for their collective industriousness.[15] But for decades, traditional media have rarely connected the model minority stereotype to business or political acumen in the Asian American community. In an updated analysis of the political characteristics and power of Asian Americans, Karthick Ramakrishnan, coauthor of the 2012 National Asian American Survey and an associate professor at the University of California, Riverside, polled over 3,000 Asian American adults.

His survey showed that the community was mostly leaning Democratic and could heavily influence congressional races in Illinois, Hawaii, and New York. Ramakrishnan said that while a few outlets covered the release of the survey, "typically the argument has been that there hasn't been enough data about Asian Americans so they don't get covered as much."

SFGate.com, the website published by the *San Francisco Chronicle*, ran a story online but not in print, he said, which was surprising in a city with a high concentration of Asian Americans and an Asian American mayor.

"The national story is that the numbers of Asian Americans are not as large as other ethnicities, but in various states, Asian Americans are becoming demographically more important," he added. When media fail to cover the Asian American community, specifically during election years, editors and reporters complain that a lack of data or limited available research is to blame. But in 2012, there were three major surveys of Asian American voters, making the lack of data argument moot.

Ramakrishnan said in a phone interview that in the past, because the Asian American community wasn't that active, journalists and other institutions didn't pay much attention to them. "But now there's more engagement, and there's still a significant lag both in news coverage and by outreach by political campaigns. It's something that states need to grapple with because Asian Americans are the fastest growing racial group in the country, and it's important to make an investment from the journalism side or from the campaign side in these communities."

The Missing Stories of Native American Communities

There is likely no racial or ethnic demographic that is as ignored in traditional media as Native Americans. Perhaps because Native Americans are a smaller percentage of the U.S. population than other ethnicities at 1.2 percent as of 2013, they are far less visible than other people of color in legacy media narratives and largely omitted from most traditional mass media unless the narrative centers on tragedy or dysfunction on reservations.

Mary Hudetz, who was president of the Native American Journalists Association in 2014, worked for years as an editor and reporter for the Associated Press before she became editor of the Phoenix, Arizona-based *Native Peoples* magazine. Hudetz, who is a member of the Crow tribe, said in a 2012 phone interview that the lack of Native American reporters in traditional media fueled a widespread misconception that reservations are very dangerous places, "like it's lawless land and everyone's a victim. That comes from the fact that there are huge gaps in the justice system that are supposed to protect Native Americans living on reservations. There are triumphs and tragedies on reservations, but somehow only the tragedies come out."

Again, lack of context has impaired the ability of traditional media to tell important community stories. Ways to improve coverage of Native Americans include news organization investment in stories like the impact of Affordable Care Act implementation on American Indians and Alaska

Natives, and more accountability reporting to review data and documents related to Indian services. Stories that receive greater coverage like whether the name of the Washington Redskins football franchise is racist overshadow more important stories that impact American Indians on and off reservations including an epidemic of youth suicide or disproportionate foster care placements of Indian children with non-Indian families, which is made increasingly possible with the uneven application of the Indian Child Welfare Act.

But generally, "Mainstream media doesn't really hold tribal governments accountable, either," Hudetz said. "There's a lot of handling them with kid gloves when it comes to covering the reservations. When it comes to local newspapers and TV, it's hard to break through. The open government laws of the state don't apply because the tribe is its own sovereign government." Without the ability to utilize Freedom of Information Act laws on reservations, media organizations that are already short-staffed and not particularly invested in delivering the kind of resources in time and reporting to Native American issues simply ignore the Native American community.

As a result, what happens in Indian Country is what has happened in communities of color all over the world: In the absence of a larger media ecosystem that includes them and stories of importance to them, they make their own. Hudetz said that a lot of tribal newspapers are dedicated to covering reservations and other large Native American communities. But that is of little comfort to communities and tribes who don't have their own newspapers. "In those cases, people have no idea how their money is being used, or what type of resources are available to them. So I can only imagine that there might be a misuse of funds, as is the case in most (abuses) of power," Hudetz said.

When Hudetz worked at the Associated Press bureau in Phoenix, she noted that there was just one other Native American journalist on staff—and even that low number was an exception to the rule. Echoing the sentiment of many generations of journalists of color, she said, "I really believe having more Natives in news would improve coverage. Yes, we tell the hard stories, about high suicide rates and a lack of law enforcement to deal with crime. But we don't just use the broad brush on those stories. We try to show the full picture of what the reservation is because we know what that is like," Hudetz said. That is preferable for Native Americans and other communities of color, of course, to have steady representation rather than reporters who parachute in during tragedy or mayhem and parachute out, which is the only way that traditional media typically cover Native Americans.

Mark Trahant, a member of Idaho's Shoshone-Bannock Tribe and Atwood Journalism Chair at the University of Alaska Anchorage for 2013 and 2014, said in a 2012 interview that he doesn't judge the media "in the singular." He pointed to a great story on oil production on the Blackfeet reservation by the *New York Times*, but also said that network television often misses stories. "For the most part, Native American stories are nonexistent, and when they are, they're usually stereotypical—poverty in Pine Ridge or extreme wealth from gambling," Trahant said. "When networks parachute in, they go to South Dakota and the Navajo nation. Locally, the institutions that cover Indian country focus on the crisis of the moment rather than the big picture. What really makes the Native American story complicated is that it's not just one about race, but one of citizenship, because you're involving nations within our nation. Very few people are taught in school how tribal education fits into city, state federal government, and so the task is left up to the media to provide that education. Yet tribal governments were here first."

Tristan Ahtone, in a 2013 *Columbia Journalism Review* article, put it simply when he said that better coverage has been eluding journalists in Indian Country because reporters lack depth and interest on "getting to know communities on a level deeper than can be found through statistics. Crime, casinos, and cultural revitalization are all important topics, but reporters could be digging deeper. Spend time with the communities you want to report on. Native communities are traditionally closed off to outsiders, and in gaining a community's trust, you'll be able to get to stories that are truly underreported and important to the people you cover."[16]

The Coverage of Race as an Event

Because, as John Hope Franklin noted as quoted in the book, *Yellow*, by Frank Wu, "this country cut its eye teeth on racism in the black/white sphere," there is frequently a disconnect between news that unfolds within the African Diaspora and the legacy media outlets that cover it. This is true for everything from cultural and entertainment stories to national tragedies. Recent examples include the 2014 Best Picture win at the Academy Awards for *12 Years a Slave*, the problematic framing of mental illness as a crime and clear differences in the way that American tragedies like Hurricane Katrina and Superstorm Sandy were covered in traditional media.

Any movie about slavery in the modern era that received the kind of ongoing coverage and accolades awarded *12 Years a Slave* was bound to underscore the limited purview of the few African American copyeditors, editors, and publishers that remain at print newspapers. It was enough of a surprise for Ellen DeGeneres, the 2014 host of the Academy Awards, to call the Oscars out on their general lack of diversity by saying that Sunday would either end with the movie winning Best Picture or "You're all racists." Intentional or not, a few news headlines missed the mark trying to even write about the Oscars side-stepping any suggestions of their racism. Richard Prince, a media columnist at the Maynard Institute for Journalism Education, noted the misfires in reporting the slavery movie's wins in headlines from California to Illinois: "*The Daily Breeze* of Torrance, Calif., and a sister paper, the Los Angeles *Daily News*, bannered, 'Slave' becomes master.' The *News-Gazette* in Central Illinois headlined '12 Years a Slave Escapes With Top Oscar' on Page A-9."[17]

Almost a decade before, the last time the Oscars had the same kind of audience they had in 2014, the traditional media were struggling with how to cover communities of color as they had been since the 1990s. Newkirk notes in *Within the Veil* that there were several attempts in the 1990s by "mainstream news organizations to counter the white-centered thrust of the news media. One of the most extraordinary undertakings was a seven-month series in 1993 by the *Times-Picayune* in New Orleans, 'Together Apart: The Myth of Race,' which brazenly tackled racism in society and in the news media."[18]

From the impact of the Rodney King verdict and subsequent violence that impacted Asian Americans and African Americans in Los Angeles to the Crown Heights riots around the same time, there was never a full or ongoing discussion of the way that communities of color live their day-to-day lives. Episodic coverage took the form of high-profile series or in-depth investigative pieces into the aughts. In 2000, the *New York Times*, widely recognized as the nation's paper of record, ran a yearlong series called "How Race Is Lived in America" that was compiled as part of an eponymous book published two years later. While the series was heralded and interesting, part of the problem with how communities of color have been covered in mainstream circles has been that people of color have been captured on television, on radio, and in print media as marginal to normal stories.

Media critic Eric Deggans put it this way in a 2013 *Columbia Journalism Review* article:

> Race is covered as an event rather than an ongoing concern. We hear regularly about the Dow Jones Average, the activities of City Hall, the latest

action by Congress. But we don't often hear about race, outside of special stories—developed over weeks, months, sometimes years—that drop into the news mix, have a brief impact, and then are gone. Small wonder, then, it is so hard to talk about race in a measured way outside of media. We are so used to talking about race in crisis, any mention of the issue in a news story leads to assumptions that there must be a crisis at hand.[19]

The result is that actual crises that emerge outside of convenient news cycles are often neglected. Reporting about minority mental health, especially in the African American community, is one example of how traditional media fail communities of color. From Metta World Peace to Rudy Eugene, African Americans confronting mental health challenges are often portrayed as isolated examples of crazy or deranged people rather than members of a marginalized community suffering from a physical disease. Though July has been designated National Minority Mental Health Awareness Month since 2008 in honor of Bebe Moore Campbell, an acclaimed author and mental health advocate, there is usually no mention of it beyond the black blogosphere and social networking events.

The dismal state of black mental health treatment and awareness is generally not covered by mainstream print, online, and broadcast media outside of tragedies that resonate far beyond the black community. Journalists, writers, and experts cite many reasons why the mainstream media don't cover African American mental health responsibly or consistently. Among them are racism, lack of context about how African Americans interact with the health care system, and stigmas that remain entrenched in the black community which discourages those who struggle with depression, schizophrenia, or other mental health problems from discussing them.[20]

"Mental health in general has been a sub-beat in the mainstream media," said journalist Amy Alexander, coauthor with Dr. Alvin F. Poussaint of the 2001 book, *Lay My Burden Down: Suicide and the Mental Health Crisis among African-Americans*. Rarely do mainstream media outlets have the luxury of assigning a reporter to cover only mental health since most are now responsible for several beats simultaneously. A prominent exception was Clifford J. Levy, who won the 2003 Pulitzer Prize for investigative reporting and a George Polk Award for a three-part series exposing sometimes fatal neglect of the mentally ill in privately run adult homes regulated by New York State.

Alexander said, "It used to be that no one would write about mental health, and the way it would be covered would be piecemeal in the context of a report coming out from the Centers for Disease Control [and Prevention] or the National Institutes of Health. Or you would see a story pop up around a horrific event." Since Alexander's and Poussaint's book was published, little has changed. The bizarre case of Rudy Eugene, 31, an African American in Miami who chewed off a homeless man's face in May 2012 before being shot to death, made "bath salts" a nationwide buzz phrase.

Eugene took his clothes off along the MacArthur Causeway from Miami Beach before attacking Ronald Poppo, 65, in what the *Miami Herald* called a "ghoulish, drawn-out assault in plain view on a city sidewalk captured by a *Miami Herald* security camera. Eugene was shot by a police officer who found him chewing chunks off Poppo's face." The head of the Miami police union publicly speculated that "bath salts," synthetic stimulants believed to be the cause of psychotic episodes elsewhere around the country, prompted Eugene's actions. But, according to the Miami-Dade Medical Examiner's office, only marijuana was found in his system.

More likely, Kristen Gwynne wrote for the online magazine *AlterNet*, is that Eugene had a history of mental illness. "But pinning a tragedy to a drug scare is easier (and perhaps more lucrative) than explaining a non-existent safety net for the mentally ill," she wrote. "Bath salts, the mainstream media naively believes, can be banned and eradicated. Treating mental illness is a far more complicated story."

Other than sensationalized portraits of individuals, the only consistent coverage of mental illness in the black community focuses on the psychological fallout of depression and other mental health issues facing black celebrities.

These portrayals are opportunities for mainstream media to explore larger questions about the escalating suicide rate among black men, the entrenched stigma of appearing weak and vulnerable in the black community by seeking help, and the dearth of African American mental health professionals. Instead, stories focus on the unique narrative surrounding individual celebrities and not the impact of mental health problems on a broader community.

When *Soul Train* creator Don Cornelius died from a self-inflicted gunshot wound in February 2012 at age 75, far more media attention was given to his legacy than his mental state. Instead, only his stoicism was noted in a *New York Times* obituary. During divorce proceedings in 2009, James C. McKinley, Jr., wrote, Cornelius "mentioned having 'significant health problems' but did not elaborate." Another friend of Cornelius simply described him as being "very private."

When Metta World Peace, a Los Angeles Lakers player formerly known as Ron Artest, has spoken honestly and publicly about his therapy for mental health issues, he has been mocked by reporters. In September 2010, a year before Artest changed his name, *Los Angeles Times* columnist Bill Plaschke referred to him as "the looniest Laker" even as Artest was addressing middle schoolers, urging them to communicate to health care professionals what ails them psychologically.

Journalist and author Ellis Cose said these examples explore "celebrities much more so than the black community." Neither the Cornelius obituary nor Plaschke's column, for the most part, was linked explicitly to race. Poussaint, a professor of psychiatry at Harvard Medical School, did suggest that Cornelius's death might launch a conversation about suicide prevention among blacks. "But his take was the exception rather than the rule," Cose wrote in an e-mail.

Even when the topic is more about black celebrity than race, mental illness, particularly in famous athletes, is viewed as "evidence of a criminal character," said David J. Leonard, author of *After Artest: The NBA and the Assault on Blackness.* "Media go immediately to focusing on the purported pathologies of the players themselves and don't want to see what the broader context is," Leonard says. "The history of race and mental health is a history of racism and the white medical establishment demonizing and criminalizing the black community through writing about their 'abnormal personalities' and being 'crazy.'"

"That history plays out in mainstream media coverage, but it also affects public discussions about mental health because it has so often been used to justify exclusion, segregation and inequality" in mental health treatment for African Americans, he said. A recent example of how this is reflected in traditional media arrived days before Christmas in December 2014, when Ismaaiyl Brinsley shot his estranged girlfriend Shaneka Thompson in Maryland before traveling to New York City to shoot two New York Police Department officers.

The *New York Times* story about Brinsley, with the headline, "New York Officers' Killer, Adrift and Ill, Had a Plan," quoted from Brinsley's Instagram account saying he wrote: "I'm Putting Wings On Pigs Today They Take 1 Of Ours. . . Let's Take 2 of Theirs #ShootThePolice," shortly after noting that Brinsley had a history of mental problems and that his family had nothing good to say about the man with a history of violence.[21] Some stories, like the one published by *USA Today,* "Social Media Posts Threatened 'Pigs,'" completely omitted Brinsley's history of mental health issues.

Over the years, there have been other challenges to less problematic coverage of communities of color, including episodic reporting on immigration and immigration reform, which reached a fever pitch during the summer of 2014 around the issue of thousands of unaccompanied minors traveling to the United States largely from Central America. In Hispanic and Asian American communities, there are a host of other issues that include language barriers between journalists and sources as well as the cultural hurdles that exist for pitching or supporting coverage in these communities to editors and producers who have virtually no experience with them.

Much of the experiences of journalists with regards to communities of color were explored two decades, or a generation, after the diversity gains of the late 1960s and early 1970s in the 1990s. Then, more than any other time in history, women and people of color appeared to be close to achieving parity in both representation and coverage in American newsrooms. It would be the closest people of color would come to such an achievement in media in history, even if it wouldn't last very long.

Chapter 4

Examples of Racism and Sexism in Legacy Media

Before the integration of women and people of color into legacy media, it was a given that coverage of minorities reflected old stereotypes and biases, and that women were portrayed according to the socially acceptable gender roles assigned to them. But the presumed goal of media integration was to establish a system of expertise whereby women and people of color became ambassadors of worlds few white men were willing or able to authentically enter. To live up to the potential outlined by the Kerner Report, racial integration was supposed to be a panacea for newsrooms that continued failing at capturing the true scope of diversity in America. The gains of affirmative action and feminism in the 1970s and 1980s were intended to also give women permanent, unfettered access to journalistic spaces, such as sports, previously considered the exclusive province of men. But it turned out that integration alone as a solution to failing to reconcile racial, gender, and class fault lines in coverage would not be sufficient.

While there were superficial efforts at true integration in social and economic spheres, media segregation would remain a stubborn constant. There is never one reason alone for the failure of systems to foster true change, but in the case of legacy media, white male ownership economically invested in perpetuating male and white supremacist narratives has consistently stood in the way of real progress. Over time, in spite of vows, programs, and coalitions designed to improve the problem of diversity, what has been most consistent has been a retrenchment of old ideas about people of color and women, one that has seeped out in language, tone, and sometimes omission on broadcast television, on the radio, and in print media.

One pointed example of traditional media's overarching discomfort or inability to confront or assess racism has become clear with the election of a black president, which in American media, at least, seemed to highlight the many ways white Americans had not reconciled the success of some people of color with the declining economic and political influence of a growing number of whites, or the ways in which insisting on a post-racial narrative only kept an authentic, ongoing conversation about race from healing the nation of racial scars it has borne since slavery. Because racism and sexism are pervasive aspects of American culture, no one text could incorporate every single example as reflected in mainstream media; however, this chapter is an attempt to look at a few major examples.

Anita Hill, Clarence Thomas, and O. J. Simpson

In 2014, I was thrilled to take myself to see law professor Anita Hill's documentary, *Anita: Speaking Truth to Power*. It tells a story that was unfolding worlds away from my own in 1989 and 1990, but with more context than I was able to process as a little girl. I was 11 going on 12 at the time, moving around a lot and without consistent access to a television. What I knew of Anita Hill was only the image of a composed, soft-spoken black woman testifying in front of a panel of angry-looking white men and I had never seen that before. She was telling them that Clarence Thomas had sexually harassed her—another first—and regardless of the veracity of her claims, they were viewed as an irritant, which was, unfortunately, not a first.

Black women are so often presumed to be sexual provocateurs in media portrayals that I did not realize until Anita Hill that it was possible to say no to any man who wanted to say or do lewd things to a woman without her permission. Patricia Hill Collins in her 2004 book, *Black Sexual Politics: African Americans, Gender and the New Racism*, wrote: "The institutionalized rape of enslaved black women spawned the controlling image of the jezebel or sexually wanton black woman. This representation redefined black women's bodies as sites of wild, unrestrained sexuality that could be tamed but never completely subdued."[1] This was a context that I knew and recognized from the real world, one that was oddly familiar, and one that was in deep contrast to the reserved, modest-looking Hill on television.

But even though Thomas evoked the language of a "high-tech lynching," earning the sympathy of men who perhaps felt threatened by the recent gains of women through affirmative action, the way he pivoted to become a victim instead of a potential perpetrator was made all the more fascinating by the fact that it was the first time in popular culture that a powerful black man and woman were pitted against one another in such a public way.

The Anita Hill film begins in present day, with a widely publicized voice message from Clarence Thomas's wife, Virginia Thomas, playing for the audience. Thomas is calling for Anita Hill to apologize for what she did. What Anita Hill had done was submit a confidential statement to the Senate Judiciary Committee saying that Thomas had sexually harassed her. Investigations into its earlier findings were "inconclusive" but at the urging of other people, Hill would go on to testify publicly after her statement was leaked to the media.

What followed was a media circus. Even though Clarence Thomas is black and blackness is assumed to align with Democratic or left-leaning politics, his conservative views made him a political enemy in the broader black community. That didn't mean that he couldn't exploit stereotypes that shaped the gaze of a largely white audience by famously referring to Hill's testimony as a "high-tech lynching" in the midst of proceedings *60 Minutes* reporter Steve Kroft described as "more titillating than the soap operas."[2] Hill was cast by Thomas and by others as a sinister, calculating woman who tried to destroy Thomas. This is despite the fact that there were witnesses and credible mentors who could corroborate her accusations.

The documentary audience is reminded of the stark contrast between Anita Hill and the congressmen who sought to discredit her while also confirming George H. W. Bush's pick for the Supreme Court. Coverage of Anita Hill's testimony, however, set precedent for media coverage in that it provided America's first public look at the intersection of race, gender, and political power. Here was a humble-looking black woman, featured in televised reports as though she were totally alone. In her face, there was no sign of conflict or deception, just the open-faced wonder that comes with sitting before a line of white men firing hostile questions at her. In the film, we see the full back story, which includes her large family lending their support in Oklahoma, the white feminist lawyers who came to her aid and spoke out in support of her to news reporters, and the sharp contrast of what happens when a powerful black woman tells her story versus a corporate media behemoth.

But traditional media coverage at the intersection of race and gender in the criminal justice system has generally been a reflection of outdated stereotypes. Some of it has to do with giving audiences what they think they want, which is content consistent with what they have always consumed. Some of it has had to do with a lack of diversity in correspondents, editors, and producers. The latter is likely more important, since developing and disseminating narratives for public consumption about women and people of color that also offer balanced portrayals are impossible without creators who know these groups intimately and are free from bias.

The consistently menacing tone of coverage of the murder trial involving O. J. Simpson is a perfect example of what happens in the absence of that balance. The Simpson murder trial became one of America's most widely publicized criminal trials and certainly the most popular trial in the pre-reality TV era.

In June 1994, Nicole Brown, Simpson's ex-wife, and her friend Ronald Goldman were found stabbed to death. The story emerged on the traditional media radar with a dramatic made-for-the-movies low-speed pursuit with O. J. Simpson giving chase in his famous 1993 Ford Bronco, which *Vanity Fair* as recently as 2014 described as "white as innocence, as a lie."[3]

Not unlike the stories that preceded it, media coverage of Simpson's murder trial revived long-standing American cultural tropes about black manhood while also managing to circumvent some. Simpson was a well-known athlete who'd grown up in a tough San Francisco neighborhood. He was a black man from humble beginnings who went on to become great. African American men of prominence who marry interracially are often portrayed as attempting to secure their status as men by marrying outside of the race; but whatever Simpson's intentions, the history of black men being romantically involved with white women in America is a fraught one.

The construction of aggressive, libidinous black men in ruthless pursuit of white women has been the justification for mass murder and lynchings, the destruction of towns and high-profile deaths like that of Emmett Till, who was murdered for reportedly flirting openly with a white woman. So the notion that O. J. Simpson had not only married a white woman but had possibly killed her and a white man certainly played into media coverage of the trial. Peter Arnella, UCLA law professor, told *Frontline*, "In the O.J. Simpson case, (the media) simply reflected back onto the white majority what the white majority already believed. Public opinion polls made it quite clear that most white Americans believed Simpson was obviously guilty before the trial ever started. Most white Americans feared that the defense would . . . use racism to get a black jury . . . to acquit an obviously guilty defendant. That was the frame of public discourse before the trial ever started. Everything was fit into that frame in terms of how the media covered the trial."[4]

In the African American press, professor Charles Ogletree said, Simpson was portrayed differently because black journalists "understood from all too many experiences African Americans [being] wrongfully convicted . . . they understood that sometimes evidence can be tainted and they understood that all too often African-American men in particular have been convicted. So we had two different versions of this trial, one through the lens of the Afro-American press and one through the lens of the white press."[5]

Among the most publicized examples of racist legacy media coverage was a June 1994 photoshopped *Time* magazine cover featuring O. J. Simpson's darkened mug shot, associating darker skin with a more menacing Simpson. After widespread criticism, then-managing editor James R. Gaines apologized and said that "no racial implication was intended."[6]

David Margolick, a staff reporter who covered the Simpson trial for the *New York Times*, told PBS that he could only remember two black correspondents reporting on the trial.

> The overwhelming majority of people covering the trial were white . . . we understood that race was an important issue, [but] I guess that we didn't think about the profundity and the depth of that issue, or we underestimated it. I mean, the racial dimension of the case was readily apparent. It was in our faces. So there was no way of ignoring it, but I think white Americans are naive about racial matters. And I think that we just don't understand how fundamental an issue this was, and our reaction to the verdict was a prime example of that.[7]

The *Washington Post*, in a 20-year anniversary piece on how Simpson's trial changed the media landscape, noted: "The case, and in particular, the not-guilty verdict, also fanned leftover racial tension from the 1991 police beating of Rodney King, which triggered race riots in Los Angeles. Race had been a key topic during the trial—a black defendant, two white victims. . . . Its conclusion quieted little of the talk that America remained divided; opinions on the case and verdict traveled racial lines, and two decades later, they often still do."[8]

Urban Unrest, Riots, Race, and Beyond

Given that thoughtful analysis of how race impacts media was born of the riots, protests, and urban unrest in predominantly black communities during the mid-to-late 1960s, there is some irony to the fact that traditional media have not evolved very much in how they fail to contextualize these events in their coverage. The same news angles reporters relied upon to report on urban unrest nearly 50 years ago persist, decade after decade, in coverage of melees, protests, marches, and riots from coast to coast. Passive language about racism has evolved somewhat from previous incarnations—"racially charged" became "racially tinged,"—but the meaning remains less than damning.

Legacy media templates for explosive racial tension that results in the death of teenagers reach far back to the birth of the press. A significant moment that underscored racial bias in traditional media emerged in 1955, after Chicago native Emmett Till was kidnapped and brutally murdered in Money, Mississippi, for having flirted with a white woman at a local store. His death and the trial of the men who murdered him were only initially covered by two black publications, even though Till's death galvanized the civil rights movement.

But modern examples include descriptions of white residents in Bensonhurst Brooklyn in reaction to the death of Yusuf Hawkins, a 16-year-old black teenager who ventured with his three friends into a predominantly Italian and conservative part of Brooklyn in August 1989. Angry youths jumped the boys, and Hawkins was shot to death. The initial *Times* report of Hawkins's death described Bensonhurst in idyllic language, even after noting that 10 to 30 white youths were involved in the incident that led to Hawkins' death. In a story that echoes that of Till, the story focuses on the neighborhood assessment of what happened—the youths who killed Hawkins thought he was dating a white neighborhood girl. So, the motive was not racism, they argued, but a lover's jealous revenge.[9]

The *New York Times*, in retrospect, described the unrest that followed this way: "The tragedy, racially polarized from the start, exploded into the national consciousness when 300 black demonstrators who marched through the neighborhood three days after Mr. Hawkins's death were confronted by jeering whites who chanted 'Niggers go home,' screamed obscenities and held up watermelons as a gesture of ridicule."[10]

The racial tension from Bensonhurst spilled over to other parts of Brooklyn and even the country. Four white Los Angeles Police Department officers were videotaped beating Rodney King, who is African American, more than 50 times with batons in March 1991. This was just a few months before the seven-year-old son of Guyanese immigrants, Gavin Cato, was struck and killed by a car in a motorcade carrying a rabbi thousands of miles away on the East Coast, touching off the three-day Crown Heights riots, which would become an American cultural touchstone.[11] Even more than a decade later, the *New York Times* summarized the events this way: "Angry residents rampaged through the streets, beating Hasidic Jews they encountered, stabbing and killing one, Yankel Rosenbaum."[12]

The Crown Heights riots were portrayed as a reflection of the unfortunate convergence of unsettled black residents in Brooklyn and their uneasy Hasidic neighbors. The traditional media depiction of the riots that followed the trial of the Los Angeles Police Department officers who beat Rodney King had quite a different tone. In April 1992, the officers were acquitted, touching off five days of rioting that left 50 people dead and more than 2,000 residents injured. The estimated cost of damages to the city was more than $1 billion.[13]

In her May 1994 paper on how television news framed coverage of the Los Angeles riots, journalism professor Erna Smith describes how television news emphasized white fear in broadcasts and downplayed important details, including the fact that Latinos were more than half of the thousands of residents arrested during the rioting. On the *CBS Evening News*, for example, Smith noted in one newscast that Dan Rather highlighted that the violence in Los Angeles was centered on communities of color, but "the fear is haunting other communities and people." One news reporter said that "fear and loathing among whites is intensifying here . . . what scares the daylights out of whites is the image of bands of marauding black youths."[14]

Smith found that the media then were more comfortable describing the riots as a black-against-whites war and that media more frequently wrote about racial minorities through a lens that viewed America through a black and white lens that excluded other ethnicities. But when Latinos, Asian Americans, and Native Americans were included in coverage, media still relied on stereotypes. Despite the fact that Latinos were the majority of people arrested and that they then made up the majority of the city's minorities, the story of the Los Angeles riots on television remained focused on African Americans as perpetrators and agitators of crime.

The minority press was less likely than mainstream media to assign blame to individuals and to inflame existing interracial tensions in Los Angeles.[15] And the minority press would be consistently objective again when it came to other examples of racial profiling—usually involving the convergence of race, gender, and the criminal justice system.

Race, Gender, and Trial by Press

There are few narratives in American society that highlight ongoing racial and gender bias in the media in the same way as stories that evoke old stereotypes, particularly when it comes to matters involving sexual assault or harassment. The most infamous case of traditional media racism, and perhaps one of the most damaging to the lives of the men who were wrongly accused, was the case of the Central Park Jogger.

On April 20, 1989, Trisha Meili, a 28-year-old white woman who worked as an investment banker, was found raped and brutally beaten in Central Park. Police gathered up the perfect suspects: Black and Latino males between the ages of 14 and 15 from Harlem. The press referred to them as evil beasts, a "wolf pack" that had been "wilding"—a term used to describe out-of-control urban youth.[16] The front page of the *New York Daily News* on April 21, 1989, read: "Wolf Pack's Prey: Female jogger near death after savage attack by roving gang" under the bold banner "Central Park Horror."

New York City was known as a site of turmoil targeted at black and Latino young men in the 1980s, before I was aware of the power of the press as my mother and I settled into the city by way of Philadelphia. Stories that featured young men as lawless marauders were a mainstay in coverage, despite the one-sided characterization of these young men as ruthless lawbreakers in a media that have always purported to be most concerned with matters of fairness.

Natalie P. Byfield, author of the book *Savage Portrayals: Race, Media and the Central Park Jogger Story*, worked at the *New York Daily News* when the story began and would continue to write about the case of the accused young men for decades to come. She describes in her book knowing from the first day of the story that it would be different from the others she covered and understanding the historical context in which the story fell. "The incident seemed to galvanize the media and the public because the teens charged with raping Meili—a white woman—were black and Latino. Even in 1989, when the civil rights gains since 1965 were supposed to have erased racial hierarchies and overt discrimination, the incident revived fears of black men preying on white women and engaging in random acts of violence," Byfield writes.[17]

She added that she felt the "sting and the heat of racism" as she covered the story, noting how the intersection of gender, race, and class defined her reporting process. The coverage, Byfield writes, "likely contributed to changes in the way we address juvenile justice, with profound consequences for the life outcomes of juveniles of color."[18]

Not until a 2013 documentary by Ken Burns, *The Central Park Five*, did the five men accused and tried in traditional media and then convicted to prison for the crime have their stories told in a fair and balanced way. The documentary explains how their convictions were vacated in 2002 after another prisoner confessed to the crime. By then, each of them had already spent the majority of their young lives in prison. It mattered little that they lost the most promising years of their lives—the presses and the film kept right on rolling. The Central Park Five did, however, reportedly reach a settlement in 2014 after filing civil lawsuits against the city of New York.

In a more recent twist involving the stereotype of a menacing, hyper-sexual black man, 2014 also saw multiple sexual assault allegations lodged against comedian Bill Cosby. Cosby has for decades been, arguably, America's most asexual black comedian, famous for touting respectability politics to America's black underclass after establishing himself as an authority on representations of the black family through *The Cosby Show*. Numerous women, from Janice Dickinson to Beverly Johnson, came forward in 2014 detailing similar stories in which they claimed that Cosby drugged and sexually assaulted them. Cosby and his lawyers repeatedly denounced accusers, but traditional media continued to publish and disseminate the stories. When Cosby broke his silence, he reportedly said, "I only expect the black media to uphold the standards of excellence in journalism, and when you do that, you have to go in with a neutral mind."[19]

What was hardly mentioned by Cosby or anyone else was the collateral damage that came from the expectation that black press and black reporters would have a different standard for reporting than others. Mark Whitaker, a former journalist who had worked at *Newsweek* and CNN, wrote a biography of Cosby that was mostly written before the comedian eventually granted Whitaker permission and access he needed to tell Cosby's story. When I interviewed Whitaker ahead of the biography's publication in the fall of 2014, neither one of us could have anticipated the media maelstrom that would culminate in Netflix canceling a Cosby series, the cancellation of Cosby's appearance on *The Queen Latifah Show* and Cosby's stubborn refusal to answer questions about the decades-old allegations on National Public Radio and with the Associated Press. Whitaker affirmed then that he only wrote things in the final version of the biography that he could independently verify; but later on, Whitaker took heat from journalists for failing to make mention of the sexual assault allegations.

The veracity of the women's stories seemed implied in part because of Cosby's silence; but in the subtext of each story published in traditional media was the presumption of Cosby's guilt. Whether or not his guilt or innocence could be proven seemed to be beside the point; and the treasured objectivity that tends to be touted by editors was notably absent. Editors and producers were able to make the most out of the long-standing and never-dispelled archetype of black men as sexual predators who prey particularly on white women through spreading the stories that could not be verified through traditional journalistic means.

It was a standard practice in newsrooms where I worked for reporters to carefully write about sexual assault: Reporters needed legal documentation and at least an attempt to get the story of the accused before newspapers could publish anything. Libel and defamation were a constant concern for newspapers, in particular, and several organizations I have written for have been sued even after taking such precautions. But one of the compelling differences between how things once were and the media ecosystem of today is that print has to compete with the Internet, which means the rules of reporting—careful, vetted reporting—are constantly being rewritten.

Black Men on the "Down Low"

There was a foreshadowing of this shift in accountability journalism and careful vetting of facts in traditional media coverage related to black sexuality in the early 2000s with a fresh angle on the few HIV/AIDS stories that were published and aired in mainstream journalism. Late in 2003, the Centers for Disease Control and Prevention (CDC) released a study showing that black women accounted for 72 percent of all new HIV cases, and that they were most likely to contract the disease from heterosexual men. But additional data collected by the CDC also found that a "significant number" of black men who sleep with men identify as heterosexual, and that black women at risk "may not be aware of their male partners' possible risks for HIV infection such as . . . bisexuality." This was long before Men Who Sleep with Men, or MSMs, were considered a group that could exist along a sexuality spectrum that didn't require an orienting label.

But the persistent tropes that characterize how black male sexuality is framed in traditional media—as predatory, sinister, and cloaked in malevolent deviance—became the only way journalists seemed able or willing to talk about the alarming prevalence of HIV/AIDS in the black community. It seemed easier to report a supposedly new trend of black men hiding their homosexual encounters from unsuspecting wives and girlfriends instead of exploring systemic, social, and structural solutions to ending health disparities in diagnoses and treatment.

The use of the term "down low" emerged around 1991 when E. Lynn Harris published *Invisible Life*, a novel about a man on the DL who infects his girlfriend with HIV. Years later, a smattering of articles and talk show episodes on the topic appeared, including a lengthy 2003 *New York Times* magazine profile of the flourishing DL scene in Columbus, Ohio. It was in 2004, though, that mainstream forums from *Oprah* to *Essence* to the *Advocate* took on the topic in earnest; the subject even made it onto an episode of *Law & Order*. As a hot topic, the DL was tailor-made: Widespread publicizing of alarming disease statistics like the CDC's that all but confirmed DL prevalence as the number-one reason black women contract AIDS, coupled with the timely emergence of a media-savvy DL poster boy and a generous sprinkling of Oprah's magic turned the down low into an outright phenomenon.

In April 2004, a convenient few months after the CDC's bombshell, Chicago native J. L. King released his first-person account of living on the DL. *On the Down Low: A Journey into the Lives of "Straight" Black Men Who Sleep with Men* not only positioned King—who for years had been an anonymous source on the DL lifestyle for mainstream media—as a bona fide expert, but it also inspired a full-blown media exploration of the trend. The book centers on King's jousts with men while he was married, and is peppered with CDC statistics and a dash of assertions that are not exactly verifiable like "Women involved with DL men are being infected with HIV because these men do not believe in wearing condoms and they don't know their HIV status." King also details how both his relationship with God and his concern for the type of man his daughter would marry led him to write the book, and then launches into flashback tales about sleeping with a married man from his church and hooking up with a male preacher.

King's tale of well-orchestrated deception, which quickly hit the bestseller list, was generally treated as a self-help book—and accepted as gospel, despite the lack of statistical information to back up his pronouncements about seemingly straight black men. It seems highly unlikely that a similar story about white men would gain the same kind of attention and acceptance without some hard data. When, in April 2004, the Queen of Talk herself tried to get some concrete answers from King, he dodged even her. Discussing the "secret fraternity" of men who sleep with men, Oprah asked, "How big is this fraternity?"

KING: This invisible population, if you just look at the numbers, if you look at 68 percent of all new cases, I'm even surprised sometimes when I meet a DL brother. It blows me away when a brother comes up to me or I find out that he's on the DL. We're like, "How-you're on the DL, too?"

WINFREY: Well, how does one know who is and who isn't?
KING: We do it by the—we do it by the eyes.
WINFREY: You do it by the eyes.
KING: We do it by the eyes. You know, I wrote a chapter about
                the signs.
WINFREY: Yes, you did. Yeah.

Though data from the *American Journal of Public Health*, among others, suggests that men of all ethnicities engage in DL sex, black men are considered the demographic most likely to live life on the down low. Because black men have been more marginalized in the economic, educational, and social spheres than other men, researchers say, they tend to be more hesitant to surrender what they may consider a crucial and defining element of their masculinity—heterosexual sex—by defining themselves as bisexual or homosexual. This behavior is nothing new, of course, but with the advent of HIV/AIDS it's taken on a different meaning.

In the 1980s, as inner-city black neighborhoods were saturated with crack cocaine and President Ronald Reagan responded with a war on drugs, millions of young black men were sent to jail. It is suspected that, while serving harsh sentences, some men participated, willingly or not, in the don't-ask-don't-tell, sex-as-power-brokering culture of the prison-industrial complex. Since condoms aren't exactly widely circulated in penitentiaries, it makes sense that at least some of the ubiquity of both DL behavior and HIV infection originated behind bars. Other significant contributing factors are the rampant and largely accepted homophobia in the black community, the overwhelming silence of most black churches around HIV and sexuality, and widespread misinformation about HIV.

But rather than use the troubling CDC statistics and memoirs like King's as a chance to open up a potentially painful yet necessary dialogue about race, sexuality, and behavior, legacy media, as usual, seized upon the most sensationalistic aspects of the issue. The news stories that erupted in the wake of King's book resembled slipshod tabloid journalism far more than they did serious exploration of a social phenomenon: In most of the stories, men engaging in DL sex weren't characterized as complex human beings, but as sexual culprits and perpetrators of bad behavior; the women in their lives were presented as innocent pawns. The structure and substance of many articles centered around denial, the futility of prevention efforts, and the lack of sexual integrity in the black community. Many pieces focused on individual women who were shocked to discover, upon having blood rejected at the blood bank or being turned down for health insurance, that they had contracted HIV from their men.

A lengthy 2003 *Orlando Sentinel* piece is a prime example: It profiled a woman who discovered she was HIV-positive during a blood test to determine her eligibility as a bone-marrow donor. When she realized she had contracted the virus from her husband, she became suicidal. The article suggested that the woman's husband was both a drug addict and on the down low. Though the article stated that her husband had no idea whether he'd contracted HIV from a man or a woman, the reporter went on to describe characteristic DL behavior in some detail. (Two weeks later, the paper ran a correction saying the woman's husband had died in 1999 but had never tested positive for HIV.)

Many of these articles led with King's book, treating him as an HIV-prevention activist brave enough to come forward and tell his story. Taking their cues from King, journalists and TV producers pretty much agreed: Men on the DL—who were referred to mostly as "closeted bisexuals" and men who just had trouble coming out of the closet—were killing black women with their denial. "A New Kind of Brotherly Love" read one newspaper headline. Not juicy enough? *USA Today* got more specific, even if it missed the whole point: "The danger of living 'down low': Black men who hide their bisexuality can put women at risk." A two-part series in *Essence* was titled "Deadly Deception." It was never clear, in these dozens of stories, whether the coverage was geared toward getting black women informed or simply preventing legions of men who have sex with men from ever telling the truth to anyone.

Still, a handful of publications—including *Newsweek*, *Colorlines*, and the *Village Voice*—turned out sensitive and respectable articles of their own on the subject, noting that many of King's claims were unsubstantiated. An April 2004 *New York Times* article profiled a group of black women who'd seen a musical about men on the DL and explored their resulting sense of urgency about it. Other pieces, including one in the *Denver Westword*, examined HIV-prevention classes or ways that information about the DL was changing the way black women felt about relationships.

The *Colorlines* article was one of the few to be penned by an out bisexual black man without a pseudonym. In it, Juba Kalamka, a member of the queer hip hop group Deep Dickollective, shared a refreshingly astute view of black identity and sexuality: "While gay and straight white academic communities and the popular media continued to engage in rote, inflammatory, sensational and racist demonizing of black sexuality, the black community, gay and straight, has not been able to get a handle on the discussion either. This failure is largely due to the dynamic overlap of homophobia and class privilege that has stunted most discussions of the way unchallenged patriarchy and sexism are integral to the experience of those on the DL and those they may infect."

Kalamka's article underscored two questions largely ignored in all the media coverage: Why hasn't the black community shed the idea of HIV as a gay white man's cross to bear, and why, even though blacks contract the disease at a rate many times that of whites, do many still feel invincible in the face of it? It is reasonable to conclude that the majority of media outlets weren't concerned with constructing a nuanced, ongoing dialogue about black sexuality and American culture. "It's just so irresistible for the press to have something to say about black men that is in some way demeaning or embarrassing," says Brenda Wade, a San Francisco–based psychologist and host of the TV show *Black Renaissance*. "One, it's about sex. But two, it's about the myth of the black man as a stud being blown apart. So people are saying, 'Ah ha! A lot of them are actually gay men.'"

Black men—already vilified in the media and canonized in pop culture as immoral thugs, sexually insatiable mandingos, and big, scary bogeymen—are easy targets when it comes to sensationalism. When those same black men are declared to be disease-infested vectors, the result is a psychoanalyst's playground. Wade, who wrote a practitioner's response to King's book for *Black Issues Book Review*, was one of the few levelheaded voices to emerge amid the hysteria. She suggested that black folks simply grow up, so that individuals can talk frankly about sexuality instead of sending men deeper into the closet.

What was lacking in all this coverage, according to Phill Wilson, executive director of the Black AIDS Institute in Los Angeles, was a real story, with real facts and numbers. Apart from Gary Dorsey's June 2004 article in the *Baltimore Sun*, which expressed some ambivalence about the tangible connection between the DL and HIV-infection rates in women, and the extent to which DL men were to blame for black women contracting the disease, few people have asked the important question: Just how many men are we talking about here?

"No one has quantified this phenomenon," says Wilson. "We don't know if it's a big deal or a little deal; we don't know if it's 100 percent of black men or one percent of black men. And no one has done any research to ascertain whether men on the DL are indeed having unsafe sex with their male partners." But lack of evidence didn't stop some publications from enhancing their arguments with shoddy reporting. *Jet* erroneously reported that 60 percent of black men who were having sex with newly infected black women were living on the DL. The *New York Times* magazine article about the DL scene in Columbus, Ohio, devoted just two paragraphs to a connection between the DL and HIV in black women, and the statistics the reporter cited raise more questions than they answer.

While intravenous drug use is a large part of the problem, experts say that the leading cause of HIV in black men is homosexual sex (some of which takes place in prison, where blacks disproportionately outnumber whites). According to the CDC, one-third of young urban black men who have sex with men in the United States are HIV-positive, and 90 percent of those are unaware of their infection.

The most troubling aspect of the DL media frenzy was that it placed the blame directly on MSMs for a burden that is too big for any one group to carry. Can we be certain that black women are not contracting HIV by willingly having unprotected sex with heterosexual men? If women are socially or culturally programmed to have sex without insisting on condoms, whose fault is that? Instead of asking the hard questions, many articles stuck to the same old easy-to-regurgitate story: Black men will do anything—even kill—for sex.

There was more thoughtful exploration of black sexuality in traditional media after the initial stories about the down low began to subside. During the otherwise tepid 2004 vice presidential debates, moderator Gwen Ifill asked candidates Dick Cheney and John Edwards to comment on the government's role in ending the AIDS epidemic in the United States, specifically mentioning the high rates of HIV infection among black women. Predictably enough, neither was familiar with the statistics Ifill cited, and neither had an intelligent response. But it did give debate commentators a chance to present the DL as one of many factors related to the deaths of hundreds of thousands of black people from AIDS. In February 2005, Keith Boykin published *Beyond the Down Low: Sex, Lies, and Denial in Black America*, which could bring some balance to what had previously been a rather one-dimensional story.

Meanwhile, J. L. King published *Coming Up from the Down Low: The Journey to Acceptance, Healing and Honest Love* in 2005, which was in part about the overwhelming response to his best-selling memoir. When asked about his first book and its exaggerations of the scope of the DL phenomenon as well as its connection to HIV and AIDS in black women, he said, "I tell people to do their own research and find out what's going on in their state and go to the Centers for Disease Control. Don't take my word for it. I'm an activist, not a health educator. I'm just telling my story."

A Tale of Two Disasters: Hurricane Katrina and Superstorm Sandy

In a 24/7 news cycle, inclement weather and natural disasters that hit the United States are covered, particularly by cable news channels like CNN, as though they are international events of epic proportions—for better or worse. When Hurricane Katrina made landfall on August 29, 2005, it also made history as one of the most devastating storms in U.S. history. More than 1,200 people died and estimated damages to the city totaled approximately $200 billion. The Bureau of Labor Statistics estimates that in the months following the storm, the city lost $2.9 billion in wages.[20]

In the immediate aftermath of Katrina, however, in the absence of important information about the number of residents who were stranded in the deluged city, when the government would respond to them and what next steps would be, some journalists did they best they could to communicate facts in a city where logistical problems made reporting almost impossible. I had just arrived in the *Austin American-Statesman* newsroom a little more than a month before Katrina hit New Orleans, and I remember distinctly watching Anderson Cooper's outrage unfold on CNN from the desk where I worked the night shift.

His impassioned response to the condition of New Orleans, portrayed largely in the immediate aftermath of Katrina as a city provoked into a state of black depravity, lawlessness, rampant sexual assault, looting, and murder in the dark corners where police were unable to respond—for the early days, that meant the entirety of black New Orleans in the audience imagination—underscored what Steve Classen described as a "Reporters Gone Wild" feeling, first coined by the online magazine *Salon*.

That the first reporters sent to the scene were white male reporters like Cooper and NBC's Brian Williams reinforced the macho, gendered newsroom roles that have added to mainstream media's mounting irrelevance. That was the case at the *Statesman*, at least. These correspondents were considered journalists as heroes, willing to walk into danger zones while others desperately wanted to flee, all to deliver the news.[21] I was immediately interested in how we could tell stories that contextualized race and class in ways that were totally absent from most traditional media coverage from the start, but my editors were not interested in my perspective.

Instead, reporters like NBC's Brian Williams, who would later be suspended for embellishing accounts of coming under fire while reporting in Iraq in 2003, took advantage of a lack of verifiable facts and made some up. Williams reported that his Ritz-Carlton, for example, was overrun with gangs, according to the *Washington Post*, a claim that, like a few others he made, was later found to be untrue. The most damaging aspect of the racist and sensationalized coverage and narratives that emerged after Katrina is that they diverted attention from the most significant, pressing problems that New Orleans residents were facing and would continue to encounter as the city struggled to rebuild.

The class implications of those who had remained in the city despite multiple warnings, for one, were alarmingly apparent but most traditional media were mute on how poverty had led to death for thousands in New Orleans. In legacy newspapers, on television and on the radio, there was little acknowledgment that many of the people who stayed in New Orleans had not left not because they were being disobedient citizens, but because they did not have the means to do so. Save for stories like a front-page *New York Times* article examining a chasm of race and class in New Orleans, most coverage framed black residents as unworthy victims of a fate of their choice. By and large, race and class was omitted from broadcast television news discussions. Jack Shafer, *Slate*'s former editor-at-large, wrote: "By failing to acknowledge upfront that black New Orleanians—and perhaps black Mississippians—suffered more from Katrina than whites, the TV talkers may escape potential accusations that they're racist. But by ignoring race and class, they boot the journalistic opportunity to bring attention to the disenfranchisement of a whole definable segment of the population. What I wouldn't pay to hear a Fox anchor ask, 'Say, Bob, why are these African-Americans so poor to begin with?' "[22]

The language used to describe black Americans in New Orleans was the first indication that coverage of the disaster was going to do more harm than good. Images of black people stranded on rooftops, spray-painted pleas for help beneath or around them on small sections of dry land, or destroyed houses were heartbreaking enough. Then, the stereotypical descriptions of black people as thugs and criminals began.

They were further marginalized not just from being New Orleans residents but American citizens when they were immediately referred to as "refugees." In one frequently cited example, photo captions of a black person clutching food from a store was described as "looting" while a white couple doing the same was characterized as them "finding food."[23] One of the authors of a caption, Chris Graythen, told the *New York Times* that he had given his caption quite a bit of thought. "Now is no time to argue semantics about finding versus looting," he wrote in an e-mail. "Now is no time to argue if this is a white versus black issue."[24]

But it turned out to be the perfect time to examine word usage and language, since the finer details were of the utmost importance. Rumors, reported as truth in an information vacuum, emerged for weeks into coverage of response to Katrina including stories about gangs of armed blacks attempting to shoot down rescue helicopters, descriptions of vile acts of sexual assault inflicted on babies and adults at the Superdome and Convention Center. In one particularly egregious case of journalistic malpractice, reports circulated that 40 murder victims had been discovered in a refrigerator. It was later discovered that the number was four, with one person being a murder victim.

This distancing of the press from the real needs and tragedy of what had befallen longtime residents of the city had a lingering impact, potentially inhibiting more immediate relief efforts in historically black and poor neighborhoods and may have hindered having more lives saved.[25] In an experiment involving 2,300 people, Stanford University professor Shanto Iyengar and *Washington Post* staff writer Richard Morin found that most responded to racial cues in coverage by expressing their desire to award lower levels of hurricane assistance after reading about looting or after encountering an African American family displaced by the hurricane.[26]

It would take years before the kind of careful, considered coverage in New Orleans that could have helped those who died without it would surface in the form of books, articles, and most notably, filmmaker Spike Lee's 2006 *When the Levees Broke: A Requiem in Four Acts.*

Several years later, in October 2012, when Superstorm Sandy struck the outer boroughs of the media capital of the United States, the intersection of race, class, and gender again defined how the media framed its coverage. What was notable this time was the absence of a full range of stories, including more substantial coverage of a black mother whose two children drowned in the storm.[27] Power failures and gas shortages made Sandy, like Katrina, logistically difficult to cover, but Occupy Sandy—a volunteer and information hub—covered the impact of the storm with more coordination than traditional media.

Jeff Yang, in an interview with the *Columbia Journalism Review* said, "I feel disgusted to even be saying this, but I think that the way that disasters are covered in the media—and ultimately, how they play out in larger society—often comes down to the colors of the corpses. I personally heard uttered that Sandy was 'white people's Katrina,' which defined the context of both disasters: Sandy was discussed as an issue of decaying infrastructure and overwhelmed or underestimated civic planning. New York is a place where a lot of powerful white people live, and they were inconvenienced by Sandy. Their interests drove a disproportionate amount of the narrative." The solution to this kind of coverage, Yang says, is diversity in establishment media.[28] Latoya Peterson, a veteran journalist, said that she looked to social networks for breaking news and major news outlets for context during Superstorm Sandy, another major difference in the coverage of Sandy and Katrina.

The Power of Representation: The Single Black Woman Story

One of the key stories at the intersection of racism and sexism in legacy media that played out for some time as a kind of trend story in print and broadcast media was one that later might be rightly considered concern-trolling. It centered on the growing number of black women who were unmarried and who were mismatched in terms of mating options if they were to rely solely on available, equally educated black men. It was a story entrenched in the belief that African American families are embroiled in Moynihan's description of the "tangle of black pathology" (in the 1965 Moynihan Report). Moynihan lamented that matriarchal black women were one of the key problems with the black family and that women-led households were responsible for the economic and social ills in the lives of African Americans.

In the form of archetypes and stereotypes of black women as emasculating, seething, long-suffering, and hypersexual, the notion that masculine black women who were thrust in unnatural circumstances—including poverty and a system of criminal justice and economic policy that made it more likely for a black woman's brother, husband, or son to go to prison than that of her white peers—were ultimately responsible for those circumstances was an old one. It was revised for the twenty-first century when the story of the upwardly mobile African American woman who was too independent and statistically endangered to get married began making headlines.

I witnessed this from personal and professional experience. As my reporting career moved from Texas to the West Coast, the release of data from the 2000 Census inspired a wave of demographic stories about a seismic shift that was imminent for the United States. Many of these stories were about diversity. One persistent story was about the alarming number of black women who were single through some combination of factors that included the following: African American men were many times more likely to be incarcerated than to be enrolled or matriculate from college and black women were outpacing them academically and economically; black women were far less likely to date interracially than black men; and finally, black women were representative in some ways of the challenge of the modern single woman—their romantic lives made them victims of their own successes.

In *Newsweek*, the February 23, 2003, cover story bore the headline: "From Schools to Jobs: Black Women Are Rising Much Faster Than Black Men. What It Means for Work, Family and Race Relations." The *New York Times* on January 16, 2007, went with: "51% of Women Are Now Living without Spouse." Even *Nightline* weighed in on April 21, 2010, with "Face-Off: Why Can't a Successful Black Woman Find a Man?"

The focus on the single black female condition wouldn't have been so odd if black people weren't just between 12 and 13 percent of the American population. Given their small percentage, shrinking print newsrooms, and fewer people to do more work, work that is important to the democracy of the country, why and how had it become so important for journalists to point out that there are a lot of unmarried black women in America who were statistically unlikely to ever marry?

I felt targeted by these stories, especially because I was a working print journalist who considered it my professional duty to stay aware of news trends not just in the cities where I worked but also throughout the nation. As the Internet evolved, I became swept up in the reactive conundrum that has become the modern news pundit and consumer's fate in a digital media ecosystem. I could simply not avoid think pieces or Op-Eds about the topic, no matter how hard I tried.

Whether I believed that the potential for black women to find true love and happiness in a marriage to a black man was good or not didn't matter as much as the fact that American culture was fixated on it. Eventually, the *New York Times*, the *Economist*, the *Wall Street Journal*, and many, many others would chime in about single black women. I blame journalistic curiosity for my inability to walk away from thinking about the story in terms of what it meant about black popular culture.

And, as a black woman, I was directly impacted by the veracity of these stories and statistics. These stories shaped the contexts in which I would date throughout my 20s into my 30s. Not only was I hypersensitive and nerdy, I had also been largely self-parented through reading material since the 1990s. So all my cues about how to live life came from external sources like magazines, newspapers, books, and television.

The stories I used to learn how to live shaped how I was in the world, which was not always bad. But it meant that I started dating as a woman who believed that the odds of finding love with a man in her community were already stacked against her. I believe life coaches and relationship experts refer to that as baggage.

I can still see the February 23, 2003, *Newsweek* cover mentioned earlier. Beyoncé and Star Jones were on the cover. This was five years before Beyoncé's hit song made "All the Single Ladies" and "Put A Ring On It" global phrases. ("Single Ladies" is still one of my favorite songs of all time.)

Beyoncé Knowles, a pop star, had given a celebratory twist to an ongoing sociological rift, not just between black people, but between the unsatisfied single women in the world and their would-be suitors. It was fun to sing along with my friends, but the educational and financial inequalities among black women and black men only started to worry me on a personal level when I considered that *Newsweek* cover.

It meant that what I had always heard referred to as black America's dirty laundry was officially on America's front street. The Q&A inside included a publishing professional who joked—if, in fact, it was a joke—that she was going to start going to prison to find a mate. In November 2014, when I thought these kinds of stories had finally stopped appearing in traditional media for good, someone forwarded me an awful opinion piece by David Kaufman at the *New York Post* about the chief of staff for New York City's first lady, Rachel Noerdlinger, with the headline "No Scrubs? The Dilemma of Modern African-American Women."

Kaufman portrays Noerdlinger as a frustrating symbol of black women who are "educated, upwardly mobile women" that "have earned the right to choose their own spouses. But tethered to their pasts by baby-daddies and preachers, they may be no more emancipated than their sisters stuck in the 'hood.'"[29]

In the past decade, the number of mainstream news stories circulated in traditional and new media about the masculinity crisis and its impact on the state of marriage has continued to multiply. These stories center around blaming millions of American unmarried women directly or inadvertently for their upward trajectory in mainstream life since the advent of feminism and affirmative action. Even though less than half of those women are black, in a nod to the Moynihan Report, the bulk of mainstream news media coverage in the past decade has increasingly scrutinized the bleak and hopeless plight of the educated single black woman unable to find equally successful black men to marry because of high incarceration and low matriculation rates.

The best-selling publication of comedian Steve Harvey's 2009 book *Act Like a Lady, Think Like a Man: What Men Really Think about Love, Relationships, Intimacy, and Commitment* eventually spawned a subgenre of literature focused on solving the conundrum of black single women. As usual, alternative and ethnic media like *Essence* or *Ebony* along with the *Root* and *Bitch* magazine lent corrective voices to the media chorus. But along the way, a slew of black male celebrities R&B singers, journalists, and bloggers have started cashing in on the popular misconception that single black womanhood is a plague to be remedied.

The advice became so popular that it became a part of what writer Samhita Mukhopadhyay called the "romantic-industrial complex." I wrote about the response trend to books like Harvey's for *Bitch* magazine which, at some point, appeared to be published by the dozens in an unlikely subgenre: Romantic advice penned almost entirely by unmarried black men.

These tomes range from satirical dating advice to fidelity how-to books, but what they all share is the condescending sentiment: That everyone but all the single black ladies know how to be in committed relationships. Ray J, Brandy Norwood's little brother who co-starred in a sex tape with Kim Kardashian, wrote a relationship book called *Death of the Cheating Man* with Maxwell Billieon in February 2012. Billieon is an executive-turned-"lifestyle guru" who outlines steps to help men consider the consequences of cheating. In the book, Ray J writes explicitly about his affair with a woman (enigmatically referred to as "KK") and how he learned to stop cheating using Billieon's techniques.

But that's just for starters. Journalist Jimi Izrael published *The Denzel Principle: Why Black Women Can't Find Good Black Men* in 2010. "Some black women say they have trouble finding the right guy, but the truth is, some of them manage to find a new one every night, and word gets around. Or they find great guys—legitimately good brothers with jobs, benefits and all their own teeth—and stay happy for about 15 minutes," wrote Izrael, who probably chuckled at his clever combo of slut-shaming and the stereotype of the angry, insatiable, uptight black woman. "Then they wear them out emotionally (rarely sexually), get bored, step out of the relationship and throw the proverbial dice in hopes of an upgrade. . . . They end up spending their golden years with 50 cats and 150 ceramic collectibles, trying to lure the mailman inside with a plate of food." Joel Dreyfuss published an excerpt on the *Root* (where he was then editor), assuring readers the excerpt was not an endorsement but still reminding ladies, "We can't all be Denzel."

Actor and author Hill Harper tried for a more tender approach with *The Conversation: How Black Men and Women Can Build Loving, Trusting Relationships*. "We are growing jaded, cynical, tired, and world-weary before our time," Harper wrote. "[Our] lower expectations are making us unfulfilled and taking us farther from each other. The walls between us do not serve us." Felicia Pride, writing for the *Root*, described the book as a typical dating how-to book. But she also added the important critique that many of these books focus on heterosexual relationships and ignore all same-sex and alternative forms of partnership.

Popular relationship bloggers Damon Young and Panama Jackson published *Your Degrees Won't Keep You Warm at Night: The Very Smart Brothas Guide to Dating, Mating and Fighting Crime* in 2011. The book is the rare collection of funny dating stories about black men and their female friends, and I read the entire book the day it arrived in the mail. I loved it, but I was also several years into reading about how undesirable and untenable black women were when it came to love and relationships. Since when did relationship advice to black women become so funny? Who was meant to benefit from the sexist and heterosexist perpetuation of the notion that a woman could not be considered fully successful at life or womanhood unless she married a man or the racist insinuation that the only proper and natural mate for a black woman would be a black man?

The relationship-book bandwagon continued far past its prime with singers like R&B singer Musiq Soulchild's *1 4 3: Love According to Musiq*, a book based on his perspective as a musician whose music affects some people's relationships. (That these books found publishers during such a time of upheaval in the publishing world is certainly another area worth further analysis.) While he told the *Root* that he didn't want to be mistaken for a love guru, Musiq's contribution joined a glut of dating and romance books penned by unmarried black male authors. In an era when Lil' Wayne can croon about never learning how to love, the cadre of irritatingly mundane black creatives who honed in on pretending to sell solutions to single black women only seemed to grow.

Harvey, the comedian, radio show and *Family Feud* host, remains king of these published shenanigans. *Act Like a Lady, Think Like a Man* inspired a sequel (*Straight Talk, No Chaser: How to Keep and Understand a Man*), a feature film (*Think Like a Man*), and a movie edition re-print of the *New York Times* best seller. In October 2014, Harvey went even further and launched his own dating site, Delightful.com, to, in his words, help women "become more dateable," and "find love and keep it."[30]

In the meantime, Harvey's movie was a box-office hit for two weekends in a row when it debuted, proving that audiences were clamoring for more dating insight and entertaining anecdotes from Harvey. The secret to his popularity may be that while he seemingly writes for a black audience, women of all races and ethnicities have also taken note of his folksy intent to "empower you with a wide-open look into the minds of men," as promised in the dedication for *Act Like a Lady*. Despite the fact that the book is written with Harvey's trademark wit, it hardly prompts readers to consider the source of their information—in this case, insight from the mind of a man who has been married three times. In *Forbes* when he launched the dating site, Harvey explained that his knowledge base came from that failure. "I've come to learn in my life that failure's a wonderful teacher. I've scooped a lot of the dog poop off the sidewalk so you wouldn't have to step in it."[31]

While that certainly distinguishes Harvey as a chivalrous man in some respects, what makes the expansion of his dating advice empire so problematic is that Harvey makes no startling or revolutionary suggestions about how women behave in relationships. He writes that too many women have been talking to their female friends about relationships, which is why they can't get a man. He tells women to make sure they ask all the questions they have about potential dates instead of waiting until later, and to wait to have sex for at least six months, if not longer. His book includes lines like: "Encoded in the DNA of the male species is we are to be the provider and protector of the family, and everything we do is geared toward ensuring we can make this happen. . . . This is all a man wants; anything less, and he doesn't feel like a man."

But how sexist is it to continue to perpetuate the notion that if only women could act right, they would be in relationships? What are we to make of the mixed messages that women should be more level-headed like men are in relationships, but that they should at some point disavow themselves of the emasculating and/or masculine attributes that are part of the foundation of their economic success? The success of these books—and why I refused to pay money to see *Think Like a Man* (besides Chris Brown's casting)—is that the messages embedded within them demean the success of black women. Doubly oppressed by race and gender, black women continue to succeed academically and economically—but they are still stumped in matters of the heart. What, no celebration over the academic degrees? Black women didn't get to learn how to read legally for centuries. Where's the bestseller-turned-blockbuster about *that*?

Instead, popular culture narratives leveled at black women—particularly those penned by black men—are typically demeaning, snide, childish, humorous at the expense of successful black women. In his post "Where the Hell Are All the Good Single Black Women?" The Champ (coauthor of *Your Degrees Won't Keep You Warm at Night*) points out a few factors that might "discredit the relationship eligibility of women" including how often they cry at the end of the movie *The Color Purple*, whether they've "dated" a professional athlete or rapper in their adult lives, if they refuse to have sex the week after they've gotten their hair done, and if they're completely uninterested in hobbies.

These works debase black female readers by way of black male condescension. It's a kind of intellectual bullying and a Catch-22: If women consume it, they are under black male control, if they dismiss it, they are fulfilling the stereotype of emasculating, hard-headed black spinsters who don't know how to treat a man, which is why they can't keep one.

Thankfully, some women have had their say about the omniscient relationship experts who continue to tell them how to behave if they want to be partnered. In 2010, radio host Shanae Hall co-wrote a book with her mother Rhonda Frost, *Why Do I Have to Think Like a Man? How to Think Like a Lady and Still Get the Man.* Hall told *USA Today* she wrote the book to address the holes in Harvey's book and premise. Hall maintained that *Act Like a Woman* was wildly successful "because women are desperate. They want answers. What he does is give them hope. At least someone is trying to explain why we're all going in the direction that we're going in." But Hall and Harvey share the presumption that all women are desperate and that without the right advice, they're headed in a direction that will leave them alone and lonely—a key element of the romantic-industrial complex that has sold millions of books.

Harping on female desperation not only sells books, but it also sells movie tickets. *Think Like a Man* made $37 million in its opening weekend and, at one point, outsold *The Hunger Games* according to the *Los Angeles Times*. Either much of black America is immune to the backhanded compliments informing the narrative that single black women need to rely on other people to figure out how to date or they just don't care because entertainment is worth a few jabs to the self-esteem.

The stories that black people tell about themselves and to the world about black love are still as important today as they were during the days of Jim

Crow, when interracial marriage was both illegal and a social taboo. But exactly how these stories are being told need to be examined. Oft-quoted statistics about America's estimated 19 million unmarried single black women (the Census reports there are about 100 million single people altogether) harp on the intersection of class, race, and gender dynamics in the black community, but are rarely contextualized. Most black male relationship experts see those numbers and say these women are too materialistic, demanding, or independent for them to be marriage material. Almost none of these books address the fact that black women largely choose to date black men exclusively—the Pew Research Center reported in 2008 that 22 percent of black male newlyweds married a nonblack woman, while only 9 percent of black women married interracially. So even if single black women fix themselves, it's a crap shoot.

The proliferation of these books also plays on the race loyalty and insecurities of black women and others who buy into them. Since at least the 1970s, the modern story of black love has been embroidered with a debate over women-led households and matriarchy. In his seminal 1965 report, Senator Daniel Patrick Moynihan referred to the black family as a "tangle of pathology" because women providers were an aberration from the traditional family structure.

The report's legacy has fostered the idea that black women are to blame for undermining black masculinity in America—despite the impact of the systemic violence of slavery, deindustrialization, unemployment, and the prison industrial complex on the black family. Moynihan's report also perpetuated the idea that when black women become powerbrokers of their families, they emasculate black men to a devastating degree. The sometimes-underlying, sometimes-overt thread tying these relationship books together is that black women are too domineering to be good partners and unless they learn tricks to be more submissive, they are doomed to be alone.

The cumulative effect of these messages means emotional and psychological turmoil for black women. Ralph Richard Banks in his 2011 book, *Is Marriage for White People?*, documents the factors that lead to low self-worth including man-sharing among black women that leads to high STD rates and a proliferation of baby daddies. This is where relationship books by black men intersect in a sick Venn Diagram with mainstream relationship books.

As Samhita Mukhopadhyay writes in her book *Outdated: Why Dating Is Ruining Your Love Life*, dating how-to books play on (and sell well because of) women's perceived insecurities. But this trope has added implications for black women, who deal with specific expectations when it comes to hair, weight, body confidence, and motherhood. Depictions of black women in America have, for centuries, portrayed them as overweight with unruly, exotic and/or strange features (namely, their hair), and bad attitudes. Any media depicting black women, especially those who have strong African features—brown skin, full lips, high cheekbones—typically portray black women as sassy, mean, overbearing, and overly confident.

A recent example of this was a 2011 *Psychology Today* article written by evolutionary psychologist Dr. Satoshi Kanazawa entitled "Why Are Black Women Less Physically Attractive Than Other Women?" Kanazawa wrote that black women had more masculine features than women of other races, which is why they were viewed "objectively" to be less attractive. *Psychology Today* later ran an apology.

But the damage had been done with just one more example of the ways that black women's bodies and presence in their culture is considered undesirable. And despite the popular movie featuring Simon Baker, *Something New*, the idea that black women are desirable to eligible people of other races is still treated as the exception and not the rule. With so many demeaning messages from media, it's no wonder so many black women truly believe that if they want to be married, a black man is unlikely to be attracted to them. This is also why self-proclaimed gurus continue to sell books: They offer love advice that doesn't come packaged with a bonus self-loathing soundtrack. Their messages overlap with mainstream relationship book messages that suggest that only if women change themselves will they be worthy of the love of a suitor.

For women seeking rational voices on black women and love, sisterhood has remained a powerful force. Women writers and bloggers of all races have actively tuned out barbs aimed at their success and independence, and remarked intelligently on this trend to mitigate the damage.

Gina McCauley, founder of the website What About Our Daughters, consistently recommends that black women "defund foolishness" and otherwise refuse to support media that demean them. When comedian and *Think Like a Man* co-star Kevin Hart insulted black women by posting an offensive cartoon online, McCauley wrote a post on the star of "Act Like a Lady, Think Like a Man, Crawl Like a Lizard and Slither Like a Snake" that wryly addressed women who are "[prepared] to prop up yet another movie whose success is totally dependent on you and your sister friends traveling en mass to 'support' folks who kinda sorta don't like you very much." Kaneisha Grayson published a book called *Be Your Own Boyfriend*. Michelle Callahan, Ph.D. and author of the 2009 book, *Ms. Typed? Discover Your True Dating Personality and Rewrite Your Romantic Future*, has also offered an alternative narrative that uplifts black women instead of treading on them. In online spaces like *Clutch* magazine, Racialicious, and Think Progress, women of all races are intelligently critiquing the notion that black women are in dire need of men and instructions on how to keep them.

The future looks necessarily complex for popular culture portrayals of relationships between black men and women. The appearance of black healthy love between Barack and Michelle Obama, a modern-day love story of intellectual equals who don't seem to level power plays against one another, sets an example for what's possible. Witnessing it allows the black community a model for healing a history of tension between black men and women. Seeing the most famous couple in the world exchange sweet nothings or dance in elegant attire may be the most visible and tangible black love story of our generation. But appearances aren't everything. And there can only be one Barack and Michelle Obama, for better or worse.

The voices of reason are out there. The question is whether or not those voices will be heard over the latest racket from the advice squad or self-appointed relationship gurus. R&B singer and actor Tyrese coauthored a book with Reverend Run called *Manology*; this is from an entertainer who had one-hit song in the 1990s, a few Coca-Cola commercials, a starring movie role as an adult-sized fetus, and who once told happily single women they were going to "independent [their way] into loneliness."

Ideally, publishers and movie producers will stop publishing and promoting books and movies that perpetuate the sexist and racist notion that black woman are incompetent in matters of the heart. Since self-love, acceptance, and approval don't translate to best-selling books or movies, the end of the black male relationship book subgenre is probably not near. But if black women could embrace the clearly unpopular idea that they are fine and loveable exactly as they are, the joke would be on the clowns who make money trying to convince them otherwise.

Women and Sports Journalism

Another underreported aspect of sexism in traditional media involves women journalists covering or participating in the hypermasculine world of sports. There is perhaps no mold more traditional and no remaining bastions of white male privilege as remarkably stagnant as sports coverage, especially in the talk radio realm. This was certainly the case when women who "invaded the temples of male supremacy—the press box, the sidelines, and, most sacrosanct of all, the locker room," in the 1970s through the 1990s, when things changed dramatically with the steady erosion of sexism from athletes and male colleagues and the creation of groups like the Association of Women in Sports Media, reporter Sherry Ricchiardi wrote in the December/January 2005 issue of the *American Journalism Review*.[32] Female pioneers in sports media recall humiliating antics and hostile locker rooms that led many of them to move on to different beats within journalism.

One of the most jarring instances of blatant sexism occurred on September 17, 1990, when 26-year-old Lisa Olson was mugged by a group of New England Patriots players in what Ricchiardi called a watershed moment for women in sports journalism. As Olson conducted a practice-day interview, she was accosted by naked football players who made lewd gestures and vulgar comments as she tried to do her work. She referred to it as "mind rape," and the incident resulted in a 108-page report from the National Football League. When the news broke, Olson received hundreds of obscene phone calls and pieces of hate mail before she fled to Australia. She later settled a civil harassment suit against the Patriots.[33]

While there have been some improvements in media with regards to hiring women journalists in sports, there are still very few women working as sports editors or senior producers in sports journalism, which continues to impact coverage. In its annual report, *The Status of Women in U.S. Media 2014*, the Women's Media Center reported that the ranks of sports editors were 90 percent male and 90 percent white. "Despite recording an increase in the number of women of color who are sports journalists, the Institute for Diversity and Ethics in Sports' most recent report card, nonetheless, graded the more than 150 newspapers and websites it evaluates an F, overall, for the third time in a row for their hiring practices among women."[34]

The immediate impact of this is that the power of representation which defines and spans traditional media is nowhere as palpable as it is in sports coverage where the absence of that power is revealed in coverage of women athletes and sports. Stories about women in sports tend to center on the wives and girlfriends of male sports figures more than centering women athletes. And given the dearth of people of color and women in sports editing, producing, and reporting positions, it is almost a given that stories will be framed as though the athleticism of black people is a biological advantage at the expense of intellect or strategy. In the case of Asian American athletes like Jeremy Lin or the now-retired Yao Ming, such stories take on an odd tone supported by stereotypes as old as the ages.

This is especially true when it comes to black female bodies. Examples of stories fixated on the black female body as the exotic other instead of amplifying unique ability include a 2009 *New Yorker* magazine story about Caster Semenya that centered on the debate about whether Semenya should compete with women and as a woman when the then-world track and field world champion was in the news. News leaked about Semenya suggesting that she had three times the testosterone of a woman, and thus an advantage over other women. Ariel Levy, the writer of the piece, described Semenya thusly: "Semenya is breathtakingly butch. Her torso is like the chest plate on a suit of armor. She has a strong jawline, and a build that slides straight from her ribs to her hips."[35]

Nowhere in the story is the societal or social context important to framing a story about an African woman's gender-testing to level the playing field between her and "real women," but black women are continually presented in news coverage as manly, unattractive, and animal-like. The origins of depicting black women's bodies as the site of freakish deviance are as old as the story of Sara "Saartjie" Baartman, or the Hottentot Venus, whose unusually large buttocks and color were displayed for Europeans to gawk at in the 1800s. The South African woman was placed in a cage alongside animals for entertainment purposes as Europeans who presumed themselves to be racially superior to Africans regarded her body with amazement.

The same kind of objectification of black female bodies in sports sometimes emerges in the most unlikely circumstances. It arose, for instance, in a 2013 story published in *Elle* magazine about WNBA player Brittany Griner. The profile, by a former basketball player named Laurie Abraham, is mostly fine, but it goes off the rails with one paragraph:

> What surprised me, what with my familiarity with jocky women, was, off court, as I trailed Griner from appointment to appointment, how much she felt like a guy to me. Not because of the style of her clothes and the lack of makeup, and not because I thought she was "really" a man, whatever that means: Is it genitals, is it learned behaviors, it is hormones in utero and beyond? It's all three, biologists and psychologists who study gender formation say. But some combination of sensory stimuli screamed *boy* to me. So much so that I did a cognitive double take each time I heard someone refer to her as *she*: Yes, yes, Brittney is a girl, I'd think. She *is* a girl.[36]

This kind of assertion is only mildly annoying, since it is an extraneous, almost internal dialogue inserted in a piece that otherwise aims to celebrate

Griner's individuality. The preceding passage shows that while the writer wants to normalize and center Griner's experience, she herself is still grappling with the context of fluid gender expression. This kind of othering of black women is not confined to the pages of glossies like *Elle* and is particularly ugly when it comes to talk radio and broadcast television coverage.

In 2007, on his eponymous MSNBC show Don Imus referred to the Rutgers University basketball team as "nappy-headed hos" and former sports announcer Sid Rosenberg as a guest on the show said the team of young black women looked like the Toronto Raptors. Rosenberg had previously referred to tennis star Venus Williams as an "animal" in the past.[37] By themselves, these are not surprising developments or utterances, but what has changed over the years has been widespread and often swift reaction to them.

Imus was fired several days after the show was broadcast. Gwen Ifill, one of the nation's most prominent black journalists, wrote an Op-Ed in the *New York Times* noting that Imus had once referred to her as a cleaning lady to illustrate that while she was tough enough to handle his insults, talk radio personalities should pick on people who were equipped to handle them—not young people. One of the great paradoxes of traditional media is that as their impact and influence among youth, women, and people of color has quickly declined, the need for relevant and timely content has provided a forum for each demographic to react and respond to bias in ways that were traditionally closed off to them. "Every time a young black girl shyly approaches me for an autograph or writes or calls or stops me on the street to ask how she can become a journalist, I feel an enormous responsibility. It's more than simply being a role model. I know I have to be a voice for them as well," Ifill wrote.[38]

Race Baiting for Page Views and Ratings

Without voices like Ifill's, the loudest voices are those that degrade women and people of color in traditional media formats and are sometimes far less forgiving. Rush Limbaugh and conservative media figures like Bill O'Reilly, Glenn Beck, and Sean Hannity have made their careers spewing bigotry and hate speech in exchange for ratings. Limbaugh has argued that feminism is ruining women and has argued that there is "scholarly research" to support his contention that Mexicans are lazy in comparison to Cubans.[39] The best example of how Fox News and its stars have disregarded journalistic ethics arrived in 2010, when out-of-context excerpts of a speech Shirley Sherrod made before an NAACP group were posted by conservative blogger Andrew Breitbart.

Bill O'Reilly called for Sherrod to resign the job she'd only held as a U.S. Department of Agriculture official for 11 months.[40] Media critic and author Eric Deggans wrote that the viral video clips of Sherrod consumed 14 percent of coverage in major news outlets, second only in coverage that week to news about the nation's worsening economy.[41]

Sherrod told Deggans: "It wasn't all media, it was Fox [News]," the channel that, by way of Glenn Beck, had also been responsible in part for the 2009 resignation of former White House advisor Van Jones. "I don't know all that Fox was doing behind the scenes to get the effect they were looking for, which was to get me to resign. . . . I started receiving hate mail right away. . . . They had to know what they were doing."[42]

From claims of reverse racism to calling the First Lady Michelle Obama the president's "Baby Mama"—a term usually applied to unwed mothers—Fox has a long history of race-baiting and sexism.[43] But in other traditional media, the way that people of color and women are represented is also often lopsided. This is so pervasive that it seems designed to draw page views and attention. For decades, magazine coverage of women and people of color has continued to draw protests.

In 2013, *Sports Illustrated* was the target of criticism for its annual swimsuit issue featuring mostly white models posing in ethnic countries, using Africans in particular as primitive backdrops. That same year, a *Bloomberg Businessweek* cover featuring minorities holding fistfuls of money drew criticism from readers and media critics.[44] Tanzina Vega with the *New York Times* quoted Ryan Chittum at the *Columbia Journalism Review* as saying the cover was " 'clearly a mistake' because of 'its cast of black and Hispanic caricatures with exaggerated features reminiscent of early 20th-century race cartoons.' What made it even more offensive, Mr. Chittum wrote, 'is the fact that race has been a key backdrop to the subprime crisis.' "[45]

Incidents like these are reminiscent of what made the O. J. Simpson cover so appalling, and that they continue to crop up is disheartening for news consumers and subscribers who are waiting for a media landscape that includes them. When, in February 2013, a writer with the online *Clutch* magazine questioned the incoming *New York Times T* magazine editor Deborah Needleman about the first issue of the magazine she edited that didn't feature a single person of color, Needleman reportedly responded by saying, "It was something I noticed and regretted as we were putting the issue together. We are a global magazine and so would like the content, subjects and geography of stories to reflect that. . . . A majority of fashion models are still unfortunately mostly white, but it is our aim to celebrate quality and beauty in all its diverse forms. We can and will aim to do better, but our goal is first and foremost to deliver the best stories we find, and it is my belief that quality and good journalism appeal to all of us regardless of our specific ethnic origins."[46]

It is this kind of refusal to validate and respond specifically to reasonable points brought by readers that continues to lead to problematic coverage in traditional media. This is true of the 2013 cover story for *Philadelphia Magazine* called "Being White in Philly," where the writer even invites an international racist perspective instead of staying purely local. In it, Robert Huber quotes Anna, "a tall, slim, dark-haired beauty from Moscow getting out of her BMW" who says: "I've been here for two years, I'm almost done. Blacks use skin color as an excuse. Discrimination is an excuse, instead of moving forward. . . . It's a shame—you pay taxes, they're not doing anything except sitting on porches smoking pot. . . . Why do you support them when they won't work, just make babies and smoking pot? I walk to work in Center City, black guys make compliments, 'Hey beautiful. Hey sweetie.' White people look but don't make comments."[47]

Michael Brown, Trayvon Martin, and Media Portrayals of Black Youth

Another persistent example of racist coverage in traditional media underscores an ongoing and fraught relationship between law enforcement and black men that has been even more evident in an era where traditional media are late adapting to the digital era. Traditional media coverage in the 1980s and 1990s displayed how black men who are typically lionized as sports figures can be demonized in media as easily as teenagers who would be deemed guilty first by the press before evidence proved them innocent decades later. So it is unsurprising that even into the twenty-first century, media coverage of high-profile incidents involving slain black youth would continue to underscore more than any other media narrative how racism narrows the scope, trajectory, and accountability that is supposed to be the spine of serious, timeless journalism.

This is as true in the case of Yusuf Hawkins as it is for the case of Michael Brown or Trayvon Martin or legions of young black women and men who have been killed by white people—especially white police officers—but are ultimately blamed for causing their own deaths by being black. In the past three decades alone, there have been dozens of stories detailing police brutality among blacks and Latinos and a number of black men who have died at the hands of police. Unfortunately, there have been so many cases that a separate book could be written about the composite of those cases alone. Here, I will write only about a few recent examples.

Traditional media are skilled at portraying African American youth, especially black men and boys, as criminals even when they are victims of crime. This became more evident in 2012 and in 2014. The fatal shooting of Trayvon Martin in Sanford, Florida, and Michael Brown in Ferguson, Missouri, in addition to the deaths of Eric Garner in Staten Island and Tamir Rice in Cleveland to only name a few, highlighted racial difference as a marker of how modern media fail at objectivity in part because of a persistent lack of staff diversity. The result of viewing these stories through the lens of racial difference does not begin and end with the stories of the shootings, police investigations, or trials themselves, however: It extends to coverage of protests, boycotts, witness statements, and even the context into which a story is placed.

Story selection, placement, and context serve as examples of how racial profiling extends to legacy media. In many cases, the black press or people of color reporting or blogging from the ground take the lead elevating each story to legacy and new media outlets, which is probably a symptom of fewer reporters of color in traditional media as well as a diffuse media landscape.

Trayvon Martin's shooting was being reported online and in the black press days before traditional media picked up the story of the black teenager who was shot on February 26, 2012, by a rogue neighborhood watchman named George Zimmerman. Initially, the story was reported marginally in mainstream media. But in alternative media, the story's racial elements and the fact that Zimmerman was not immediately arrested helped catapult Martin's case into international legacy media, prompting a renewed conversation about racial profiling, gun laws, and self-defense. After controversial delays, Zimmerman was arrested and charged with second-degree murder in Trayvon Martin's death. He was ultimately acquitted of second-degree murder or manslaughter in Martin's death.

Another amplifying aspect of the story of Martin's death involved a little-covered case involving Florida's "Stand Your Ground" gun laws when in May 2012 Marissa Alexander, a black woman, was sentenced to 20 years in prison for shooting a warning shot to keep her abusive, estranged husband at bay. Despite the fact that no one was injured, a jury convicted Alexander in 12 minutes.[48] In November 2014, Alexander accepted a plea deal and pleaded guilty to three counts of aggravated assault that would allow her to leave jail in early 2015.

The way that violence in communities of color is oddly covered doesn't only pertain to African Americans. When two Tulsa men randomly killed three black people and wounded two others on April 6, 2012, the traditional media coverage had a distinctly different tone. Jake England, a 19-year-old alternately referred to as Native American and white in the press, had used racial slurs to vent about the black man who had killed his father just over two years ago. His roommate and accomplice, Alan Watts, was also white. Andrew Beaujon, in a Poynter critique, wrote: "Maybe it's the Trayvon Martin case, or maybe it's just the system working as it should, but news organizations are moving cautiously on the story of this weekend's shootings in Tulsa, Okla., which may—may—have been racially motivated." The men were ultimately charged with first-degree murder, shooting with the intent to kill, and the Oklahoma version of hate-crime charges, malicious harassment, according to the *Los Angeles Times.*

But Tom Rosenstiel, director of the Project for Excellence in Journalism, said the incidents received different coverage in part because of the nature of the stories. The Trayvon Martin story, he said, "has gotten a lot of coverage at a time when race and racial divisions generally are not getting significant or a substantial amount of attention in the media. We measure what subjects get covered and don't get covered on a regular basis. For five years, since we began tracking, race hasn't ranked very high. There are occasional stories that have emerged as an event, but not as a thesis, that will bring race to the fore. The Martin case is the first in a while."

It would, unfortunately, not be the last. The subsequent police-involved deaths of Freddie Gray, Walter Scott, Eric Garner, Michael Brown, Akai Gurley, John Crawford, Jr., and Tamir Rice in the years to follow—and widespread protests that would lead to both nonviolent demonstrations and disruptive, damaging riots in response to perceived law enforcement apathy—would ultimately give race a more central role in traditional media coverage, at least ephemerally.

But in 2012, given the historical context of the Tulsa Race Riots in 1921, there was a missed opportunity to explore current and ongoing interracial tensions not just between blacks and whites, but also between blacks and Native Americans in Oklahoma or between blacks and Latinos in Sanford, Florida, where Zimmerman and his family insisted that he was both white and Latino. At least one story included an interview from one of England's relatives dismissing the fact that he could have been racist because he was Cherokee; A *Colorlines* piece debated the merits of exploring Zimmerman's racial identity as white and Latino.

Much of the insightful, quick analysis of racial context in news events is provided online in what are known in the vernacular as think pieces—800–1,000 words composed of little reporting or context that generally rely on the intellectual resources of the author. Where racism and sexism have truncated opportunities for growth in traditional media has to do with the unfortunate demise of and appetite for what Rosenstiel called the Sunday story treatment.

In the past, newspapers used the additional space afforded their pages by generous advertising—and broader circulation to subscribers— to cover multiple dimensions of a story that had unfolded during the previous week like the shootings in Tulsa or the Martin case. The luxury of the Sunday story treatment was that it offered reporters and editors time to pause after breaking news developments slowed to consider answers to questions that remained unanswered and to fill in knowledge gaps with more in-depth reporting and dedicated resources. This kind of opportunity no longer exists. "The media culture moves so quickly now. If you're going to do it, you can't wait until Sunday. There isn't space, there isn't time and there is the perception that there isn't enough patience on the part of the audience," he said.

It may also be that there isn't enough patience on behalf of readers and viewers to discuss race at length. Jill Lepore's *New Yorker* story, "One Nation, Under the Gun," about the role of guns in the Trayvon Martin case was lengthy, well-reported and did not mention racial factors that impact legal gun ownership at all. (Some of this may be related to publications knowing their audiences well, since the eight-page article was the most-read article on the *New Yorker*'s website soon after it was published.) What was clear in the Martin case in particular, Rosenstiel added, was that race hadn't been such a significant part of a news story in many years—whether or not mainstream media outlets addressed it. Bob Butler, vice president of the National Association of Black Journalists, said that he didn't think mainstream media outlets did a particularly stellar or poor job of handling racial elements in the case.

But two years later, when Michael Brown was fatally shot in 2014 in Ferguson, Missouri, traditional media again had an opportunity to show how far or little they had progressed regarding the tension between law enforcement and tensions in the black community. Again, it took the voices of the black community in Missouri and around the country to elevate attention to Michael Brown's story, prompting increasing national interest.

Brown's case involved a white police officer named Darren Wilson who shot the unarmed teenager several times. Brown's death was the latest in a spate of high-profile fatalities of black men at the hands of white men, especially police officers or auxiliary police, covered by an increasing number of outlets, though in traditional media, still predominately white reporters. Those fatalities included the death of Eric Garner who was put in a chokehold by a police officer, but a grand jury still failed to indict the officer. The same was true for a police officer who shot a black man in Milwaukee who was not charged in an announcement that made headlines briefly in December 2014.

The first fact most audiences learned about Brown's case suggested police misconduct; Brown's body was left in the street for hours before his body was taken from the scene. Still, in most traditional media coverage, Brown was covered as an unworthy victim in ways that Martin and other black men had also sometimes been characterized. Later media reports disclosed that the St. Louis suburb of Ferguson was predominately black and living below poverty level; but the majority of police officers were white—a typical scenario in America's cities, and one that seemed even more likely to stoke racial tensions.

Early profiles of Zimmerman and Wilson, in contrast, were thin on details, since both men went silent after coverage became a daily media obsession in the summer days following the shooting. In contrast, traditional media profiles of both Brown and Martin described them as wayward-leaning youth who were likely to provoke fear in their neighbors or police, with particular attention paid to their marijuana use. Responsibility for their respective deaths were cast as reflections of poor life choices, not systemic, ongoing policing issues that are emblematic of interactions between police officers and black and Latino youth.

The *Los Angeles Times*, for example, thought it appropriate to publish a story about Brown's rap music—even though for traditional media audiences which are now predominately white, over 40 and male, hip hop and rap are considered synonymous with criminal activity.[49] The *New York Times* framed a story around the fact that Michael Brown was "no angel," angering African Americans across the country.[50]

Darren Wilson was not arrested or charged in the death of Michael Brown; additionally, in November 2014, a grand jury did not indict him in connection with Brown's death.[51] (The FBI and the Justice Department had also started two separate investigations into the incident, in which an autopsy showed that Brown was shot six times.) Media coverage of the decision in November 2014 centered on what was described in multiple outlets as mounting racial tension in the predominantly black St. Louis suburb. In cities around the United States, nonviolent protestors took to social media.

When the grand jury's decision was announced late in the evening on November 24, the news that a grand jury had declined to indict Darren Wilson for shooting Michael Brown at least six times resulted in riots erupting in Ferguson, even as Michael Brown's parents called for peace—more than a dozen businesses were destroyed by fire and thousands of National Guard troops were deployed to the area. Protests developed around the country for days afterward.

But long before the decision was rendered, the common pattern of vilification that distinguishes coverage of young black men was at play. Even before the ascent of hip hop as a mainstream code to discuss race, class, and gender in black and Latino communities, popular culture became increasingly desensitized to one-dimensional portrayals of black youths. The notion that young black men are more ruthless, menacing, and lawless than their white, Latino, or Asian counterparts has long been a part of the American entertainment complex, not only based on the words and images that reporters use to describe them—words like "marauding" or "wilding" that were used in the Central Park Jogger case or the characterization of peaceful protests in Ferguson as the equivalent of riots—but also based on other media and entertainment sources, including the Internet, movies, and video games.

The legacy of people of color as inferior is rooted in a legacy of racial hierarchy in the United States—a system of stratification based on the belief that skin color makes whites superior. Another factor that contributes to embedding these stereotypes is that even as U.S. Census data shows a growing number of nonwhites in America, fewer people of color are in decision-making positions at daily newspapers, television and radio stations, and online news organizations.[52] With a more diverse array of editors, producers, and information gatekeepers as well as decision makers, criminalized portraits of young black men would at least also offer the context in which those young men find themselves—as the most disproportionately criminal justice system-involved youth in the world, as explained brilliantly in Michelle Alexander's book, *The New Jim Crow*. When such stories appear, they often appear in a vacuum that disregards the systems in which many black men and boys are disenfranchised by high unemployment, unfair housing practices, educational institutions that are biased against them from the beginning and neighborhoods where poverty and violence are embroidered into day-to-day existence.

At the center of questions about the deaths of both Trayvon Martin and Michael Brown were issues related to race and self-defense. It seemed plausible to traditional media reporters that both Zimmerman and Wilson would be rightfully afraid of Martin or Brown, and that these young men would have aroused a life-threatening fear that justified their deaths. That's how reporting in each case quickly shifted from the possibility of Martin's or Brown's innocence to the likelihood that they each likely deserved what they got.

An Associated Press story from Orlando, Florida, began: "Trayvon Martin had marijuana in his system. He was shot through the heart at close range." Other media stories portrayed Martin as a thug because he had been wearing a hooded sweatshirt the night he was fatally shot. The same was true of Michael Brown. Reports about autopsy results underplayed the fact that Brown was shot at least six times and centered on the fact that he was an amateur rap artist.

The presumption of guilt in traditional media stories also applies to some coverage of young black women. When Rekia Boyd, 22, was fatally shot in the back of the head by an off-duty Chicago police detective in March 2012, her death was largely overshadowed in mainstream media by the Martin case. Boyd was with friends on a street near the detective's home when words were apparently exchanged and he fired several shots, one of which struck Boyd. Boyd's family filed a civil lawsuit against the city and the detective, who was charged with involuntary manslaughter. In its report on the shooting, one Chicago television station insinuated that Boyd was a victim unworthy of sympathy by pointing out she had been hanging out with a group "at 1 in the morning."

Stories about black youths that don't reinforce stereotypes, that don't involve celebrities, and that tell narratives about everyday lives of black people haven't been a priority in news coverage. In the case of Ferguson, Missouri, broadcast and cable networks contributed as much to the story as any other factors. As Marc Fisher and Wesley Lowery wrote in the *Washington Post*, and as President Obama acknowledged the inevitability of a negative reaction, television networks provided a split screen emphasizing violent protest over peaceful demonstrations. But that violence was "so widely and persistently predicted that it seemed as much a self-fulfilling prophecy as organic expression of rage."[53]

After news of the Brown case spread, nine residents were arrested for looting. Although peaceful, nonviolent protests were more prevalent, there was more widespread coverage and reaction to the looting, portraying African American rage as the volatile byproduct of a wrongfully-vilified white police officer, Darren Wilson, doing his job. But on social media and elsewhere, youth and people of color showed a different side of the story: Peaceful protestors on Instagram, Twitter, and Facebook with the saying "Hands Up, Don't Shoot." A group of black women coined the phrase and hashtag "Black Lives Matter," which sparked divisive conversations about the value of all lives and in the case involving Ismaaiyl Brinsley, was co-opted by police officers to say that "Blue Lives Matter."

Despite minimal actual damage from the spate of looting that proved the exception rather than the rule, ahead of a November 2014 grand jury decision in the case, the state's governor declared a state of emergency, dispatching the National Guard into the city as a preemptive reaction to potential rioting.

In one of the more bizarre takes on racial animus in Ferguson, CNN ran a story about a white woman with a black husband and young son who were afraid of reactions to them in a town where racial tension had been brewing under the watchful eye of journalist outsiders. Stefannie Wheat, a transplant to Ferguson, told the story of struggling to raise her son in a "biracial home. . . . She wanted Christopher to grow up colorblind, even though America wasn't."[54]

Coverage of these volatile events in Ferguson and New York showed that even in cases where race is clearly a factor, journalists of color are expected to prove their capability as objective reporters that are at least as competent as their white male peers. This partially explains why diverse hiring and retention in traditional media has not necessarily led to coverage that is more sensitive to difference or cultural nuances. In order to succeed as reporters of color, assimilation to newsroom mores is essential.

As Touré put it his 2011 book, *Who's Afraid of Post-Blackness?* when he recalled a racist comment from a magazine editor who suggested that his status as a black male writer made it impossible for him to write well about a white musician like Eric Clapton, "It was assumed I was unable to write about a musician because he's white. This was the curse of affirmative action: We need you to talk about Black subjects but we won't use you in the larger conversations about non-Black subjects. This was the glass ceiling. . . . Even though I had written about Black music intelligently, my skin remained a cloak of inferiority."[55]

Within the span of a week in November 2014, 12-year-old Tamir Rice was fatally shot by a Cleveland, Ohio, police officer for brandishing a BB-gun on a playground, and Akai Gurley, described by William J. Bratton of the New York Police Department as a "total innocent," was shot and killed in the stairwell of a project apartment building in Brooklyn. (These headlines were unkind to black men across the board and mingled with escalating reports of women coming forward with accusations that legendary comedian Bill Cosby had sexually assaulted them and the death of Marion Barry, the beloved Washington, D.C., mayor that TMZ tastelessly called a "crack mayor.")

Reports of the Tamir Rice shooting said that to the rookie police officer, the toy gun looked real. Some media coverage focused on a 9-1-1 call, where the woman described the boy as a "guy"—as if it was impossible to tell that he was a child. Coverage of Gurley's death in the *New York Times* was framed in a less offensive way, though early on it characterized the police officer who killed Gurley as being rightfully afraid—as if the kind of fear he felt justified accidental homicide that had not yet been determined even by a police interview.

The prediction and forecasting of violence in Ferguson and elsewhere in response to the cumulative impact of these events on black communities was indicative of a media system where publishers, editors, and producers responsible for story and source selection, as well as timing, often don't prioritize narratives that humanize or contextualize lives of black youths. In journalism, not only are decision makers generally predominantly white, but they tend to be middle class or wealthier, and disconnected from the narratives that comprise a broader swath of the American public.

A 2011 study by the Radio Television Digital News Association and Hofstra University showed that while the percentage of people of color in the U.S. population had risen since 1990 from 25.9 percent to a projected 35.4 percent, the number in television rose 2.7 percent and fell in radio. TV news diversity, it noted, "remains far ahead of the newspaper."

"The way that journalism is currently practiced and structured doesn't allow for the telling of stories of underrepresented people," Malkia Cyril, founder and executive director of the Center for Media Justice said in a phone interview. Privatization of corporate media is one reason that continues to be true.

In 1983, 50 corporations controlled U.S. media, according to *The Media Monopoly* by Ben Bagdikian, a longtime journalist and media critic. By 2004, in his revised and expanded *The New Media Monopoly*, Bagdikian wrote that the number was five—Time Warner, Disney, News Corp., Bertelsmann of Germany, and Viacom, with NBC a close sixth.

"The way that journalism is on the open market means that stories are for sale, and what sells is stereotypes," Cyril said. "Market-produced coverage will tend to misrepresent youth."

The implications of "this charged environment can result in the dehumanization of black life and regressive political decisions that can lead to violence, as the Stand Your Ground Laws resulted in the shooting death of Trayvon Martin," she added. "Otherwise, the story gets framed as coverage leads to bad individual behavior, and the systemic piece gets lost."

When media producers in journalism and popular culture media like movies, television series, and video games are mostly white, chances that young people will be humanized and fully represented are slim, said Eleni Delimpaltadaki Janis, public opinion and media research coordinator for the Opportunity Agenda in New York, in a phone interview.

"You see few images of black men and boys being good students or being good fathers," Janis said. "They're really fewer images of men in those roles compared to reality. It's not just the news coverage. It's also every type of media, but also in entertainment media, including video games. They all do a good job at using negative images of black boys and men for entertainment."

Solutions include reporters intentionally incorporating black youths into everyday or evergreen stories like those about Christmas shopping, Janis said. Eileen Espejo, director of media and health policy at Children Now in Oakland, added that producers across the media spectrum should seek ways to avoid stereotypes. "We don't want there to be a quota," she said. "But we want you to think more creatively about the roles that people of color can play, and break out of the traditional mold."

At work in media coverage of the premature deaths of black boys and men is one of the most damning and foreboding aspects of white supremacy: A society always poised to defend itself against black masculinity. It is a media portrayal that informs popular culture narratives and perpetuates media bias, but it also reinforces the irrelevance of traditional media outlets that rely on such lazy portrayals. The ultimate impact of that laziness would be the migration of attention from women and people of color away from traditional media to social and new media.

In most coverage of women and people of color, making the distinction between relying on a singular authoritative voice versus finding factual context in one place and breaking news in another would begin to define the cracks in the foundation of the house built by traditional media systems. At the most diverse and fascinating time in the modern journalism era, when the Internet and multiculturalism were dovetailing, when print media were unaware that it was about to spiral quickly to near extinction, it became clear that eventually the stories of all Americans were going to have to be told somewhere. The questions were how those stories would be told, by whom, and at what cost?

Chapter 5

The Apex of Inclusion for Traditional Media

The Rise of a Multicultural Narrative within and Outside of Legacy Media

The 1990s were the glory days for traditional media and the apex of inclusion for women and people of color in newsrooms. This decade represented a full generation since the advent of serious widespread social contemplation related to identity politics and the meaning of America's growing diversity. It also reflected the maturity of women and people of color who had utilized the total spectrum of legal actions available to them to respond to legacy media stalwarts determined to exclude them in hiring and coverage.

The money companies made as the society they covered was raking in largely borrowed cash was sometimes used, too, to augment newsroom staffs with diverse hires or boost diversity programs and training to get predominately white institutions to commit to making their staffs look more like their audiences. While the money was flowing, diversity for audiences who so craved it seemed assured.

Nearly two decades after affirmative action became a codified part of the American social infrastructure, newsrooms were also making a concerted effort to make newsgathering more of a public, "citizen journalist"-friendly zone. Print editions, additional products, and shows geared toward a multicultural audience cropped up, even as affirmative action backlash proved a deterrent to these items. As media grew increasingly corporate and profit-focused, the alternative press, along with subculture product that accurately covered the marginalized, began to proliferate. This included but was not limited to the emergence of zines as grassroots media spaces where women, people of color, and people with alternate gender identities could explore everything that was generally missing from corporate media—from transgender bias and mental illness to rape culture, sexism, and personal transformation stories.

Zines were an outgrowth of Riot Grrl culture and a subset of the alternative press that flourished as a precursor to widespread use of blogs and social media. Zines also emerged during an American apex for ethnic and cultural magazine publishing and growing cultural acknowledgment of hip hop as a legitimate global and organizing force, including and apart from its commercial aspects. These shifts coincided with a growing move toward race and ethnicity as a focal point for stories instead of as afterthoughts.

As the analog predecessors for the power of individuals telling their stories before the Internet became ubiquitous, zines and their proliferation in American culture made a statement about the ability of the traditionally marginalized to center their narratives and define themselves outside of the mainstream. These publications reinforce the notion that when women, youth, and people of color frame their own narratives, the topics are myriad, relevant, and a significant departure from how stories are framed about them in traditional media spaces where their voices are largely absent. These are stories of protest, whether related to war or inclusion in movements where women of color are generally ignored.

It has to be noted that this is not the type of media, like social media or blogs, that are financially viable or particularly sustainable. The power of corporate, traditional media lies in their ability to attract advertising to pay for news production and staffing. This is a luxury that small or independent publications cannot afford, and it makes the investment in diversity even more remarkable.

Zine themes run the gamut but include narratives about the able-bodied versus those who have physical handicaps; the hard of hearing and deaf community, those who cut or self-mutilate who are often viewed as white women and not women of color; the ancillary discussion of the transgender community and people of color in the history of LBTQ rights, and so on. Zines also allowed multiple spaces for correctives to stereotypes or misconceptions circulated in mainstream narratives.

That included *Homos in Herstory: "Work-in-Progress"* 1980s edition by Elvis Bakaitis, which critiques early erroneous articles about AIDS like a *New York Times* article that referred to HIV as a "homosexual disorder." In Mike Funk's *Stonewall 1969*, he wrote, "Media coverage of Stonewall brought Queer oppression to the mainstream. But many publications wrote about it as an uprising of white gay men. Journalists picked an angle, and soon, so did history."[1]

That last sentence is true for most events, if not all, in American history. What makes zines so remarkable is the range of topics they cover, especially for the publications created by and for women of color. Topics range from fat shaming to anarchy; authors and audiences range from mixed raced women in Portland to Filipina punks in Oakland. The creation of zines, both as a way to critique punk culture and to make space for individual narratives within a larger, marginalized narrative, is inspiring but it also is necessary for a full, accurate view of women and communities of color. In her zine, *Yellow Kitty*, journalist Anita Chan wrote about the racism she experienced as an Asian American in predominantly white and male newsrooms.

In the first volume, she wrote about racial assumptions. A few weeks after she started working at 1010 WINS an editor singled her out to read an article in the editorial section of the *New York Times* entitled "Asian American Achievement Rooted in Family Values. 'I was an Asian American, after all, and articles on fellow Asian Americans, especially when they appear in the *New York Times* (has the annual average surpassed single digits yet?) should concern me . . . naturally.'" I was most interested in Chan's article, "Mediated Disillusionment: Stories about Nanking and Beyond," published in *Yellow Kitty No. 2*.

Chan wrote about the sanitization of her reported story about the mass murder and rape in Nanking beginning in 1937 and her frustration with her colleagues. She had interviewed locals with intimate knowledge of this event, though their memories were deemed too graphic for the newspaper and eventually omitted from the published version of her story. "Here, I knew, was a chance to bring coverage to a community that remained virtually invisible in the pages of the paper, and to do so without mentioning either lion dances, red lanterns, or chop sticks," she wrote. "I only wondered how many of the paper's editors—all of whom were self-identified 'Americans,' and only three of whom were of color (African American) were conscious of the same thing."[2]

In *Yellow Kitty* and online, Chan published the story with the significant details from survivors that her editors had taken out. She also offered a warning to readers about news literacy, specifically as it relates to people of color. "Never believe what you read in the news," Chan wrote. "Or if you do, always remember to ask yourself whose story is missing on the page. Because without question, there's always an Other story missing, buried in the back pages of paper, crammed into the corner of a page, or shoved into the margins—that is, if it appears in the paper at all."

Excessive Spending and Room for All?

The notion that traditional media could become truly multicultural and more gender balanced did not seem far-fetched in the 1990s, in part, because of the excesses of the time. Affirmative action was still young, and it was not yet obvious that the clearest beneficiaries of the federally enforced program to dismantle old boy networks would not be people of color but white women. At the pinnacle of a monopoly on the attention of viewers, listeners, and readers before the Internet became ubiquitous, there was money to be made and spent.

These were the decades when newsrooms were not only flush with cash but were also operating as if they were intoxicated with an unlimited notion of what journalism could become. As journalism professor Christopher Daly has noted, before media became concentrated in the hands of just a few, and before the disruption of the Internet, traditional media were the way to go. Print journalists are perhaps the easiest to document: *Time* magazine was paying writers $10 a word, the *New York Times* writer R. W. Apple expensed $400 bottles of wine and news organizations paid for some to be flown back and forth by plane, train, and, in some cases, helicopter. (For perspective, as of 2014, most print and online outlets paid a standard essay fee of $150 for a piece between 800 and 1,000 words and reporters would have to consider themselves lucky to be reimbursed for mileage, let alone a plane trip.) The media industry took a page from the Wall Street business playbook, which is why the 1980s and 1990s had so much money to throw around. It was borrowed money, spent on borrowed time.[3]

These two pivotal decades reflected a kind of cultural and material decadence, as television, radio, and print outlets were expanding their audience through mergers, not just good old-fashioned popularity—although they had that, too. The corporate consolidation of journalism would eventually coincide with a growing appetite for constant, mobile-delivered, friend-approved news amplified via social networks, breaking open the definitions of news and journalism. But in the purgatory between legacy media domination and its accelerated collapse beginning in the late 1990s was a media monoculture, uniformly concentrated and largely family-owned companies run almost entirely by elite white men.

Simultaneously, particularly by the 1990s, it became evident that there would be both real and figurative costs for marginalizing people of color. In his 2014 book, *Who We Be*, Jeff Chang writes, "With cable's rise, advertisers began to adapt to media fragmentation. In 1990, the University of

Georgia's Selig Center estimated the combined buying power of nonwhites at $455 billion. The same demographic shifts that had unleashed the culture wars were also huge business opportunities."[4]

More than a decade since civil rights legislation had made a significant difference diversifying the faces reflected in newspapers and magazines, on broadcast airwaves, and in voices heard on radio, what looked like a tidal wave of progress gained significant momentum. The birth and expansion of multiculturalism "was about recognizing and representing how Black it was to be an American, how Latino, how Asian, how indigenous it was to be an American. Being American was a thousand narratives, not just one," Chang writes in *Who We Be*.[5]

Black Entertainment Television was one example of how media were beginning to reflect the many narratives in America. Robert Johnson started BET in 1980, showing reruns, old movies, and infomercials on a part-time basis. When the channel started, 75 percent of its programming consisted of music videos for millions of blacks in the United States. In 1993, 60 percent of BET's audience was non-African American. In 1999, Johnson sold BET to Viacom, the media company that also owns MTV along with other cable networks. Viacom eliminated newscasts on the channel to save money. By 2004, 9 out of every 10 African American cable households subscribed to BET.[6]

At the time, Johnson was one of just a few early media moguls of color. The other, Oprah Winfrey, got her start as a broadcast journalist and was just becoming well known in what seemed at the time like a crowded daytime talk show lineup of personalities that included Phil Donahue, Geraldo Rivera, Sally Jesse Raphael, soon to be followed by Jerry Springer, Richard Bey, and Montel Williams.[7] Oprah's astounding international reach and popularity became notable not only because she was an African American woman, but also because of the diversity of her content and reporting, the influence it had among women and people of color, and how it helped Oprah build her ubiquitous brand, which originated in local news but expanded to softer features.

Elsewhere in media and outside of news, television shows targeting and featuring African Americans expanded after the success of the best known sitcom featuring a black family in television history, *The Cosby Show*, which ran from 1984 to 1992. The Fox Network, in particular, honed in on its largest underserved audience—minorities—by counterprogramming, or pitting successful shows like *Seinfeld* and *Friends* with shows like *In Living Color* and *Living Single*. Author Eric Deggans says that by NBC and

Fox pitting popular shows against one another, two things happened—Fox made black Americans 25 percent of their market and "produced a schism among audiences . . . on-screen segregation, inspired by the economics of TV, was producing a similar reality in the lives of television fans."[8]

It was that schism that I navigated as a consumer first, while coming of age, and later as a young journalist. The scope of media targeted to black people and women seemed enormous, even though it would not last long. Niche media publications offered some promise with ultimately disappointing results. In 1989, Time Inc. launched *Emerge*, a news magazine focused on black issues around the world. Only 12 years later, the award-winning publication was folded into *Savoy* in 2001, when BET gave publishing control to Vanguarde Media.[9]

The Impact of Media Consolidation on Multicultural Progress

Years later, news editors and producers would lament the rise of infotainment or popular media that offered "truthiness" to better reception than hard news. In retrospect, this kind of news was the natural outgrowth of an unsustainable media ecosystem, one that could not afford the exorbitant costs of gathering and reporting hard news. Infotainment has two huge advantages over traditional news: It relies on the popularity and perceived integrity of an individual person or brand and it draws a wider audience than objectively reported content.

The seeds of infotainment, best embodied now in shows like *Last Week with John Oliver* or Jon Stewart's *The Daily Show*, arguably began with the consolidation of media that began in earnest in 1985. Media consolidation placed more and more journalism properties inside giant companies that sometimes had little interest in news—a trend that has slowed only because there are so few companies left to buy. That year, Capital Cities Communication (a company previously unheard of in the news media) bought ABC for $3.5 billion, and General Electric bought RCA and its NBC division for $6.3 billion."[10] This consolidation started a trend that would continue until only nonprofit organizations and the wealthiest news companies like the *New York Times*, CNN, and National Public Radio were producing regular national news in the 2000s.

ASNE reports and data show that this was the best of times and one of the most diverse in the history of America's print press. This was probably also true for broadcast news and television, along with radio, but it's hard to measure the impact of diversity efforts in those areas because of their connection to the Federal Communications Commission (FCC). The FCC, which licenses the use of public airwaves, required that broadcasters respond to the needs of their audiences. Lawsuits in the mid-1970s toughened the requirements for integration and programming.[11]

"The historic coincidences of calls for more diversity began as press ownership began to consolidate," Mercedes de Uriarte wrote in a report, *Diversity Disconnects*. "Both increased over time. But as corporate power grew, minority participation in newsrooms crept along and in 1990 plateaued. Indeed, in terms of parity, minority participation later shrank in relation to the overall population."[12] ASNE's census showed 5.75 percent minority participation; RTNDA reported 9 percent participation in radio and 15 percent in television, including those in Spanish-language media. There has been little real change since 1972.[13]

There are many reasons that multiculturalism as a diverse-hiring principle and a directive for content framing slowed in the 1990s before grinding to a halt. Among them: The school-to-newsroom pipeline at that time operated much like it always had and has continued to follow suit. Producing reporting as a broadcaster or print journalist first required resources and luck above all else to acquire an unpaid internship, even for students who were journalism majors or enrolled in graduate journalism programs, known in the industry as J-School. And the professionalization of journalism at the academic level would only, unfortunately, replicate the same predominately male and white networks of the past.

The Accreditation Council on Education in Journalism and Mass Communication in 1984 added a standard requirement to its accreditation process that required organized efforts from accredited journalism schools to recruit, advise, and retain minority student and minority and female faculty members.[14] Generally, the two standards introduced to recruit and retain minorities and women and also teach a more diverse curriculum have been mostly ignored. The ranks of journalism faculty in most places consist of women and minorities at the yearly contracted and adjunct/instructor level, while tenure-track positions are usually awarded only to white men and sometimes women with a combination of PhDs and journalism experience.

I experienced this firsthand as a part-time lecturer at the University of Texas Austin, where I attended graduate school and earned a library school degree. I had about a decade of journalism experience when I was asked to start teaching an Introduction to Newswriting course, while also working full time at the *Statesman* and freelancing when I could fit it in. I joined a staff that had three other African Americans—two men and one woman, all tenured professors who had not been reporters for many years—and two other white women—both former journalists and adjuncts. The rest of the staff, and the majority, was white and male. This was not surprising in Texas, but it also is a reflection of the lack of diversity in other journalism schools.

There have been few professional endeavors that I loved as unequivocally as teaching journalism. It is something that I did in the Bronx in the summer between high school and college, when I walked to the nearest community center and asked if they needed a writer and they ended up paying me and a few younger kids to make a neighborhood newsletter. I knew nothing about reporting except that they should write and photograph what they saw.

Years later, my students at the University of Texas loved me and I loved them. From what they shared with me at the end of each semester, they especially appreciated that I had recent and relevant newsroom experience as a reporter who knew how to blog, Tweet, use Facebook—for both my personal and professional life without mixing the two—and that I could give them timely information that my tenured and colleagues with PhDs were not able to share because by and large they didn't have the same wealth of recent, relevant experience. My classes reflected a student body that was more diverse than its faculty, and my students also benefited from learning about journalism from a woman of color who had worked as a journalist in several cities.

When I left newspaper reporting at the end of 2011, it was also the end of my career as a lecturer at the University of Texas. The woman who hired me suggested that this had more to do with the fact that the curriculum was changing. But later, a white man with fewer credentials and no teaching experience (but also a colleague that I had grown fond of) was hired into a full-time position. Several of my displaced colleagues from the *Statesman* were hired at University of Texas in full-time positions with benefits and salaries.

These kinds of actions and hiring decisions in academia, as well as in newsroom employment practices, perpetuate institutional racism and sexism that ultimately impacts the quality of journalism audiences pay for. This kind of systemic bias in higher education is perpetuated when students enter newsrooms that have not changed much since before the 1970s.

Another factor that slowed the momentum and progress of multiculturalism was the disappearance or scaling back of diversity initiatives and programs geared toward people of color and women that operated outside of traditional journalism education in order to make significant inroads, like the Hearst Fellowship that was my pathway into newsrooms. Disney has a program for minority screenwriters. The *Los Angeles Times* recruited minorities and women through its Metpro program. Scripps Howard, *Dow Jones*, and others have joined the mix.

At the end of the 1990s, as I was finishing up my undergraduate career at Vassar College, I dreamed of becoming a college professor some day, or writing novels, but it had never occurred to me that I could write for a newspaper and someone might pay me to do so. Part of this stemmed from the fact that until I went to college, newspapers had fallen far off my radar since I was a little girl in Philly.

I cared about music and surviving the Bronx, where I grew up, in that order. At the tail end of Generation X, hip hop culture offered me a cultural and creative context from which to operate that nothing else did. When I learned about reporting, it was through that empowering lens.

The Rise and Fall of Niche and Hip Hop Journalism

As a teenager growing up as hip hop also came of age, the culture created by blacks and Latinos, second-generation immigrants and urban youth, the 1980s and 1990s were a crash course in watching traditional media fail to reckon with an influx of difference. I was too young to understand how significant it was that Michael Jackson was deemed the King of Pop in a world that largely gave such monikers solely to white musicians. By the time I was 14, however, I was used to raising myself mainly on a steady diet of popular media—the sitcoms of the day, from *Diff'rent Strokes* to *Good Times*, *Growing Pains* to *The Jeffersons*. I listened almost exclusively to Hot 97, a rap station, and WBLS, dedicated mostly to R&B.

Print, however, was my weakness—magazines in particular. The first time I saw a black man from my generation in a dignified pose on the cover of a glossy magazine that wasn't *Ebony*, *Essence*, or *Jet* was the day I was walking with my mother through the Port Authority bus station and I spotted *Vibe* magazine. Treach, a rapper with Naughty by Nature, was on the cover, arms crossed as he stood in the seminal B-Boy stance.

The cover was a powerful statement because it meant, to my Bronx-girl brain, that despite money or class or geography, I could one day become a journalist. Not just for a so-called black publication, but for outlets that I hadn't even allowed myself to imagine would some day exist.

Some of this was timing and kismet. As hip hop grew in popularity and influence, a few key media organizations were able to tell the story of the culture as insiders—something that was completely inaccessible for white suburban audiences, whose main entry point for the culture was the nascent cultural programming of MTV with *Yo MTV Raps!* What insiders like me knew about hip hop was that it had emerged as a cultural example of creative ingenuity; that while arts funding had been cut for public school students, which meant no music, dance, or art classes, black and Latino kids were painting murals in brilliant colors that were criminalized as graffiti. People of color were writing poems and rapping to beats of their own creation. They were determined to make beauty out of otherwise bleak lives, and it would eventually have universal resonance.

Founded by Quincy Jones and Scott Poulson-Bryant, *Vibe* would become a heavy-hitting hip hop industry bible that attracted talented, innovative writers like Joan Morgan, Jeff Chang, and dream hampton. While there were other hip hop publications of note, including its competitor the *Source*, I was partial to *Vibe* for its beauty, for the quality of its writing about the next big thing, and for the voice and shape it gave to a zeitgeist before anyone else seemed to acknowledge it or see it coming.

Bay Area native Danyel Smith eventually rose through the ranks to become *Vibe*'s editor in chief before going on to publish novels, edit *Billboard* magazine, and become a Knight fellow at Stanford. In 2014, she and her husband Elliott Wilson—another industry heavyweight and editor, were producing a publication called HRDCVR with the tagline "For the New Everyone." The idea, funded by a Kickstarter campaign, was to offer a one-time, beautiful, and inclusive print magazine to audiences that are too frequently left out.

Smith said of the 1980s and 1990s in a phone interview, "Understanding that it may have never been easy, was it easier then to get into the industry." There were clearer paths of entry in traditional media and less staff turnover. There was broader acceptance of writing about different demographics.

As a reader, it appeared as though race was an intrinsic part of what *Vibe* was selling without being the whole story and without being a negative defining feature. Never before had I seen people of color and women look so loved in the same publication, in a publication that appeared targeted at me. From the looks of *Vibe* it seemed like there was now a vehicle for the stories of people who looked like me and were interested in the same things I was interested in. It looked like race was not an inhibiting force from a glance at the bylines and the masthead, which boasted women and men across ethnicities.

I asked Smith if she thought race or racism impacted her work. "I don't like to think about it, so I don't like to imagine that it has had any affect whatsoever on my personal career," she said in an interview. "Of course, it has affected my career in every way at all times. If I stopped to think about it 10 years ago or 20 years ago, I don't think that I would have done the things that I've done. One, to have a byline. Two, to manage a section and three, to run a publication and to be in rooms where the long-term decisions were made about publications."

Most of the writers who were journalists during hip hop's golden era didn't have what is referred to in the industry as "traditional newsroom experience." That meant that they had skipped the unpaid internships and glorified indentured servitude that is still prevalent in media today which generally requires young reporters to work for free in exchange for access to an ever-dwindling network of people who will be likely to pay them a small salary at some point to continue their work. This was a tangible divide even within organizations that reflected the demographic makeup of its audience, Smith said. "Within the profession there are class issues, whether you're a (National Association of Black Journalists) journalist or another type of journalist—culture journalists versus those who cover active news. If you are the type of journalist who came up as a 'hip hop journalist' and even excelled in that way, a lot of times there are issues with those in the professional organizations."

The rich narratives of multicultural audiences for advertisers in traditional media—mainly magazines that focused on niche audiences like people of color—seemed to offer an unending payday. There were some caveats. In his 2011 book, *Who's Afraid of Post-Blackness? What It Means to Be Black Now*, journalist Touré writes that trying to get his start as a magazine writer was like "trying to get deaf people to notice you in a pitch-black room."[15] Those narratives dovetailed with a few noteworthy attempts by mainstream news organizations to counter the white-centered thrust of the news media by attempting to write about race through the framework of hip hop. Generally, they missed the mark except for when they began poaching hip hop journalists from niche publications like the *Source* and *Vibe* in the mid-to-late 1990s.

As much money as there was for advertisers, it became much harder for writers to sustain a career for themselves as writers outside of hip hop culture or hip hop journalism. "As much as I love writing, I knew that writing wasn't going to be enough for me," Smith said. "And if I wanted to be towards the top of the masthead, there were things I couldn't let get in my way. There weren't a lot of role models for me. A lot of the people I reached out to weren't terribly supportive. It's very hard to get and maintain any sort of power within an organization and it makes you very nervous about the people who come up behind you."

What in two decades would become defined as journalistic entrepreneurship actually began with pioneers of hip hop journalism like Smith and her husband, a subset of minority reporting and journalism that ended up offering a groundswell of journalists who would go on to work for mainstream, or traditional outlets like their colleagues in the black press. They told the stories of people who would never get print space or air time outside of niche media except as outcasts, thugs, and worse: Tupac Shakur, Christopher Wallace, and Suge Knight among them. As hip hop matured, so did the journalists who covered it, and they went on to work in other industries or work independently as the media landscape changed beneath them. The same was true for other targeted publications like *YSB*, *Honey*, *Black Issues Book Review*, and others that struggled to find long-term investors as late as 2003 and 2004.

The Decline of Multiculturalism in Traditional Media

In traditional media, minorities were not faring better. People of color were starting to leave the journalism industry at a much faster clip than they were entering it, which coincided with a growing backlash against affirmative action. Some of this backlash was evident in reporting such as that which appeared in response to the publication of *The Bell Curve*, which outlets like the *New York Times* and the *New Republic* gave credulous coverage like much other legacy media. In a 1994 *Times* review, Malcolm Browne praised the controversial book for making "a strong case" of a "smart, rich" elite polarizing with an "unintelligent, poor" population—meaning racial and ethnic minorities.[16]

The FCC, which had been aggressive in enforcing diversity policies for broadcast license holders, started "finding race-based hiring considerations constitutionally untenable."[17] One of the most vocal critics of diversity policies, author William McGowan, claimed that affirmative action in newsrooms suppressed networks and other media from disseminating unfavorable information about people of color. It was a criticism related to the notion that it was impossible for journalists of color to be objective or for reporting about them to be something other than advocacy. McGowan complained that newsroom diversity efforts "undermined basic principles of good journalism and subverted venerable guiding principles of neutrality and objectivity."[18]

The idea that objectivity and neutrality were compromised by gender and racial diversity was a widespread sentiment that directly flew in the face of any potential progress. There would, eventually, be a space for advocacy journalism—the Solutions Journalism Network, for instance, is one example of a group steeped in results-oriented reporting to inspire change. In the meantime, the old notion that journalists across ethnicities are unfairly biased toward their communities when writing about the communities they know best was perpetuated as the main faulty justification for calls for diversity.

Unfortunately, it was as clear then it is now that if women and people of color do not produce those stories, they often will never see the light of day. The simplest explanation for that is that newsrooms are notoriously resistant to change. One of the many journalists who know this firsthand is author Minal Hajratwala, who worked as a copy editor and reader representative in California after graduating from Stanford University in the 1990s.

Hajratwala went on to write multiple books, and is the award-winning writer of *Leaving India: My Family's Journey from Five Villages to Five Continents.* Hajratwala was my instructor at a writing workshop for writers of color in California called Voices of Our Nations or VONA. She told me in a Skype interview that she remembers well the benefits and drawbacks of the rise and fall of multiculturalism as a former journalist in legacy media.

After working at a couple of tiny newspapers as part of a diversity program, she went on to work at the *San Jose Mercury News* as a copy editor in 1994. Like a number of other journalism organizations, the *Mercury News* developed a diversity audit with an eye toward improving its coverage. And like many young people of color who enter the news business, Hajratwala became the head of the diversity committee even though she was one of the most junior staff employees. When a report of the findings was released, she said, the paper didn't change too much on race, but they did add a youth reporter whose job was to cover young people.

At the time, "We had decent levels of people of color in the newsroom," Hajratwala said. The chairman and publisher at the *Mercury News*, from 1994 until 2001, was Jay T. Harris, widely regarded as the highest-ranking African American newspaper executive in the United States at the time and a diversity champion. While Harris was publisher, the *Mercury News* built one of the industry's most diverse staff and management teams—the newspaper's newsroom was more than 30 percent minority and women were more than half of the officers of the newspaper when he resigned in 2001 to protest planned layoffs—and posted record profits, according to Harris's bio at the USC Annenberg School of Communication and Journalism where he has been a member of the faculty since 2002.

When Hajratwala started working at the *Mercury News*, the newspaper had a race and demographics team, along with Spanish- and Vietnamese-language editions of the paper. Diversity audits were a popular enterprise with newspaper executives, so Hajratwala, along with many others, continued to do that work, to no avail. What audits revealed were one thing, but, she said, "We were finding that it really wasn't translated into coverage. The diversity in hiring was happening, but it wasn't really changing the coverage because the coverage was all aligned with this old beat system—City Hall, Police. Whether or not those reporters were people of color, they were locked into what the coverage was."[19]

The entrenched pattern of coverage in traditional media along the beat system has always offered organization to outlets that once seemed to be a structure dedicated to keeping editors, producers, and writers from missing important news in a variety of spheres. Examples of typical beats include sports, style, music, books, crime, religion, or international news produced from a bureau. Because most gatekeepers in the traditional media realm—later to be replicated on the Internet—are white middle-class and upper-class men, their purview decidedly influences coverage. In other words, what they believe is newsworthy along these coverage lines determines what goes on news broadcasts, radio segments, and on the front page of newspapers and magazines. It is a continuing feature of racial disparities and white privilege that the stories with the greatest relevance to people of color and women are generally buried in newspapers and magazines, if they are featured at all.

This is why Hajratwala noted that the paper's sporadic diversity audits ultimately didn't make much of a difference. "The data was the same. It didn't shift from year to year. The problem was structural, in terms of what the news priorities were and how the front-page decisions were made and the whole system of how people decided what was worth covering and promoting." There might be projects, like a series produced at the *Mercury News* on Mexican Americans with stories about the challenges of sending money home to Mexico, for example. "But it wouldn't affect the day-to-day coverage."

The most significant challenges to impacting day-to-day coverage were manifold. They included what Hajratwala called "subtle levels of racism," archaic, and hard-to-understand systems of promotions and resistance—particularly from senior white male reporters—to make the extra effort to reach out to women and people of color in stories that were not specifically centered on race or gender. Why not interview a few women for a story on a piece of legislation or interview an Asian American family about Back to School or Black Friday shopping, for instance? Reporters of color didn't want to be pigeonholed by being required to solely cover their respective communities and often white reporters charged with quoting any random person on the street "just didn't want to add diversity, they really didn't," Hajratwala said. "They expressed that as a fear of compromising the objectivity or the purity of the news."

It was both affirming and disappointing to hear that Hajratwala experienced the same things I did when I became a full-time reporter at the *San Francisco Chronicle* in 2002. At the end of my fellowship with the Hearst Newspaper Corporation, I was 24 years old. I had worked at the *Houston Chronicle*, the *Beaumont Enterprise*, and the ill-fated *Seattle Post-Intelligencer*, which stopped its print edition and went online-only in 2009. When I was hired as a features reporter at the *San Francisco Chronicle* in 2002, it made me the only full-time staff writer at the paper who was a black woman. I was also the youngest person at the paper, aside from the editorial assistants, prompting a colleague to say, with a half-smirk, "I have sweaters older than you."

Not only were many of my colleagues probably collectors of a number of ancient sweaters, but they were largely white and male, especially at the editor level and on the metro, sports, and investigative desks. The *Chronicle* had just merged with the *San Francisco Examiner* a few years before I was hired, so there were a number of people of color at the paper, including a couple of women of color editors, a handful of Asian reporters and editors, and a couple of African American writers working in the East Bay bureau. I immediately began to write stories that I would've wanted to read about emancipating foster youth, profiles of well-regarded artists like Alice Walker and Spike Lee and much more.

It didn't take long for me to notice that editors took full advantage of the fact that I liked writing about women, people of color, and youth. Coincidentally, these were the kinds of stories that had been largely missing from the paper in one of the country's most diverse media markets. In addition to writing all kinds of features, I was enlisted at the beginning of my time at the *Chronicle* to write a story about the "culture of death" in Oakland. (This after I was warned not to venture alone into the predominantly black neighborhood Bayview Hunters Point by myself, implying that it was a dangerous neighborhood because it was predominantly black and poor. Unsurprisingly for a woman with my background, it turned out to be the place I felt most comfortable in San Francisco.) I worked on the story with a white colleague, who did some reporting from the bureau while I went to the flatlands of East Oakland to attend the funeral of a teenager who had been shot to death in front of a memorial for another teenage boy.

The story, "On Sorrow's Turf," would be my sole front-page byline during my three-year stint at the *Chronicle*. It was, by far, the most celebrated piece I produced there. While I would like to credit my writing skill, I also understand why so many people loved it—and it still makes me nauseous to have that understanding. The story reaffirmed the perception of African American culture as centered on dysfunction, death, and pathology that traditional media have continued to focus on throughout my generation. I wrote what I saw and what I experienced in reporting the story as someone from a similar place, but it took me years to process that my value as a reporter at the *Chronicle* came at the expense of telling stories that I deemed important as a human being, not just as a black woman who was raised in poverty in New York City.

I felt a double burden, described by author Joan C. Williams and others as "double jeopardy," which is the intersection of bias that accumulates against a person for being both black and a woman. You could argue, too, that my youth was an added burden. Young journalists have the energy and heart to pursue important stories with verve and vigor, but when it comes to driving intentional coverage, young reporters lack the gravitas to advocate for the kind of changes to coverage of women and people of color that truly matter: How stories are situated in coverage, where they are placed, what they include, what the headline conveys about the stories, and more.

Above all, I felt increasingly confused and frustrated by my experience. My white mentors told me that I was lucky to be where I was as a black woman in her 20s who was working for a destination paper—a phrase that is code for the place where old reporters go to work until they retire or die, whichever comes first. But I knew I didn't want to stay at the *Chronicle* for nearly that long. When I worked with another Hearst fellow and photographer on a story about three generations of a middle-class African American family in Oakland, the story ran inside despite meticulous reporting and beautiful photographs. My white male editors found it to be quaint, but without newsworthiness.

During my time at the *Chronicle*, I was also pulled into a diversity audit similar to that Hajratwala described at the *Mercury News*. A diversity committee was established with the partial attention of the *Chronicle* editor at the time, Phil Bronstein. Under the leadership of the Maynard Institute, we analyzed a week's worth of newspapers to confirm what we knew, which was that there was very little coverage of relevance to the diverse Bay Area in our pages. Dori Maynard gave our newspaper suggestions for how to improve its coverage, line by line and story by story.

Unfortunately, nothing changed.

The Beginning of the End

Instead of encouraging young people, women, and people of color to stay in their ranks, traditional media have often made the work of these journalists so untenable that they have left the industry for less demanding and less emotionally taxing work that also offers more financial stability and upward mobility. Though traditional media have been ailing for many years, cracks in the foundation of gender and race diversity that had been laid in the 1970s and 1980s began developing rapidly after 1995, when Roger Ailes and Rupert Murdoch joined forces to create Fox News, the FCC began allowing more and more media monopolies to collapse an array of print, radio, and broadcast sources and a backlash against affirmative action joined forces with general economic turmoil.[20]

A report by the Freedom Forum issued in 2000 showed that between 1994 and 1999, print newsrooms had collectively hired an average of 500 minority journalists a year. An average of 440 a year had also left. By 2000, the gap had widened to 600 hired, 698 departed.[21]

Though I tried hard to get to a point in my reporting career where I would feel the romanticism and nostalgia for newspaper reporting that my white male colleagues expressed effusively as the business began to collapse, I never got there. Like many women and people of color, I always felt like an unwelcome visitor in a foreign land where even if I learned the language, no one would really listen to what I had to say.

This is why in 2003, when the *New York Times* seemed to implode after Jayson Blair was found to have been a serial plagiarist, I wrote about it. "When a young person causes a glitch in the proverbial ladder-climbing matrix, he or she makes us all look suspect," I wrote at the time. "But the system is faulty: The fewer of us there are—young, black or other—the more pressure there is for us to be exceptional and prove that the rest of our ilk aren't so bad, so that eventually, the higher-ups will feel comfortable throwing the door of opportunity wide open. . . . Perhaps if more of us were allowed to get our feet in the door in the first place, there wouldn't be so many extreme examples of young people ditching their ethics in the name of success."[22]

I wrote a good game, but I was also struggling under the pressure and I nearly worked myself to death. I had four editors in the span of three years, including a woman who refused to read e-mail or use the newspaper's content management system to edit stories. That meant that I had to print out double-spaced copies of my stories and deliver them to her by hand. Her glorious edits were often returned to me in the same fashion.

After losing 15 pounds from the stress and anxiety of working so much, I retreated to my tiny apartment in Oakland to work from home, where, for weeks at a time, I was never contacted by anyone at the newspaper as long as I handed in my stories on time. The combination of the ongoing bad news about the financial state of the newspaper—the *Chronicle* lost more than $60 million in 2005—and my general unhappiness led me to move back to Texas to shift careers. I thought about the end goal—which was to find a job that would pay me well enough that I could support my expensive writing habit—and decided to try another profession: Librarianship. Like journalists, librarians are defenders of free speech and democracy; they know how to find vast amounts of information quickly.

My friends were worried. One said that it sounded like I was trying to hide. It was the first time in my life I took a risk that felt completely right for me even if most people disagreed. I ended up working at the *Austin American-Statesman* for several more years, which turned out to be the highlight of my reporting career. There, I started at the bottom, making cop calls to dozens of public safety officers twice a shift. I pioneered the newsroom's breaking news cops morning shift, which began at 5:30 a.m. and ended around 2 p.m., so I could take graduate classes at the University of Texas' School of Information in the evenings.

Between 2006 and 2009, I am not sure when I slept eight hours a week, let alone a night. But earning my graduate degree helped me feel secure enough about finding another job while the increasing instability of newspaper life continued to crowd e-mails in my inbox and headlines around the world. It gave me the credentials I needed to be a lecturer.

I tried actual librarianship, but it wasn't for me. I needed to write for a living. I needed the interaction, the adrenaline of a deadline, of breaking news. I missed the ornery dynamism of my newsroom colleagues when

I was working a part-time shift on the reference desk at a community college in Austin. When I left the newspaper business in 2011, it was clear to me that there were far more options for advancement, lower stress levels, and less entrenched bias against women and minorities in other fields.

My mother had fallen ill and was dying. My father had died by suicide the year before. Grieving my father and worrying about my mother while also fretting over the future of my profession and the status of my job proved to be too great a load to carry, so I made another unpopular decision and left. There were many who left after me, either through buyouts or just from being fed up. There had been many before us who had made a similar decision. "To some extent, minority newsroom exodus responds to the general newsroom environment," de Uriarte wrote. "By 1993, overall morale had declined sharply." One example of this was one of the early rounds of newspaper buyouts at the *Los Angeles Times*, where 659 journalists took early retirement instead of a predicted 200.[23]

At the end of the 1990s, ASNE was a perfect example of a media organization that was still trying for diversity while acknowledging that it would never reach the parity it was searching for. The organization initiated "Time Out for Diversity," a coordinated nationwide effort for more inclusive coverage after realizing in 1998 that newsroom parity in 2000 would not be attained. Only four years later, ASNE would be further from its 1978 goal than it was when it began.[24] In 1996, Betty Medsger's "Winds of Change" study showed the growing distance between the professional press and journalism educators.

If there was one person or journalist who could be said to have contributed to increasing attention to women and people of color for better journalistic representation, it would be Oprah Winfrey. There was no greater success story for a journalist of color, and there may never be again. Boston University journalism professor Christopher Daly put it this way in a talk at the Library of Congress called "Covering America: A Nation's Journalism": "Above all though, there is Oprah, the ultimate . . . high-impact, cross-over, all-platform media mogul. . . . Every weekday for 25 years she had a chat with the millions of American viewers of her TV show—mostly women, mostly white, and millions more in the 119 other countries where it appeared or continues to appear. . . . Her ratings, sales, and earnings were so vast at her peak that they made the case for at least the beginnings of a post-racial media universe in America. Even Oprah never could have amassed such a record if it were based on African-American readers or viewers alone."[25]

One could make the argument that Oprah's success came from the sheer breadth of her audience and the universality of her shows. The other thing was that no one person, outlet, or organization would make significant gains without diversity in a nation that was increasingly nonwhite. It was a diversity that she reflected in nearly everything she did.

Throughout the 1990s, America's immigrant population grew by more than it had during any other period: 11.3 million. Women were beginning to make inroads as pioneers at the helm of a few Fortune 500 businesses, in the military and in journalism, after decades of journalists-turned-activists like Gloria Steinem and Betty Friedan had paved the way.

But the multiculturalism in journalism that paralleled hip hop's golden era was complicated by the rise of the Internet, a dot-com boom and bust that led to the creation and extinction of several media brands and a shaky economy that was just beginning to recover when September 11, 2001, changed the nature of journalism coverage and the Internet was becoming a more ubiquitous news delivery system. Now, it became clear that it was not only important to talk to diverse subjects or to reach out to diverse demographics—there was an imperative for a diversity of news dissemination whether or not editors and producers liked it.

Chapter 6

How Social Media Replaced Traditional Media for Women and People of Color

The Global Power of Twitter

I joined Twitter as a newspaper reporter who was trying and failing to quit journalism. I learned of Twitter's power for global storytelling in real time as a library student at the University of Texas Austin while I was also a full-time cops reporter at the *Austin American-Statesman*. At the time, I had been in Austin for two years and in graduate school at the School of Information for almost six months.

It was the afternoon of April 16, 2007. Hundreds of miles away, Virginia Polytechnic Institute and State University student Seung-Hui Cho had killed 27 people on campus before shooting himself in the deadliest shooting rampage in American history. I knew from my experience in journalism to expect comparisons to other events in places like Columbine. But what was new for me was the ability to see the reactions of my peers around the world.

At the front of the classroom, a professor had projected a global map of Twitter reactions to the shooting. Like my classmates, I was transfixed by our ability to see the reactions of others to a news event as the details unfolded. While it was clear to me then that Twitter had the potential to change news and news delivery, I wasn't quite sure how that might happen.

Journalism, after all, was concerned with authoritatively delivering the news to readers. What would happen when the audience controlled news delivery? I also couldn't imagine a world where news was user-generated, in part because I was so used to editors vetting questionable facts or sources in my stories. Who would control media generated by their audience? Who would check for errors or stop the spread of wrong information? While these were valid concerns, the obvious benefits to users were also clear.

Instinctively, I could feel the difference between reading the thoughts of my peers in their words and my daily experience of editing commentary as part of a corporate intermediary. There was something powerful about the eye-witness accounts that were unfiltered by reporters, something liberating.

It was an exciting difference for me, since my motivation for becoming a journalist stemmed from wanting to be a witness for marginalized voices that were seldom heard in mainstream journalism. So Twitter, like all of social networking, to me, seemed not just revolutionary but also like a natural progression of the kind of storytelling I wanted to be a part of: Unfiltered, authentic, and global. Facebook, which became available to non-academic audiences in 2006, had the same kind of potential, and the *Statesman* was one of a few newspapers I noticed that was an early adopter of social networking as a vehicle for news before the social network became savvy about its potential to operate as its own news delivery system. I would always have problems with the opaque power structure of what one can see on Facebook, the murky manipulation that lurks just beyond the "News Feed," and the domination of Facebook when it comes to website traffic. But when both Twitter and Facebook emerged, they were revelatory: Social media provided a new way of thinking about how to tell stories, particularly to women and people of color who were so often condescended to or ignored in traditional media.

The irony of sitting in my library school classroom thinking about the future of journalism was that I knew deep down that I was too passionate about telling stories for a living to ever be satisfied changing careers. But I pursued library science as a practical way to potentially feed myself while the traditional print media business grew increasingly unstable and unsustainable. Daily, my e-mail inbox brimmed with the heartbreaking stories of layoffs, buy-outs, and shutdowns. It was only a matter of time before journalists like myself were replaced with younger, cheaper bodies that could and would, in the words that every employee loathes, "do more with less."

In print journalism, Vanguarde Media, helmed by Keith Clinkscales, went under. Time Warner merged with AOL and deleted AOL from its title. Radio, especially in its urban format, was significantly impacted by the consolidation of companies, and soon, most stations fell under the umbrella of Clear Channel Communications. In his excellent 2004 book, *The New Media Monopoly*, Ben H. Bagdikian noted that most television, radio, and print media—expanding then to include large swaths of the digital landscape—were owned by five global media conglomerates who had a total of 141 joint ventures with one another, giving them "more communications power than was exercised by any despot or dictatorship in history."[1] The Federal Communications Commission would, as always, play a key role in the deregulation of rapidly consolidating companies, which changed the diversity of legacy media by narrowing the scope of content and political views to which audiences were exposed.

The narrowing of scope in content that followed had made it nearly impossible to get space or interest in the stories of people who lived outside of the mainstream—in-depth pieces about stories that impacted women and people of color—and our deadlines were no longer 4 or 4:30 p.m. Our deadlines seemed to be at the top of every hour. In reality, our deadlines were even more frequent than that, requiring us to update new details in court cases or breaking news events as they occurred. We were expected to blog, shoot video, edit the video, field calls from sources, conduct interviews, edit our blog with updates, and so on. We learned when we had local major breaking news—like the 2009 Fort Hood shooting about an hour north of Austin when Maj. Nidal Hassan shot 13 people—that our audiences were looking for the overview, narrative, and analysis at some point. But they also expected constantly updated, accurate news on the web, too.

Another aspect of audience expectation was a regular stream of updated Twitter and Facebook statuses, which regularly drove traffic to news websites. This seemed futile at first. How would we make money by tweeting? Was the future of the only profession I had known as an adult truly going to be determined by and described in 140 character missives?

It turned out that I was missing another great irony. When I began tweeting in 2008, as a cops reporter who would soon be writing about religion and education among other topics, I noticed that I was growing an audience not only because of the information I provided, but because I was suddenly part of a growing tribe of women and people of color who could talk to one another at any time of day or night from their mobile phones anywhere in the world. As part of a media company that awkwardly navigated the new space of individual brand creation combined with news company brand creation, my tweets were stale, bland, and not particularly fun to read. Before "Tweets do not equal endorsement" or "Tweets are my own" disclaimers began to be a staple of Twitter bios, reporters who tweeted false information or had stepped over the ever-shifting line between being a persona and being a representative of a media company were fired or reprimanded.

As early as 2001, I was connecting with my peers on Internet message boards, experimenting with online dating and finding a virtual tribe that seemed completely detached from legacy media. Finally, I had the virtual tribe of my dreams. The only down sides were that I was petrified of overstepping unclear boundaries and I was working—for free, I might add—all the time.

The Expectation of Free News

The conversation about the piracy of music that emerged around Napster and other sites that allow for the illegal, free download of music, movies, and books in retrospect had serious implications for attitudes about news and journalism. A society that believes that everything that is expensive to make should be free will certainly not want to pay for news, especially not information that isn't particularly digestible like property tax increases or bond measures. This is especially true for digital natives, whose definition of news has been understandably different from the definitions of their parents and grandparents.

News for a digital native is aggregated from multiple sources, both paid and free. It may look like what journalists call editorializing, opinion, or a simple charticle (the combination of a chart and an article, or the prehistoric version of what most people refer to now as an infographic). But if it conveys a story that has not yet been told, and if one's friends are sharing it, it is news. And if you can get news that is already filtered by people you care about and available widely online via social networks and blogs, why would you pay for a subscription?

Traditional media organizations hoped that readers and cable subscribers would care enough about the quality of news networks, newspapers, and magazines have been producing that they would pay to sustain legacy media in spite of having so many sources of information at their disposal. It was a matter of tradition. They were wrong.

With the exception of print newspapers like the *Wall Street Journal* and the *Economist*, both of which put up paywalls requiring subscriptions relatively early, most traditional media seemed slow to understand the catastrophic impact that this new model of news-sharing would have on their flagging business models. Most newspapers had also underestimated the power of the Internet to completely decimate their advertising base while also destroying their hierarchy-based news delivery system.

A good case in point: The year that I left, the *San Francisco Chronicle* reported that it had lost over $60 million in part because of the lack of advertising sales. In newspapers, advertising pays to keep the lights on and it pays staff salaries. In the Bay Area, important context was and is that Craigslist had begun to gut advertising and classified revenue because who wants to pay for a print newspaper with finite space for ads when you can go online and see an unlimited number of up-to-date listings for free? It astounded both me and my sources that the *Chronicle* could lose so much money in such a diverse place and fail to see how failing to diversify might have also cut into its ability to make a profit, but this was also an operation that had a permanent split between its online presence, SFGate.com, and its print product.

The very foundation of legacy media's authority was presumed to be imperiled by the encroaching, hierarchy-leveling presence of the Internet. The sentiment of publishers seemed to be, "Why should we worry about what people are doing for free online? All the money is out here in the real world." The arrogance of my former employer was shared by many other newspapers and media outlets. In some ways, it still is, because the people in power at legacy organizations came of age during a time when authority trumped what *Everything Is Miscellaneous: The Power of the New Digital Disorder* author David Weinberger calls social expertise—the value of groups gathering on social news sites like Digg or Reddit, which allow audiences to bond socially while also deciding for themselves which news is more important instead of leaving that decision to mostly white men gathering each day to decide what should go on the front pages of newspapers.

"This binding is certainly different from the way broadcast media have formed one nation, under Walter Cronkite," Weinberger writes. "With everyone seeing the same national news and reading the same handful of local newspapers, there was a shared experience we could count on." Now, as audiences molecularize and form groups that create culture, the journalism ecosystem has entered a purgatory between "the expertise of the men in the editorial boardroom and the "wisdom of crowds."[2]

The mere idea that audiences would know better what they want to read, hear, and watch and how they want to see themselves portrayed is one that has not seemed to penetrate the citadels of traditional media, with some key exceptions. With billions of users, social networks have offered media an opportunity to poll the masses, to talk to them, to convey that information in an infographic, to track trends, to pivot more quickly to give audiences what they want in order to succeed. But metrics, even good ones, are not replacements for good business models. A sound social media strategy is not, by any means, a panacea to the problem of the increasing irrelevance of traditional media—digitization of the news has not become a sustainable economic model. No one has yet figured out how to make money from the way social media help spread information, or how to mitigate damage when social networks spread inaccurate information. It certainly doesn't help that much of traditional media still operates like a stubborn old dad who refuses to trade in his dusty old Walkman for an iPod: A patriarch holding fast to the rules of yesteryear, while his children propel themselves toward the future.

An Opportunity to Talk Back

Caveats aside, the key power of social networks is that they affirm for women and people of color who are traditionally ignored or stereotyped in legacy media that they can empower themselves with a broader array of information sources that are tailored to them than has ever been possible in the past. As a result, they are utilizing the social web to have their say, to talk back to legacy media that disparage or ignore them, and to create or own the narratives they want perpetuated about them for the historical record. Social media, specifically Twitter, have also been used to amplify and promote activism around the world, creating a synchronicity between making news and being a news consumer.

This is possible because women dominate pretty much every social network with the exception of LinkedIn.[3] In traditional media, this is typically framed as women who are the living embodiment of soft features, especially as it relates to Pinterest, where early stories reported the stereotypical uses of the pinning site to share recipes or fantasize about weddings. They would not be the sole demographic to be dissected for their use of social media.

Latinos and African Americans, in particular, are heavy users of social networks of all kinds, especially Twitter: The Pew Research Internet Project reports that overall 73 percent of African American Internet users—and 96 percent of those ages 18–29—use a social networking site of some kind. Twenty-two percent of blacks online use Twitter, compared to 16 percent of their white counterparts.[4]

The latter statistics have led to the characterization of African American Twitter engagement as simply Black Twitter. This is an opportunity for African Americans who are typically portrayed in traditional media as criminals, jezebels, and worse to have a space where they can engage in dialogue with one another and call out examples of virulent racism and, in many cases, the intersectional issues of racism, sexism, and classism. I have heard Twitter referred to as a natural extension of the African oral tradition, which seems to be the best description of its organizing effect on the thoughts and opinions shared by black users.

For women, social networking can function similarly as a safe space—with some key exceptions related to online harassment that also impacts minorities—in which to dialogue with each other, to call out sexism, and to leverage their ability to forge relationships on a global platform. As an essential part of popular culture, cultivating a presence in cyberspace isn't without serious drawbacks. Just like in real life, there's always more than enough online drama to go around.

For women, though, things can quickly shift into dangerous territory offline. In "Why Women Aren't Welcome on the Internet," journalist Amanda Hess describes rape threats directed at her for simply being a woman with an Internet connection. She notes that 72.5 percent of people who reported being stalked or harassed online between 2000 and 2012 in one study were women.[5] As revealed in Gamergate, a hashtag and movement that unfolded in October 2014 when Zoe Quinn, a female game developer, came under attack by angry young men—even receiving death threats that sent her couchsurfing for weeks—sexism reaches every corner of media coverage, online and off. For women of color, the online complexities are even worse.

Two of the most extreme cases involved high-profile women of color providing commentary on controversial topics. In February 2014, professor Brittney Cooper received death threats and an onslaught of racist, sexist vitriol in response to a piece she wrote at *Salon* about a Florida jury's failure to convict Michael Dunn, a white man who was charged with shooting Jordan Davis, a black teenager. During the summer of 2013, Salamishah Tillet was attacked even more viciously after she appeared as a guest on the *Melissa Harris-Perry* show and talked about the intersection of racism and the anti-abortion movement.

Tillet, an English professor at the University of Pennsylvania and cofounder of the nonprofit A Long Walk Home, was mentioned in a segment on Fox News' *The O'Reilly Factor*—and then the first wave of attacks started. "I was flooded by letters, emails and phone calls all the way up to the Provost of my University," Tillet said in a phone interview. "My faculty colleagues and president were all contacted, and then we heard from alumni and television viewers. (Bill O'Reilly's) viewership, at least the people who contact you, is a machine. It's really a lot."

The strangest manifestation of the attacks on Tillet, though, might have been the 80 magazine subscriptions that she had to individually write and cancel, she said. "Because my credit was involved, that was more effective than the harassment. But online, people were calling me a wench, and I had to contact the police and on campus security. At least when people go after you on Twitter, you experience that as a norm," Tillet said. "But I was unprepared for both. It was really frightening."

Sometimes the scale at which women of color are attacked is not as visible. In October 2013, biologist and postdoctoral research associate at Oklahoma State University Danielle N. Lee declined an editor's request to blog at his site for free and was subsequently called an "urban whore." Lee was a contributor to *Scientific American* where her Urban Scientist blog amplified diverse aspects of the sciences and offered the rare perspective of a black woman conducting research while also drawing on hip hop culture. In the wake of her interaction with the editor, identified only as Ofek, *Scientific American* deleted her blog post about the interaction, then restored it to the site with a lengthy explanation of why it was removed. Lee also made a YouTube video in response to the incident and posted a response blog on her personal site.

"The whole thing got conflated," Lee said later. As for what others might learn from her experience, she said, "Sometimes I feel like I'm still figuring that out. What I've learned so far is that the crap doesn't end because you reach some level of success. The crap continues."[6]

University of Denver law professor Nancy Leong said she also noticed that the more visible her work became, the more of a target she became for all kinds of online drama. When Leong writes about online harassment leveled at women, as she did in a four-part series of blogs at Feminist Law Professors, she pointed out that "Internet harassers focus on identity rather than on ideas as a specific strategy for excluding women and people of color from online discourse."

Leong teaches constitutional rights, criminal procedure, and judicial behavior, among other things. But the fact that she is photogenic combined with her Native Hawaiian heritage has set off self-identified men on the Internet. This was underscored after she wrote an article published in the *Harvard Law Review* entitled "Racial Capitalism" but it got even worse when she started to blog about the other things that were happening, including someone creating a fake Twitter account using her name, her cell phone number and address being posted publicly, and the address of her parents being posted online.

Instead of garnering her colleagues' support, Leong said that she experienced a lot of victim-blaming, particularly from white men. Her experience was so far beyond anything they experienced, she said, that they weren't able to empathize. "A lot of my colleagues said stuff to me like, 'You made this worse by speaking out about it,'" Leong said. "In other words, 'If you had just gone about your business, then a lot of things that happened on the Internet wouldn't have happened.' As academics who work in the world of ideas and presumably care about what we research beyond what academics think about it, I thought it was important to raise awareness about the harassment."[7]

That harassment has grown as the number of adults online has increased steadily. The Pew Research Center reports that 72 percent of adults used social networking sites in 2013 and for a number of social networking sites, the number of women using the Internet is higher than the number of men.[8] That allows for a kind of consciousness-raising and awareness to be possible online that has generally been impossible for traditional media to foster. Traditional media are reactionary: slow-moving heavyweights that take too long to move out of the way of the svelte, real-time, quick-paced lightweight of social media.

When powerful women like Tina Brown[9] or Jill Abramson[10] are profiled by large journalism outlets like *Politico* that proceed to make them seem like harried, high-strung, emotional shrews, the sexist tinge of newsrooms where women were relegated for decades to the "pink ghettos" of feature sections are evident even to casual readers. But social media offer the opportunity for women journalists to quickly share their opinions and register their dismay via comments on the story itself or by voicing their opinions on social media. This is particularly important because gender parity for women is still elusive across media, both traditional and online.

At the end of 2014, the masthead of the *Washington Post* was all-male. The Women's Media Center reported in 2014 that men composed 63.4 percent of all journalism coverage compared to 36.1 percent of women. It is no wonder, then, that women have taken to social networks like Twitter, Pinterest, and Facebook to talk back to outlets and to assert, with the currency of their attention and through leveraging their many networks, why ignoring them is a huge mistake.

One of the best examples of this arrived during the summer of 2013.

On June 25, 2013, Texas senator Wendy Davis was cheered on by protesters via social media around the world, helped by livestreams on YouTube and the *Texas Tribune* website. Davis led a more than 10-hour filibuster in pink sneakers as she attempted to stall the Texas Senate vote on Senate Bill 5, a Republican-backed abortion bill that would close most clinics in the state. But most national mainstream news outlets were curiously silent on her historic act of defiance. (Notably, CNN aired a segment during the filibuster about the caloric content of a blueberry muffin.)[11] She aimed to filibuster until midnight, but the Texas GOP interrupted, at least as the story was reported and captured by the hundreds of her supporters and activists who had gathered outside and in the gallery at the state capitol to cheer her on.

Tweets noted the failure of mainstream media in the face of social media to deliver the coverage that others were looking for. "The revolution will not be televised," a number of people noted. Evan Smith, editor of the *Texas Tribune*, wrote in a tweet, "Last night it was livestreamed." In an interview with Ann Friedman for *Columbia Journalism Review*, Smith noted that 180,000 people watched the livestream from his nonprofit site. The end result wasn't just that the *Tribune* used existing technology to deliver to audiences what it wanted: delivering the livestream to so many and beating legacy media also came with financial benefits. Days later, Smith reported that the *Tribune* had received 419 memberships—99 percent of them new—from people in 35 states and collected $23,571 in donations.[12]

It was a pivotal moment showing how important news filtered by individuals is becoming for a younger, more diverse group of news consumers, many of whom didn't have television and were viewing the Senate procedures live on smartphones and laptops. For the length of her filibuster, Senator Wendy Davis was trending on Twitter, and she inspired Texas women to change their Facebook profiles—her #StandwithWendy hashtag was only slightly obscured by national coverage of the Supreme Court's 5–4 vote to invalidate the heart of the Voting Rights Act of 1965 by allowing nine Southern states to change their election laws without advance federal approval.[13]

Five years after I joined Twitter, and not long after Facebook and Instagram started utilizing hashtags, I noticed that the use of this popular Internet vernacular was becoming what librarians refer to as metadata—or information about information. In nonlibrarian speak, hashtags became information about information, an organizing principle around which advocates, activists, writers, journalists, or anyone else could start a conversation or join one.

While anyone can make a hashtag, it was the whirlwind protests of Arab Spring and Occupy Wall Street that raised the global visibility of hashtags as a way to start and sustain global interest in a topic. This was true in the aftermath of Superstorm Sandy as well as for #StandWithWendy and hashtags like #Solidarityisforblackmen, which went nowhere and

#Solidarityisforwhitewomen, which inspired a *Salon* series on feminists of color. #NotYourAsianSidekick, started by freelance writer Suey Park, became so popular that she was profiled in the *Washington Post*, *BBC*, and *Al-Jazeera*. In the wake of a grand jury's failure to indict the police officer who was responsible for the death of Eric Garner in New York City, #ICant-Breathe and #BlackLivesMatter kept the issue of community policing, racial inequity in criminal justice decisions, and an international spirit of protest in the news.

But like everything else on the Internet, hashtags are not all serious all the time. They can make important points about problems of racism and sexism while also being funny or entertaining. The #Racethemed hashtag, for instance, was inspired by *USA Today*, when it fumbled a headline in November 2013 about black movies, referring to them as diverse films that are "race-themed" in a story about *The Best Man Holiday* making $30 million in opening box office weekend, surpassing industry expectations. When *Lifetime* aired a biopic about Aaliyah that was considered poorly cast, Black Twitter made merciless fun of the network.

It is these frivolous moments that are sometimes considered the whole of what social media offer, particularly to an older demographic that considers social networking to be solely about vapid content like cat photos and wacky memes. But there are real financial gains for leveraging social media reach for audience growth, and the opportunity for consumers to talk back to news creators is one that television networks have taken advantage of with amazing results. Especially considering that African American buying power is set to top $1 trillion in 2015,[14] there is no better business case for brands that are still holding out on engaging social networks like Twitter. The BET Awards in 2013, for example, accounted for 51 percent of all social chatter and drew 7.6 million viewers.[15] Popular TV shows, particularly those with diverse characters like Shonda Rhimes's *Scandal*, or Mara Brock Akil's BET show, *Being Mary Jane*, also have a significant social reach that grows only with successive episodes and displays how much money businesses leave on the table by failing to consider diversity as a business priority.

The Benefit and Shortfalls of Circumventing Mainstream Outlets

The democratization of news sharing via social networking sites like Tumblr, Pinterest, Twitter, and Facebook has allowed niche audiences to circumvent mainstream media to place news they find of interest on their virtual timelines and front pages. In particular, Facebook has been a top referral engine for news organizations, as audiences continue to express their preference for news they discover by way of their friends. This is particularly important for minorities, who outpace whites when it comes to social technology use. A 2010 Pew Research study found that among all adult Internet users, 7 in 10 blacks and English-speaking Latinos use social networking sites—a rate significantly higher than the 6 in 10 whites who do so. While only a third of white Internet users go to a social networking site daily, half of all African Americans do. That number is particularly high on Twitter, which a quarter of African Americans who are online consistently visit, compared to 15 percent of their white counterparts and 20 percent of English-speaking Latinos.[16]

Millions of blogs are published each day around the world, and while sites like the *Root*, *New America Media*, *America's Wire*, and the Maynard Institute for Journalism Education aggregate from mainstream websites, news wires and other sources, they also have taken a page from the pioneering alternative ethnic press by producing separate content for community stories. This becomes essential for branding on social media, allowing audiences to find the stories they are searching for that are of relevance to them easily, especially utilizing growing mobile technology to stay informed.

Universal acceptance of social media as a valid news source only seemed to arrive after Barack Obama won the presidency in 2008, after leveraging social networks to rally his base while most Republicans failed to engage women and minority voters in any comparable way. In late 2014, as speculation about frontrunners for the 2016 race began, there was some discussion about Republican shifts in an online strategy. But if this late 2013 tweet from the Republican National Committee declaring "Today we remember Rosa Parks' bold stand and her role in ending racism"[17] is any indication, there is still more work to do. Thankfully, in May 2014, Republicans launched the Latino Victory Project with celebrity Eva Longoria, to considerable media fanfare, a fact covered in both ethnic and mainstream media.

Speaking of politics, since social media tend to skew liberal with more than half of all users identifying as Independents or Democrats, Fox News has become the Republican equivalent of social media for women and people of color. Media critic and author Eric Deggans describes the audience at Fox as a bit older as well as more male and white than other outlets. While only about 36 percent of the general public considers itself conservative, more than 70 percent of the audiences for Bill O'Reilly, Glenn Beck, Sean

Hannity, and Rush Limbaugh call themselves conservatives,[18] underscoring a kind of self-segregation that falls along gender and racial faultlines.

Another kind of self-segregation underscores some of the inherent contradictions of social media and the pitfalls of circumventing mainstream media outlets. Citizen journalism is a sexy concept for traditional media because it allows for user-generated content in a new media system without the high cost of investigative reporting. All that is required on the surface is a smartphone, a Wi-Fi connection, and the right timing on the proper platform, and story can go viral. But citizen journalism is less appealing when factors that shape the central role of journalism—such as ethical conduct or integrity in newsgathering—in American democracy are imperiled by the uneasy, and sometimes downright hostile relationship between citizen journalism and legacy media.

In short, journalism is becoming a profession that favors strategic amateurs, or accidental reporters who learn about journalistic ethics and more as they stumble into their new hobby instead as part of a system geared toward streamlining news literacy. Everyone thinks they can be a journalist now, and while they have the power of documentation and timeliness as key assets, important newsgathering standards are falling by the way side.

Some of this is shaped by an Internet that makes it unclear who owns the content that citizen journalists ultimately produce and share. While in traditional media, it is clear that corporations own content developed by journalists, on the Internet, things are a bit more fuzzy. In her 2014 book, *The People's Platform: Taking Back Power and Culture in the Digital Age*, Astra Taylor explains the power of the infrastructure of the Internet, along with the benefits and drawbacks of that structure. The Internet gives consumers power over their consumption, but it isn't nearly as transparent a process/system as it could be. The problems that disrupted the old media system—commercialism, consolidation, and centralization—have carried over into the digital sphere. "Networked technologies do not resolve the contradictions between art and commerce, but rather make commercialism less visible and more persuasive,"[19] she writes.

Speaking of making commercialism less transparent, there is perhaps no social network where this is more in evidence than Facebook. Numerous incidents involving the network tinkering with what users see in their news feed have surfaced—whether it is related to Facebook's mood experiment involving more than 700,000 of its users without their knowledge or consent or it concerns their likelihood to vote. What Facebook has in common with all social networks to some degree (and with legacy media in particular) is the question of power. The power of social media is that it allows citizen journalists to circumvent mainstream media outlets and, sometimes, scoop them. But as New York University professor Jay Rosen cautioned journalists in an April 2014 blog: "Facebook has all the power. You have almost none."[20]

When it comes to power, which translates in journalism to influence, reach, and visibility, citizen journalists can have an outsized proportion of all three to their reporting experience. Lack of formal or on-the-job journalism training can be more of a weakness than a strength. Reporting the news is not only expensive and exhausting, but it also has legal implications that are ever evolving in the digital realm. Media organizations like TMZ, for example, are well known for breaking a traditional media taboo by paying sources for stories. This sets up a conflict of interest for any citizen journalist who might follow suit in search of a scoop. Along with the costs associated with independent reporting, there is the important matter of accuracy. Errors go viral as quickly as celebrity deaths and are not as easy to retract and correct as they once were.

Though hoaxes have become easier to discern as all journalists adapt to the new news literacy that social media require in order for them to keep from destroying their credibility as journalists and/or brands, it takes critical thinking and collective maturity for audiences to cultivate a reporter's instinct for sussing out inaccurate or implausible stories. Brevity is both a tremendous asset and a detriment to social media where oversimplification of complicated matters like race and gender is rampant.

There is also the danger in new media of replicating old stereotypes: One current example is the viral street harassment video featuring actress Shoshana Roberts produced by the organization Hollaback. When the video went viral in late 2014, Hollaback issued an apology in reaction to criticism that editing of the video made it appear that the actress had only been harassed by men of color in New York City. If that seems like an oversensitive reaction, it's because of a long history of hypersexualization of black and Latino men in media that a century ago would be likely to end in lynchings for the mere suggestion that a white woman was approached by anyone other than a white man.

Still, nothing has yet been able to compete with social media for timeliness, diversity, reach, and accessibility. This is the main threat that social media pose to legacy media, despite the fact that no one has yet figured out how to monetize and sustain this evolving model. But that combination explains how the story of Wendy Davis went viral while CNN and other mainstream media outlets ignored her and what she represented in Texas and nationally; how trending hashtags have fostered important dialogue outside of legacy media circles and later informed think pieces, a kind of reactionary opinion journalism hybrid easily found at sites like *Salon* and the *Week* (I have, admittedly, contributed think pieces to both these and to other outlets). But the overriding power of social media is what they share in common with their analog predecessors, zines. Social media allow consumers, activists, and citizens alike to circumvent corporate-controlled centers of information and deliver critical information directly to one another. This is a powerful model even with all of their technical flaws.

James Carey is quoted as saying that the soul of democracy is conversation and conversation is journalism.[21] The main flaw of social media, like any other alternative medium, is also their prevailing strength; they are anti-authoritarian, allowing citizens in conversation to elevate their opinions and actions to the attention of journalists instead of operating the way news always has, which is the other way around. This is true not just in America, but around the world, where 59 percent of journalists use Twitter,[22] up from 47 percent in 2013. This becomes particularly important in the case of incendiary stories like those showing a pattern of police brutality in black communities in cities like Ferguson, Missouri; Cleveland, Ohio; and New York City.

The great irony of all of the angst related to the collapse of print and traditional media hierarchies is that the bulk of the concern is related to how to stay profitable after years of inequitable (some might say outrageous) pay scales for editors and producers versus reporters. Top heavy traditional media business models, like all others who follow an old system based on faux-meritocracy, are no longer sustainable now that hierarchies have been flattened by the Internet and there's no going back. Gone are the Watergate days, where a journalists' career could be defined and secured by an amazing scoop.

The most compelling narratives, the ones that history will sustain, have turned out to be those stories that are not dependent on commercial success. They are narratives about human beings that rarely register the kind of traffic of pet photo galleries, bloody beheadings, or scary riots. Now that audiences can talk to each other 24/7 about their feelings and day-to-day experiences, they are able to do so without intermediaries, and, increasingly, they prefer that to traditional media.

Chapter 7

Conclusion: The Progress of Women and People of Color since Integration in Journalism

Societies get the journalism they deserve. This is one way of saying what the Kerner Commission put forward back in 1968, and a call to action for anyone who cares about making a long-term investment in the future of media. Put another way, the journalism of the future will have to reflect the investments that the industry decides to make, collectively, as it transforms. If those investments do not include a serious, coordinated effort to make news organizations reflect the racial, ethnic, and gender diversity of their audiences, journalism will continue to suffer financially and in terms of how the profession is viewed by the public.

It is, of course, hyperbole to suggest that traditional media have died. The death of journalism, particularly after the economic challenges that rocked every industry after 2001, has been widely reported and forecasted, but there are still some signs of vitality if not competitive rigor. The eulogies written for traditional media mostly reflect the malaise and concern of journalists who have dedicated their lives and invested their livelihoods in a profession that is, at best, noble and at worst a reflection of inability of the United States to rise to meet the many roads that lead to long-term social progress.

The future of a strong and inclusive media will require, then, that powerful white men take stock of the overall lack of true progress the industry has made elevating the voices of the future minority-majority and women, who by and large are outpacing men as American breadwinners. It will also mean considering the notable improvements that women and people of color bring to journalism and the value they add. This is true for most arenas of public life, even if more than 60 years after signature legislation such as *Brown v. Board of Education* and the Civil Rights Act of 1964, collective attention to the significance and importance of equitable treatment has waned.

This is where the power of technology can be leveraged to improve the future of journalism, and where opportunity lies to make the future more inclusive for women and people of color. Digital news models, metered paywalls, and the like are still evolving. The future of journalism appears to rely more on either amplifying the individual brand or obscuring bylines and journalistic ownership altogether, but reporting is also increasingly personal.

One example of how this played out was in the summer of 2014 when *Washington Post* reporter Wesley Lowery, a black male reporter, was reporting from the Ferguson frontlines. Lowery utilized social media in the same ways that activists did, alerting his thousands of followers of police harassment—the same that was being examined in connection with a grand jury that failed to indict police officer Darren Wilson for shooting Michael Brown. He and other journalists reported hostile reception from officers in Ferguson became one facet of a multilayered and ongoing story with national reach. They also displayed the growing chasm between what reporting used to be—a story with three or four sources at the most—and what it has become: An evolving narrative that can include not only the voices of those interviewed and who participate in the story but many more.

While Lowery was reporting the story, people interested in Ferguson developments were also able to follow protestors and city council members who told their own stories. Activists took to Instagram, Tumblr, Facebook, and Twitter to share photographs and video from protests and marches around the country. This is just one recent example of how technology increasingly allows the audiences journalism is supposed to share the stories of import with one another without looking to media organizations to do so.

But journalism that offers reciprocity to its audience is a discomfiting notion, for reasons that are both valid and hypocritical. The main power of traditional media has been in their legitimizing authority, economic dominance, and size. As these three aspects of legacy media have dwindled and died, all that remains is nostalgia for what media once were and the potential they once held. As baby boomers and Generation Xers who grew up subscribing to newspapers and watching one or two television networks begin to mature and pass on their traditions to the rest of us, vehicles for news consumption are not on the list. Subscriptions are way down across print media, and print advertising was once the spine of the print business model; there are no Walter Cronkites or Barbara Walters of our era—not for lack of talent but because there is no one media outlet that has built up the same currency of attention that was once possible.

Now that we know and have become comfortable with the fact that the journalism of the future can be captured via a smartphone, tablet, or mobile device and the pillars that once defined mainstream media are beginning to dissolve, most of what remains of media consists of stubborn nostalgia for a national narrative that was never endangered by the myth of post-gender or post-racial successes. That is a narrative that is perpetuated by brands like Fox News and other right-wing media and will remain profitable as one of the sole alternatives to so-called liberal and elite establishment media. The popularity of that narrative is less about quality journalism than it is resistance to change.

The Failures of a Post-Racial Media

As University of Texas at Austin history professor Jacqueline Jones and others have noted, the belief that the problem of racism has been solved because America elected a black president is an understandably attractive but dangerous narrative. Pointing to the presidency of Barack Obama as an indicator of racial progress eclipses persistent problems many Americans have with immigration, or acknowledging the pervasive attitudes of white superiority and the damaging legacy of white supremacy, along with the presumed diminishing power of white men in America.

Post-racial rhetoric, which was undermined by the ongoing attention of race in 2014, is particularly damaging when making the case for media diversity. If we are supposed to be beyond race, then the importance of a racially diverse staff can be quickly invalidated, especially during a time of continued journalistic upheaval. But in 2014, a poll of 85 Associated Press editors voted police killings of blacks to be the top story of year, signaling a shift in determining the news value of black lives. Experts and academics forecast that race would continue in 2015 and beyond to be a story of significance for media, especially since in police-involved deaths of Michael Brown and Eric Garner, among others, officials had launched federal investigations.

Meanwhile, most Americans think that the United States is actually more diverse than it really is,[1] and organizations like the Pew Research Center look granularly at the differences in how white consumers view news developments that involve race—such as in Ferguson—compared to blacks. The combination of this truth and a look at America's media producers 50 years from the high point of the civil rights movement is a good reminder that there is still a long way to go. Minority representation among the ranks in the press corps and in top editing jobs for both racial minorities and women is still depressingly low and hiring is stagnant. In 2014, Pew reported that two-thirds of women were represented in top editing jobs in journalism but there was little change in the preceding 15 years in newsroom composition and the jobs that women in journalism generally hold.[2]

Denise Oliver-Velez, one of the pioneering journalists of color at the Corporation for Public Broadcasting in the 1970s, noted how little has changed since that era on public television airwaves in an article bemoaning the 2014 ending of National Public Radio's sole show related to diverse programming, *Tell Me More*, with Michel Martin.[3] Television, radio, and print media continue to employ mostly white and male editors and producers, senior staff, and interns. The number of black journalists in traditional media dropped 40 percent since 1997[4] in a profession that had in its ranks a little more than 36,000 employees by the 2013 count of the American Society of News Editors. Even a Radio Television Digital News Association survey that noted the victory of an increase in women and people of color in radio and television noted that the high was still "pretty low."[5] And a 2012 RTNDA diversity study reported that 86 percent of television news directors and 91.3 percent of radio news directors are Caucasian.[6]

This is startling because demographers have noted that five years ahead of predictions, in 2015, people of color will comprise the largest number of children born in the country. In the fall of 2014, the U.S. Department of Education reported that for the first time in history, it enrolled its first minority-majority public school classrooms. And by 2043, if not sooner, the entire country is expected to be majority-minority. Still, media critic and author Eric Deggans noted that in early 2012, no major cable news channel employed a person of color, journalist, or otherwise, as an anchor in the primetime hours of 8 p.m. to 11 p.m. weeknights.[7]

For a sense of how print publications have fared, it is helpful to look at the position of the *New York Times*, which former editor Howell Raines described in an article for the *Atlantic Monthly* magazine in 2004 entitled "My Times" as the "indispensable newsletter of the United States' political, diplomatic, governmental, academic and professional communities" and a place where the culture requires "mass allegiance to the idea that any change, no matter how beneficial on its surface, is to be treated as a potential danger." Raines said that circulation for the *Times* had peaked at 1.2 million daily and 1.8 million for the Sunday edition in the early 1990s. Digital was a growth area for the company in 2014, but the newsroom reported another round of layoffs in the same year, in part because reported gains were far more modest than the $1 billion print advertising revenues in 1998.

Back in the 1990s, Raines added, a marketing survey had shown that there were more than 80 million like-minded *Times* nonreaders in the country—or people who should have been reading the *Times* but didn't. By going after the smartest, most affluent readers, Raines wrote, the *Times* was "offering one-size-fits-all journalism to very different audiences."[8] Fast forward to 2014, and the *Times* continued to be emblematic of a pervasive legacy media problem with episodic shifts in coverage.

Newsroom Politics and Angry Women

One of the key ways that lack of gender and racial diversity continue to play out in media is in how hiring and promotion practices, as well as double standards when it comes to retention and pay, end up impacting how legacy media cover or fail to cover stories of significance.

In September 2014, for instance, Alessandra Stanley, a cultural critic at the *New York Times*, wrote a roundly criticized and racially tinged article about *Scandal* showrunner and writer Shonda Rhimes. Rhimes's shows feature a groundbreaking number of black women in lead roles and she was poised to dominate Thursday evenings on ABC in the fall of 2014 with a new show starring Viola Davis called *How to Get Away with Murder*.

Stanley's article about Rhimes led with a sentence that struck me and many others as offensive and racist: "When Shonda Rhimes writes her autobiography, it should be called 'How to Get Away With Being an Angry Black Woman.'" The thesis of the article was that Shonda Rhimes created characters in her own image, which will of course resonate with journalists of color as related to the tired argument that people of color are not creative or objective, and they are merely advocates only capable of conveying opinion or versions of their personal stories for popular consumption.

The piece sloppily tossed in mentions of pretty much all the black women on Rhimes's shows that are "angry" as Rhimes was purported by Stanley to be. The idea that Rhimes was just rewriting versions of herself as new characterizations did a disservice to her immense creativity and ability to write compelling characters. But the main problem with the angle was that it seemed untrue. In reality, Rhimes didn't seem to be very angry.

Rhimes's shows, *Scandal* and *Grey's Anatomy* together pull in 5 percent of ABC's revenue each season. She signed her first book deal to release a yet-untitled memoir in 2015. When she responded to Stanley's article on Twitter, her witty response was that she was going to do some yoga—not a particularly rage-filled response.

But the characterization of Rhimes, which was off base, was coming from a reporter who has had a troubling history of errors. In traditional media, journalists are judged harshly for a high correction count, since credibility is at the heart of a reporter's identity. I have worked in newsrooms where part of the annual review process included the number of corrections one had to write in the previous year, and how the following appraisal period would be different.

In 2009, the *Columbia Journalism Review* chronicled many of the odd mistakes Stanley has made as a cultural critic, including a story about Walter Cronkite that had several errors and required a lengthy correction and other odd mistakes. Craig Silverman, the author of the piece, put it this way: "Too often, her articles include errors about information that should be common knowledge to someone who makes a living writing about TV."[9] This was underscored again in 2012, when Stanley published a critique of a highlight reel from the *Today* show that had aired the year before.[10]

Stanley's 2014 story about Rhimes also had to be updated to correct its errors, and *New York Times* public editor Margaret Sullivan weighed in because of the large-scale response to the piece, asking Stanley and her editors about why it wound up in print. "In the review, I referenced a painful and insidious stereotype solely in order to praise Ms. Rhimes and her shows for traveling so far from it. If making that connection between the two offended people, I feel bad about that," explained Stanley.[11]

Instead of coming across as praise, that line felt like a display of the kind of white liberal racism that has made the *New York Times* irrelevant to some readers. Sullivan pointed out that problem in her exploration of the story, noting that the article "delivered that message in a condescending way that was—at best—astonishingly tone-deaf and out of touch" and ending with the fact that at the *Times* "it's troubling that among 20 critics, not one is black and only two are persons of color."

An e-mail from a black woman named Patricia Washington who works as a lawyer in Maryland also published on Sullivan's blog, exemplified the universal irritation at Stanley's latest flub: "I am a black woman and a lawyer," she wrote.

> I have worked very hard to achieve in my profession and earn respect. I live in a very nice suburban community in Maryland. And yet, none of that makes one bit of difference because a *New York Times* writer can make whatever offhanded, racist opinions about a successful TV producer who is a black woman she cares to make, and because she has the protection of *The New York Times* behind her, can publish it. Because Ms. Stanley is a *New York Times* writer, her story has reached a national audience. Why is Ms. Stanley allowed to characterize Ms. Rhimes as she did and get away it? Why is she allowed to characterize Viola Davis as she did in her story and get away with it?[12]

There were some good points in Stanley's piece, like when Stanley noted that Rhimes "has done more to reset the image of African-American women on television than anyone since Oprah Winfrey." But it was hard to reconcile that insight with inaccurate descriptions of characters like Kerry Washington's Olivia Pope—a powerful Washington player, for sure, but someone who is better known among *Scandal* fans like me for a curious lower-lip quiver that makes her look about as angry as a puppy. There is no evidence that Rhimes has drawn on the Angry Black Woman at all for her characters. Instead, tagging a black women as angry is an easy (read: lazy) description of women with power. It is a characterization that, combined with her history of corrections, would have likely been punished if Stanley were a reporter of color. In this case, Stanley was just reprimanded by the public and her editors.

The Status of Women in Traditional Media

Not long after Stanley's piece about Rhimes was published, Dean Baquet, the first African American executive editor of the *Times*, announced that he was promoting four white editors on the staff. That this announcement came on the heels of widespread criticism of the newspaper's diversity problem was one example of how traditional media seem to be moving further away from connecting with audiences instead of closer to providing them with the journalism they want. You might expect more sensitivity from a guy whose entrance to the newsroom was marred by outrage over Jill Abramson's unceremonious ousting as the first woman to hold his position.

Jill Abramson led the *New York Times* as its first woman executive editor for more than two years. Reports about Abramson's dismissal centered on leadership conflicts and speculation that she was vocal about a pay disparity between her salary and that of her male predecessor. When she was fired in May 2014 in what the *New Republic* editor Rebecca Traister called one of the most humiliating she'd ever witnessed, Abramson's public departure was regrettable on several levels. "But what's also sad, and important to note, is what it means to have so *few* women and people of color in these positions," Traister said. "Because the paucity of representation makes each one of the representatives come to mean so much more—both when they rise and when they fall."[13]

The 2014 Women's Media Center annual report, "The Status of Women in the U.S. Media," showed that as newsroom staffing declined overall 6.4 percent between 2011 and 2012, the overall tally of women staffers continued to hover at 36 percent, a figure largely unchanged since 1999. At the nation's three most prestigious newspapers and four newspaper syndicates, male opinion page writers outnumbered women 4 to 1.

While there is still time and potential for digital publications to fare much better on the diversity front, the fact is that by and large the same resistance to hiring, retaining, and promoting women and people of color has been replicated in the digital news landscape.

In 2014, Jezebel readers and fans expressed universal dismay that Dodai Stewart had been passed over for an editor position for a much younger, less experienced young white woman. News media were still fumbling diversity online: *FiveThirtyEight*, *Vox*, and other digital upstarts were taking a crack at making the newsroom of the future while looking a lot like the pre-1970s newsrooms that were sliding toward extinction: Heavily white and male. New media were actually not as new so much as they were the same old media in a different format, a reiteration of a tired hierarchical system that had failed to work for audiences in the first place.

In a piece about women who had been erased from previous mentions of digital media startups and pioneers, Meg Heckman wrote about women who led online news initiatives in the 1990s for the *Columbia Journalism Review*: "Women in digital media, I learned, are both under represented and less likely to receive credit for their work. Bell's observation that 'the new micro-institutions of journalism already bear the hallmarks of the restrictive heritage they abandoned with such glee' echoes what I discovered during nearly two years of counting and interviewing women involved in new media. Despite early prominence in digital journalism, female leaders are the minority in virtually all its corners today, and the women who do launch innovative publications aren't getting the same attention as men. That has implications both practical and rhetorical, making journalism's future seem as homogeneous as its past."[14]

Statistics underscore Heckman's point: "When ASNE surveyed 68 online news organisations on the minority percentages of their newsrooms in 2013, 43 sites reported zero minorities. Twenty-five of the online sites had minority representation from a low of five percent at KyPost.com in Cincinnati, to 100 percent minorities in the newsroom of The Natomas Buzz in Sacramento, California," journalist Michael A. Deas reported for Al-Jazeera.[15]

There were few media outlets that were beginning to harness increased diversity. BuzzFeed—a site that I have contributed to—made news for being more diverse than the average online site while also trying to earn the same kind of gravitas and authority that traditional media once had in spades through aggressive hiring and social promotion. In 2014, Shani O. Hilton was promoted to executive editor, news, making her one of the highest ranked editors of color in a growing media space. Traditional media citadels, however, continued to view BuzzFeed as a fun site of questionable integrity because of how it pays its bills—through a confluence of native advertising, or advertorials, along with a perceived lack of transparency about content on the site that is unsponsored versus sponsored.

With its viral lists, stickers, and cadre of twenty-somethings, BuzzFeed has also presented ink-stained wretches with the prospect that it may not matter to millennials whether or not they're reading advertising copy or hard news as long as it's entertaining, accessible, and relevant. The evolution of news as an extension of infotainment and reality-based media appears to be a key and winning part of BuzzFeed's sustainable strategy and revenue model. And as Nan Robertson notes in *The Girls in the Balcony*, this porous boundary between the editorial side of media and advertisers is not something traditional media are unfamiliar with. "All the pious utterances by *Times* editors and publishers about the separation of news and advertising did not hold true for the coverage of fashion,"[16] Robertson wrote, noting that the rules appeared to be flexible when it came to some large advertisers.

As a result of abandoning diversity efforts due to budget cuts, most print newsrooms have lost enough people of color through attrition that the color of traditional media are starkly unchanged from what it was in the pre-1970s era. At the end of 2014, Richard Prince reported that even as newsroom employment declined by 3.2 percent, the number of minority journalists in daily newspaper newsrooms increased by a couple hundred in 2013, according to the annual census released in July by the American Society of News Editors and the Center for Advanced Social Research.[17] In 2015, the *Economist* named its first woman editor in the history of the publication—a sure sign of progress. As the United States gets increasingly diverse and women—while still not earning equal pay—are advancing further in business than ever before, there is more opportunity than ever for smart businesses to remake their brands to center on profitable audiences that are inclusive and that reflect the nation.

Opportunity is one way to look at it. The news about the news business, however, has mostly just worsened over time. Half a century since the publication of the Kerner Commission Report, traditional journalism outlets are no closer to reflecting a diverse country than they were in 1968. In 2009, the number of minorities in daily newspapers shrank to just 5,500; 800 fewer than the previous year, and the lowest since 1993.[18] By 2012, minority employment in newsrooms remained steady only because of the acceleration of job loss across the industry.[19] In 2012, ASNE reported that 2,600 jobs were lost.[20] There was a slight uptick in minority workforces in television and radio in 2013, but it was nowhere near matching the growth of the U.S. minority population.

In niche and broadcast media, things are only slightly better. The number of black-owned television stations declined from 28 in 1995 to 20 in 2000, so that only 10 percent of the country's larger markets featured minority-owned TV stations. An independent, nongovernment report in 2006 put the number of black-owned TV stations at 18. Several years later that number was at 9. Most of those stations are in areas lacking substantial black populations—such as Syracuse, New York; Salem, Oregon; and Rhinelander, Wisconsin—suggesting blacks may be buying stations where they are least expensive.[21] In 2014, Richard Prince reported the Federal Communications Commission approved transactions that will result in 10 new minority and female-owned television stations.

Elsewhere in traditional media, most of the large, long-term institutions owned by people of color have been sold to white owners. When Robert Johnson sold BET to Viacom in 2000 for $3 billion, he became the network's first black billionaire.[22] *Jet, Vibe,* and *XXL*—all of which have a predominately African American readership—have all stopped producing print altogether in a harbinger of things to come. In September 2014, Spin Media, which now owns *Vibe,* laid off 19 people; the fallout from a decision to stop printing the magazine and to make it online only, the inevitable direction for a magazine that in some ways epitomized the multicultural, diverse media of the 1990s which the Internet has made more accessible than in the past.

Even outside of niche and ethnic media, print publications like *Newsweek* and the *New Republic* continued to tweak approaches to a fluctuating media environment. In 2014, *Newsweek* re-launched its print edition after discontinuing the print version of the magazine in December 2012 because of falling revenues. The new print version was being sold at $8 a copy as a way for owners to rely less on advertising revenue.[23]

Layoffs and consolidations remain a steady part of news about the news. In October 2014, CNN laid off its highest-ranking African American along with hundreds of others at the company.[24] But the most damaging impact of journalism's monetary struggles has by far been the talent and diversity drain that has accompanied increased corporatization of the profession. Between 2008 and 2009, 11,000 journalists lost their jobs. Others place the number far higher—as many as 12,000 during 2008 and 24,000 in 2009.[25]

Magazines that have had a history of diversity problems both with regards to hiring and with racist content have found themselves at the center of new scrutiny. The *New Republic*, which published racist content under editor in chief Marty Peretz's leadership between 1974 and 2007 (and partially until 2012), saw the resignation of senior and contributing editors en masse in response to the firing of two white male editors. In a story for *Vox*, Max Fisher, a former intern at the *New Republic*, wrote that the "fact that many of (the resigning editors) found Peretz's promulgation of racism to be tolerable, whereas Chris Hughes's firing of two beloved colleagues was not, speaks to a larger problem of how we think about racism in American society and particularly in the elite media institutions that have badly lagged in employing people of color."[26]

Ta-Nehisi Coates, one of the most visible and respected black journalists and writers on race in the United States, wrote for the *Atlantic* that deep mourning over the passing of a great American institution followed the resignation of TNR editor Franklin Foer, but that the "family rows at TNR's funeral look like the 'Whites Only,' section of a Jim-Crow-era movie-house. For most of its modern history, TNR has been an entirely white publication, which published stories confirming white people's worst instincts." That included publication of excerpts from Charles Murray's bigoted tome, *The Bell Curve*, anti-Muslim and antiblack rhetoric and more.[27] In late 2014, the new editor in chief of TNR, Gabriel Snyder, promised readers in his first

Editor's Note that the magazine would include more diverse voices in the future and in 2015, he made four hires that seemed to back up that commitment including former MSNBC producer Jamil Smith, Sarah Lawrence poetry professor Cathy Park Hong, Bijan Stephen from *Vanity Fair*, and Elspeth Reeve.

Still, it may be too late for media brands like TNR. The cumulative impact of biased coverage, combined with the financial and market realities imposed on legacy media by digital growth, has been that audiences have increasingly turned away from traditional media as a source of news and information at a clip that has decimated the industry. Since 2000, newspaper circulation has shriveled by an astounding 25.6 percent.[28] Local networks have maintained their audiences, but most viewers who remain loyal to television networks augment their news with information they find on social media. Even large media brands and stalwarts like the *New York Times* struggle to make the same kind of money with digital properties as they did back when print was a mainstay in most American homes.

In 2014, Richard Prince, a tireless columnist who covers diversity in journalism for the Maynard Institute for Journalism Education, included an anecdote that had been solicited from journalists for the Association of Opinion Journalists but was not included in a collection of pieces meant to look at racial blinders from the past. S. Mitra Kalita, who was working as a Quartz editor at the time, recalled writing a story for the *Washington Post* on an Indian dance competition called "Bhangra Blowout" hosted by George Washington University. She wrote that "the politically correct mid-1990s taught (brainwashed) us to use our backgrounds as a lens to cover the world, especially the untold stories. Cover communities from the inside out. Make stories relevant to mainstream audiences, revelatory to the subjects."

But when she wrote the story from her perspective, she says her editor responded by telling her, "When you write these stories, you've got to think about white guys like me. Eating our bagels, sipping our coffee in the morning. We're the audience." Kalita changed the story, she said, and vowed to spend the rest of her career proving him wrong, but newspaper circulation figures beat her to it.[29]

To Kalita's point, one significant way traditional journalism could revive itself would be through the coordinated and intentional recruitment, amplification, and promotion of increased gender and racial diversity not only as newsroom and newsgathering staff but at the very top of news organizations as editors and producers. The meager and often-diluted representation of people of color in legacy media matters because these institutions, no matter how weakened, are still the standard for journalism-as-democracy and as public service catalysts in the United States. They remain the citadels of authoritative information, both as the first and final drafts of America's permanent historical records. The combination of media monopoly, digital convergence, and Internet startups that rely on models that ignore or cannibalize advertising and audience demographics has had a deleterious impact on people of color in newsrooms, which has impacted the number and quality of stories that accurately and respectfully reflect communities of color and women. As I have tried to point out throughout this book, legacy media's long history of marginalizing these groups and distorting their images through stereotypical coverage has sealed the fate of traditional media as it has been practiced for centuries. Demographic realities require inclusion and, without it, legacy media brands will continue to be replaced with forward-thinking digital news organizations.

That is true not just in journalism but also in other parts of popular culture. Motion pictures about people of color and women still adhere to stereotypes, with few exceptions. As late as 2012, only NBC and ABC had multiple prime-time shows with people of color and women represented.[30]

In addition to 2014 being a year of increased attention to race and racial inclusion on television, writers and publishers adept at social networked produced the hashtag #weneeddiversebooks to highlight a dearth of books published by authors who are racially diverse. VIDA, a literary organization, has in recent years conducted a byline count for stories by and about women writers which shows that book publication trends still skew white and male.

Signs of Progress and Room for Improvement

In a 2013 *Columbia Journalism Review* piece about the future of diversity in journalism, veteran journalist Farai Chideya asked a diverse panel of journalists and writers to discuss their thoughts about the present and future of media. Baratunde Thurston, satirist, author, and former editor at the *Onion*, jokingly forecast a magazine cover in the future which would ask, " 'What Happened to All the White People?' and it will be an in-depth multipart report on how whites willingly and involuntarily gave up power over the previous 100 years. . . . We will ultimately say that young people connected by technology and global culture helped salvage and reinvigorate the American Dream. The piece will get a Pulitzer. My granddaughter will be the author."[31]

As with all humor, what makes Thurston's point resonate is that women and people of color are clearly in a time of pivotal change with the potential for technology to expand upon what little progress they have made regarding racial and gender diversity to create a new media system that centers both these groups. With traditional media, like publishing, in flux, industry leaders continue to experiment with business models and content sharing in order to deliver hard news to audiences. There is no reason that diversity cannot be included in recasting damaged business practices. Organizations only have relevance and money to gain and nothing to lose.

While there have been some signs of progress, diversity is still not a priority in news organizations in terms of staffing or content creation; discussions around it continue to be non-starters despite the fact that there are persistent roadblocks to significant progress in the industry from journalism education to retention of women journalists or journalists of color, if they manage to get hired. The same excuses that slowed the racial and gender integration of traditional media in the 1960s and 1970s have managed to remain alive into the twenty-first century. In 2011, CNN famously announced it "couldn't find" journalists of color qualified to join its fall line-up—this after they canceled Eliot Spitzer's show. In early 2014, Buzz-Feed editor Shani O. Hilton made the case on *Medium*, an online publication that relies on a mix of paid and unpaid user-generated content, that building a diverse newsroom remained a challenge because there aren't tons of qualified journalists of any color just waiting around to be hired.

Part of a dearth of women and people of color to join the ranks of new media has to do with America's journalism schools, which are racing to remain relevant like traditional media newsrooms by attempting to move the academy to swiftly adopt digital news-making tools. It is unclear whether slow-moving educational institutions can truly prepare their students for the increasingly ethnically and racially diverse audiences their graduates will aim to write for. With few exceptions, people of color are as much in short supply in academia as they are in newsrooms, as part of a legacy news media system dedicated to perpetuating a lack of diversity by creating a mental model that relies mainly on white and male non-practitioners of media in all its forms—especially new and digital media where most people of color consume news—to shape the meaning of news for reporters of the future.

For years, industry justification for refusing to recruit, hire, retain, and promote journalists of color as well as women at news organizations has had many prongs. Explanations include that minorities and women are not audiences of import or with significant market share when it comes to consuming news; when it comes to recruiting and hiring, there are never enough qualified applicants of people of color or women and those who do manage to make it past the first two assumptions are subpar and not able to hack the business when these hires inevitably leave the business to do less emotionally-taxing but more lucrative work.

The insidious impact of racism and sexism on traditional media that has corroded journalistic integrity extends to every sphere of American life, however, making it less likely that young people of color would choose journalism as a profession if they were interested in a career that might offer long-term stability as well as decent benefits. Employment in traditional media relies on an old school model that requires young people to make names for themselves as unpaid or low-paid interns in small markets before moving slowly up the food chain at print outlets or broadcast or radio stations. Author Astra Taylor also notes that the presumed cultural democracy of the Internet has not manifested for people of color or women. Of top 10 bloggers identified recently, only one was a woman, the rest were all male. Among the top 30 bloggers in the United States, there are no African Americans, one Asian and one of mixed Latino heritage.[32]

Most media organizations are taking a patchwork approach to appealing to a diverse audience or even including people of color in their stories, but there are some signs of progress. While National Public Radio, for instance, attracted some criticism for the cancellation of Michele Martin's *Tell Me More* in 2014, NPR has also made a commitment to diversity in cultural coverage by creating Code Switch, a blog focused on race and culture. After facing criticism over a lack of diversity, MSNBC in 2011 hired Al Sharpton and Melissa Harris-Perry, among others, as black pundits.[33] Fusion, which describes itself as a news, pop culture, and satire TV and digital network, launched in October 2013 with six major cable and digital distributors. Through hiring well-regarded veteran journalists of color like Latoya Peterson and Anna Holmes, Fusion was working intentionally on its mission to engage everyday as champions of "a young, diverse and inclusive America."

That progress has extended in rare cases to promotion within legacy media of women and people of color. In December 2014, Matt Thompson, who is African American, was named deputy editor of The Atlantic. com to help oversee editorial operations and shape strategic development at the site during a time of what the magazine reported as record audience growth. Thompson had most recently directed news teams at NPR covering race, ethnicity, and culture; education; and global health and development. He joined several other diverse hires at the *Atlantic*, according to a press release from the organization.

As of 2014, the editor in chief of *Brides* magazine was an African American woman. Dean Baquet is the first African American executive editor of the *New York Times*. The *Washington Post* promoted veteran journalist Kevin Merida to managing editor and Emilio Garcia-Ruiz[34] to managing editor in 2013. In the same year, Gwen Ifill and Judy Woodruff were named co-anchors, managing editors at PBS *Newshour*.[35]

There was notable progress even for women and people of color who were operating outside of traditional media. Veteran journalists of color like Roland S. Martin and Soledad O'Brien are examples of how individual reporters can carve niches for themselves both within and outside of the ever-evolving news industry. In 2014, Martin was the host of two TV One shows and still worked as a CNN contributor. (He was suspended from CNN in 2012 for offensive and homophobic tweets).[36] In 2013, Soledad O'Brien's morning show was cancelled, and the high-profile journalist, known for producing content focused on exploring race and ethnicity, went on to develop her own media company, Starfish Media Group. Both followed in the increasingly well-tread footsteps of reporters who chose to pursue an entrepreneurial journalism model instead of relying on a full-time staff position at a TV station or network.[37]

There have also been signs of improvement as it relates to traditional media coverage in the present as well as corrections of coverage from the past. The ubiquity of social media and technology allowed for Ava DuVernay, the director of the movie *Selma*, about a significant chapter of the civil rights movement, to respond to criticisms from aides of former president Lyndon B. Johnson and others that her film had what one *Washington Post* headline called a "glaring flaw." The *Washington Post*, on its Style blog, followed up with embedded tweets from DuVernay addressing the criticisms. "The notion that Selma was LBJ's idea is jaw dropping and offensive to SNCC, SCLC and black citizens who made it so. . . . Bottom line is folks should interrogate history. Don't take my word for it or LBJ rep's word for it. Let it come alive for yourself."[38]

The truth is, when it comes to past coverage of communities of color, editors at more than one newspaper have reexamined their civil rights-era coverage and found it sorely lacking. In 1988, the *Birmingham News* admitted its coverage of race relations in the 1960s was characterized "by mistakes and embarrassment." In 2006, the paper reported that a photo intern had found a cardboard box of 5,000 images, which were taken at the height of the civil rights struggle but never published. The newspaper went on to run the photographs in a special issue and on the News' web site. Another Southern newspaper, the *Lexington Herald-Leader*, marked the 40th anniversary of the Civil Rights Act of 1964 with a front-page article acknowledging that it, too, had failed to adequately cover the civil rights movement.[39] *Herald-Leader* editors said the paper failed to meet journalism's most basic obligations. Negligent coverage had "irreparably damaged the historical record and caused the newspapers' readers to miss out on one of the most important stories of the 20th century."[40]

These acts of journalistic reparations serve as an example of how editors, publishers, and media executives can play a critical role in changing how traditional media are viewed and are, increasingly, dismissed as bastions of racist and sexist propaganda. There are ways in which these acts appear to be the very least an organization can do. While they underscore the importance of recognizing the significance of legacy media as an important organ of perpetuating the historical record, acknowledging racism is not the same as having a better plan for inclusive coverage going forward. Making a moral step forward, toward a neutral and inclusive perspective, is not the same as making a necessary investment in the future of a media organization or the journalism industry as a whole.

An Economic Imperative

A balanced racial and gender-inclusive media is often discussed as an ethical imperative for media organizations, as if it would be an act of charity or piety for news organizations to remain relevant by pivoting to adjust to the needs of their audiences. What is rarely acknowledged or discussed with sustained interest is that the business case for diversity that some companies in other industries have discovered and proved is that diversity is an economic imperative for businesses that want to survive well into the future. (The great irony of technology as the main industry responsible for the total disruption of journalism is that it's also an industry riddled with diversity problems for women and people of color.)

Pamela Newkirk, author of *Within the Veil*, said in a phone interview that the potential financial benefits for media to diversify in light of changing U.S. demographics have been contradicted by racial attitudes held by essential media powerbrokers that have remained unchanged now for decades, if not longer. "Traditional media is filled with the same people with the same mindset and the same notions of racial superiority," she said. "That's really what this comes down to. But it's still what we're talking about. Otherwise, it makes no sense. The economic imperative would tell you that you have to get over race. But that has never been the case and it still is not the case. When you're talking about the media, you're talking about a reflection of power and no one is willing to give up the reins. Here we are in 2013, talking about the same things we talked about in 2000, in 1968."[41]

As is the case with how discussions of race and gender have shifted over the years, the language of dismissing diversity is now a coded conversation that is as much a commentary on class as it is on race. Explicit or overtly biased treatment has long been considered politically incorrect, but that doesn't mean the bias is gone; it solely means that the language used to describe differential treatment is now coded and embroidered with other marginalizing decisions. In a piece for the *Billfold*, Aboubacar Ndiaye wrote about news organizations' inability to get over cultural difference even in digital newsrooms because of the way that hiring editors think about who best fits their idea of a reporter:

> The uncomfortable truth remains that white males are still likelier to report so-called hard news, while whites of either gender are likelier to graduate from the marquee journalism programs at Columbia, Northwestern, and Yale. White males also continue to benefit from the amoebous quality of looking the part. They LOOK like a reporter in a sort of a priori, unconscious way. The other part, one that is rarely acknowledged, is the sort of income/class uniformity which plagues both old and new media. It stands to reason that the high costs of the premier schools favored by new media organizations help to weed out potential hires from more disadvantaged backgrounds.[42]

That this filtering process continues to be at work in both traditional and new media is not solely a concern for the journalism industry. It is also a pipeline problem for Hollywood and cultural industries that stand to gain more than they have to lose if they can cultivate a new generation of cultural leaders and creators. A 2013 UCLA study and current television programming provides some insight into the case for an economic boon for traditional media if they can bring themselves to rededicate themselves to reflecting the true face of the United States. The study showed that the most successful television programs were those that were more diverse—not majority white—and those that had writing staffs that were also more diverse.[43] The ascendancy of African American showrunner and creator Shonda Rhimes, who is one of the only women in Hollywood who has ever had an entire chunk of a primetime line-up devoted to her with the shows she created *Scandal*, *Grey's Anatomy*, and *How to Get Away with Murder*, affirms that racial and gender diversity is marketable and what audiences want to see. Rhimes's high ratings translate into big advertising sales and her diverse casts reflect the world that we all recognize from our everyday lives.

Mara Brock Akil, who produced *Being Mary Jane*, is another black woman who is capitalizing on what *Bloomberg Businessweek* called the audience TV forgot with BET's first original scripted drama series starring Gabrielle Union. Like her other show, *The Game*, *Being Mary Jane* was a hit that premiered to four million viewers in 2013; its audience swelled to 5.8 million live-and-same-day viewers for the February 25 finale—more than the numbers for the finales of HBO's *True Detective* and *Girls* combined.[44] ABC's fall 2014 line up was especially, historically, diverse and sitcoms with more on the horizon from other networks into 2015.[45] Notably, one of the most diverse new shows on Fox, *Empire*, starring Terrence Howard and Taraji P. Henson had record-breaking ratings just weeks after it debuted in 2015.

The Journalism Minorities and Women Deserve

The future of journalism as an industry worth perpetuating and as a genuinely worthy practice depends on people of color and women to tell the narratives that truly reflect the United States. Given what is known about the realities of evolving business and marketing models, this is more than simply a hopeful hypothesis. In order to get to where journalism reflects parity and fairness, where journalistic integrity is synonymous with media that is truly multicultural, powerbrokers in media will need to leverage the authority and gatekeeping capabilities that remain at their disposal to transform what remains of traditional media into a relevant vehicle for real change. After many years of neglect, of course, this is not nearly as easy as it sounds. It will require a complete inventory and analysis of existing business practices and structures and how they distract or augment truly diverse coverage. Research has shown that diversifying the staff or even the leadership at news organizations does not mean that coverage of minorities will improve.[46] What change demands of traditional media is an intentional, holistic response to diversity as a business practice regardless of whether the staff reflects all of the audiences an organization intends to reach or not. This is of particular importance when it comes to newspapers, where minority employment has stalled for the past two decades,[47] a fact that holds true for every demographic, including Latinos.[48] Still, there's no reason that the absence of a particular demographic from media staff should determine whether or not that group is represented in coverage. A 2014 study by Columbia University showed that stories about Latinos comprise less than 1 percent of media coverage and largely focus on Latinos as undocumented workers or criminals.

The Internet, and particularly mobile technology, has the potential to transform the future of media so that representation and coverage can be more evenly distributed. Unfortunately, Juan González and Joseph Torres note that the problem of legacy media and diversity is the same as it ever was: "Much like the labor press of the 1830s, and the muckrakers of the early twentieth century, the new Internet press appears to have replicated some of the patterns of exclusion and neglect that characterized the old legacy media system."[49] In 2009, journalists of color comprised close to 20 percent of ASNE's count of people of color in online newsrooms. Only seven news organizations participated in an annual diversity survey. The Daily Beast, the Huffington Post, Talking Points Memo, and Yahoo! were among the largest online organizations that did not respond.[50]

While staff diversity may not be a panacea for damage already done to brands that have historically ignored people of color and women, it certainly is a good starting point for sustainable change. The more points of view that are incorporated and accounted for in traditional and new media, the better journalism will be, because it will refer to a world where its narratives are relevant. The sustainability of journalism depends not only on its financial future, but also on its social and cultural future.

Diversity detractors and deniers will point to the ongoing success and stability of outlets that have not made diversity a central goal for guiding future coverage. It is true that some media brands will continue to thrive without a concentrated diversity effort. This is especially true when it comes to monopolies that are best served by the current cable television infrastructure. While print and online media revenue is touch and go, author Astra Taylor notes that some media brands have actually seen their share prices go up in recent years—Disney and Time Warner were up 32 percent in 2013; CBS was up 40.2 percent and Comcast, a shocking 57.6 percent.[51]

In general, when businesses make an effort in an area where they do not see immediate success, they make adjustments that ultimately change the direction of their companies for the better while also acknowledging that they could tweak their models for future success. The journalism industry seems to be one of the few that has regarded diversity failures as evidence of a zero-sum approach. That doesn't bode well for efforts to tailor news to America's fastest-growing demographic, Latinos, which are not doing well,[52] with the exception of Univision.[53] As the attention spans of news consumers appear to grow shorter over time, the combination of an impatient, dying legacy media and increasingly apathetic audiences isn't a particularly encouraging mix.

But in 2003, U.S. Hispanic media spending totaled $2.8 billion. Buying power among African American and Asian American households is also significant. That nearly tripled to $7.9 billion in 2012. And Hispanic Internet display spending, now at $431 million, wasn't even measured a decade ago.[54]

The great gains women have made in education and in the workplace, despite not achieving pay parity with their male counterparts, suggest that women will continue to be an economic force to be reckoned with. As of 2008, single, childless women in their 20s made more than their male peers in 47 of 50 metropolitan markets. Women made up 58 percent of consumers spending online retail dollars and 44 percent of the fan base for the National Football League.[55] Those numbers across demographics suggest that continuing to experiment with ways to diversify newsrooms and media coverage of all kinds is a worthy and smart business imperative.

In the United States, *Time* magazine reported in 2010 that women held sway over 51.3 percent of the nation's private wealth and "as Maddy Dychtwald observes in *Influence* . . . 'We're on the brink of a massive power shift, a grinding of the gears of history into a new human condition. . . . It's a world where women can, if they choose, seize the reins of economic control.'"[56]

It is also a world where women are increasingly asserting themselves in traditional and online media with historic results. Television's first all-female sports talk show, *We Need to Talk*, was scheduled to begin airing on CBS Sports Network at the end of 2014. "Instead of being relegated to a sideline reporter—or the lone women on a traditional all-male sports-talk format—these women take center stage, tackling diverse topics including domestic violence, concussions and a much-maligned *Men's Health* article advising dudes how to talk sports with girls," wrote Kirsten Fleming for the *New York Post*.[57]

And while much has been made in these pages and in other places about the death of traditional or mainstream media, women are starting their own digital verticals, too, and making strides. Ann Friedman is one of few journalists to acknowledge women-led digital startups like the *Toast*.[58] In

2014, the *Toast* expanded its brand to include the *Butter*, with author Roxane Gay at the helm. And even though white male journalists have been the focus of most stories about digital startups, Meg Hackman noted in the *Columbia Journalism Review* that while women are usually not given credit, they were digital journalism pioneers as early as 1995, although the gains they made have since been lost.[59]

Sexism in traditional and new media also remains a challenge to inclusive coverage and to legacy media's bottom line. When Rush Limbaugh, a right-wing talk radio star, launched dozens of personal attacks on Sandra Fluke, Media Matters reported that the advertising fall out translated to millions of dollars in lost revenue for Cumulus Media, which carries Limbaugh's show in 38 markets.[60] In 2013, a British story about "A New Golden Age" of print media featured a roster of six white guys, showing an impressive combination of tone-deaf coverage related to both women and people of color who remain in media.[61] In 2014, when domestic violence came to the fore after a video featuring Ray Rice punching his wife in an elevator went viral, ESPN hosted a discussion that did not include a single woman. "Pretty cool of @espn to have a roundtable on domestic violence and invite 0 women to participate!" quipped writer and editor Andi Zeisler on Twitter.

The growing economic and political power of women suggests that leaving them out of decision-making processes when it comes to news or continuing to confine their expertise to soft news stories with just a few exceptions is a disservice to journalism. It also means that media that insist on excluding women or abiding sexist coverage and commentators are unfortunately committed to incomplete reporting. The future of journalism will require accuracy by way of inclusion, and acknowledging gender differences and imbalances will be key.

By and large, the people who stand to offer the future of journalism the most and are essential to saving it are often the ones who are still shut out of the process. This is not as much a function of intentional racist and sexist behavior as it is an indication of how little has changed in the minds of old white male gatekeepers in media. The cloak of ignorance under which traditional media operate has also covered some new media startups, which suggests an inherited, dangerous, and lopsided media landscape for years to come without serious industry reflection and intentional reaction.

Veteran journalist and author Farai Chideya put it this way: "Media entrepreneurs need to understand why integrated media is not 'feel-good' but essential in an America rapidly becoming majority-Latino and non-white.

Race-based stories are often precursor indicators to larger societal shifts."[62] So are gender-based stories, and without thorough ones, journalism in any form does not do its main job, which is to inform its populace.

The result of the absence of these voices and the people who raise them has been the distrust that comes from the African American and Hispanic communities, for instance, as indicated in a survey published in September 2014.[63] When the survey—produced by the Media Insight Project, an initiative of the American Press Institute, in collaboration with the Maynard Institute, New America Media, and the McCormick Foundation—was released, Tom Rosenstiel, executive director of API said, "The great worry that people of color would not have access to digital has not occurred as many feared—thanks in part to the advance of wireless. But more access has not translated into creating more content that audiences think is rich, diverse and accurate about underserved communities." Access for people of color has meant being connected to reporting that excludes them and having mostly free tools at their disposal to present their sides of the story via social networking tools or blogs. It has also meant allowing their commentary on verticals that are either niche-based like the *Huffington Post*'s Black Voices or relying on segregated community-based media in combination with established national authority legacy media like the *New York Times*.

As Rory O'Connor notes in *Friends, Followers and the Future*, "Along with losing their previously privileged position, legacy media have also lost the trust of many of their customers—largely as a result of their poor performance over time . . . With our longstanding dependence on them diminished, the legacy media and their corporate advertisers can no longer rely mainly on brand power to inspire trust and confidence." What legacy media need instead, and what will be critical to their resurrection and revitalization, is an intentional commitment to present and future audiences to recruit and retain women and people of color. That would mean actively seeking recruits and potential hires outside of their known networks and doing the reporting that marks the best journalism in order to find appropriate candidates. It would mean identifying a list of well-known bloggers and writers with potential who have significant followings on social media who might lend relevance and credibility to teams of older, more seasoned journalists in exchange for the kind of mentoring and guidance rookie reporters and journalists need. And it would require legacy media to become increasingly flexible with allowing nontraditional content—Vine videos, infotainment, Storified tweets, and more—to be situated alongside objective news stories in order to fill the gaping void where communities of color and women have been largely invisible. By lending legacy media platforms to the otherwise marginalized, traditional media stalwarts would show their willingness to adapt to a rapidly approaching future that otherwise will crush the old system before it has a chance to redirect.

America's minorities have been marginalized for so long that it is now a significant part of their identity to be invisible in most news. But with the increasing cultural changes in our country, the power to remain a meaningful part of America's historical record is well within our grasp. It is not a power to rewrite U.S. history as much as it is a pivotal opportunity to recast the nation's narrative as one that is fully committed to equal access to media that act as a mirror.

As Frank Wu writes in *Yellow*, "It is only through romanticized hindsight that we could believe we once had a cultural unity that has been compromised. It is not the appearance of minority cultures that is new; It is their power."[64] That power, as infuriating as it has been for cultural conservatives and as uneven as it may be as it relates to American institutions where true power could be leveraged more successfully—like voting or with regards to stemming minority incarceration—is continuing to grow. Dori Maynard, in a story at the *Atlantic*, put it this way: "The news media and the nation are moving in two different directions. News Media is getting whiter as the country is getting browner."[65]

If traditional media begin to move in the same direction as the country, the entire nation will be better for it. The truth is that these long-marginalized groups are now moving to the center of a conversation that no longer ignores them or pushes them to the side. They can use this moment to centralize themselves and their narratives and they can create the journalism that all audiences deserve. It helps to have meaningful help from powerful people, as President Obama showed in his final press conference of 2013, when, for the first time, a sitting president called only on female reporters.

It also helps that all Americans are starting to view racism and sexism as problems that all citizens need to prioritize. A 2014 Gallup poll showed that 13 percent of all Americans—the highest since the Rodney King trial in 1992—viewed racism as the country's most important problem.[66] As Dori Maynard put it in a phone interview, "My ideal newsroom is able to tackle the difficult questions that we as a society are facing with honesty. Lack of diversity is a century-old problem that needs to be really attacked in a vigorous and wholesome way. All of the goals of diversity aid the media in helping journalism to live up to its ideals to tell the story of communities and influence public policy for all of us." With what Astra Taylor calls a more robust support system for the Fourth Estate, which has given diversity a boost in other countries, the United States media system can be sure that journalism takes everyone possible into account. The future of American democracy depends on it.

Notes

Introduction

1. Edward S. Herman and Noam Chomsky, *Manufacturing Consent: The Political Economy of Mass Media* (New York: Pantheon Books, 1988, 2002), x.
2. Joann Weiner, "Diversity Is Good. Why Doesn't Everyone Agree?" She The People, *Washington Post* blog, Last modified November 26, 2014, http://www .washingtonpost.com/blogs/she-the-people/wp/2014/11/26/diversity-is-good-why-doesnt-everyone-agree/
3. Eric Deggans, *Race-Baiter: How the Media Wields Dangerous Words to Divide a Nation* (New York: Palgrave Macmillan, 2012), 12.
4. Joan C. Williams and Rachel Dempsey, *What Works for Women at Work: Four Patterns Working Women Need to Know* (New York: New York University Press, 2014), 26, 27.

Chapter 1

1. Juan González and Joseph Torres, *News for All the People: The Epic Story of Race and the American Media* (New York: Verso, 2011).
2. Ibid., 30.
3. Ibid., 138.
4. Ibid., 140–145.
5. Ibid., 151.
6. Ibid., 153.
7. Ibid.,12, 64–66.
8. González and Torres, *News for All the People*, 2.
9. Sally Lehrman, "Race and Ethnicity, Coverage of," in *Encyclopedia of Journalism*, ed. Christopher H. Sterling (Thousand Oaks, CA: Sage Reference, 2009), 1179–1185.
10. Félix F. Gutiérrez, "More Than 200 Years of Latino Media in the U.S.: American Latinos and the Making of the United States: A Theme Study." The National Park Service. Accessed December 19, 2014. Page 106. http://www.nps.gov/latino /latinothemestudy/media.htm#_edn8

11. González and Torres, *News for All the People*,131–132.

12. Ibid., 132.

13. Amsterdam News website, About section: http://amsterdamnews.com/about/

14. The National Women's History Museum Presents "Women with a Deadline: Female Printers, Publishers and Journalists from the Colonial Period to World War I," https://www.nwhm.org/online-exhibits/womenwithdeadlines/wwd4.htm

15. Ibid.

16. Ibid.

17. González and Torres, *News for All the People*, 149–150.

18. Venise Wagner, "'Activities among Negroes': Race Pride and a Call for Interracial Dialogue in California's East Bay Region, 1920–31." *Journalism History* 35, no 2. (2009): 82–90.

19. González and Torres, *News for All the People*, 137–138.

20. Ibid., 138.

21. Ibid., 260–261.

22. The Commission on Freedom of the Press, *A Free and Responsible Press: A General Report on Mass Communication: Newspapers, Radio, Motion Pictures, Magazines and Books* (Chicago: University of Chicago Press), 93. https://archive .org/stream/freeandresponsib029216mbp#page/n107/mode/2up

23. González and Torres, *News for All the People*, 284.

24. Ibid., 285–286.

25. Steven Waldman and the Working Group on Information Needs of Communities, "The Information Needs of Communities: The Changing Media Landscape in a Broadband Age." Federal Communications Commission, July 2011. Accessed December 17, 2014.

26. Gutiérrez, "More Than 200 Years of Latino Media in the U.S.," Page 111.

27. American National Biography entry, "Payne, Ethel Lois." Accessed December 17, 2014. www.anb.org/articles/16/16-03900.html

28. Lehrman, "Race and Ethnicity, Coverage of," 1179–1185.

29. Freedom Riders, A Production of American Experience, http://www.pbs .org/wgbh/americanexperience/freedomriders/issues/the-media

30. Audie Cornish, "How the Civil Rights Movement Was Covered in Birmingham," NPR CodeSwitch, June 18, 2013. Accessed December 18, 2014, http:// www.npr.org/blogs/codeswitch/2013/06/18/193128475/how-the-civil-rights-movement-was-covered-in-birmingham

31. Barbara Friedman and John Richardson, "'A National Disgrace': Newspaper Coverage of the 1963 Birmingham Campaign in the South and Beyond." *Journalism History* 33, no. 4 (2008).

32. Julian Williams, "The Truth Shall Make You Free." *Journalism History* 32, no. 2 (2006): 106–113.

33. William G. Thomas III, "Television News and the Civil Rights Struggle: The Views in Mississippi and Virginia," November 3, 2004, University of Virginia.

Accessed December 18, 2014, http://southernspaces.org/2004/television-news-and-civil-rights-struggle-views-virginia-and-mississippi#_edn2

34. Williams, "The Truth Shall Make You Free," 106–113, 8p.

35. Author Interview, December 2013.

36. Virginia Postrel, "The Consequences of the 1960s Race Riots Come into View." *New York Times*, December 30, 2004. http://www.nytimes.com/2004/12/30/business/30scene.html?pagewanted=1&_r=0

37. Juliana Barbassa, "Summer Program for Journalists." *Hispanic* 11, no. ½ (1998): 106. *MasterFILE Premier*, EBSCOhost. Accessed November 8, 2013.

38. Elmer Smith, "OPINION: Kerner Report Saw Racial Divides, and They're Still There." *Philadelphia Daily News, The (PA)*, March 4, 2008. *Newspaper Source*, EBSCOhost. Accessed November 8, 2013.

39. Belva Davis, *Never in My Wildest Dreams: A Black Woman's Life in Journalism* (San Francisco: Berrett-Koehler, 2010), 119.

40. Nan Robertson, *The Girls in the Balcony* (New York: Random House, 1992), 124.

41. González and Torres, *News for All the People*, 282–283.

42. Kay Mills, "Measuring Progress: Women as Journalists." Nieman Reports, January 10, 2011, http://www.nieman.harvard.edu/reports/article/102534/Measuring-Progress-Women-as-Journalists.aspx

43. Gail Collins, *When Everything Changed: The Amazing Journey of American Women from 1960 to the Present* (New York: Little, Brown and Company, 2009), 15.

44. Gwyneth Mellinger, "The ASNE and Desegregation." *Journalism History* 34, no. 3 (2008): 135–144.

45. Dwayne Mack. Freedom Rides, 1961. Accessed December 18, 2014. http://www.blackpast.org/aah/freedom-rides-1961

46. Mellinger, "The ASNE and Desegregation," 135–144.

47. Pamela Newkirk, *Within the Veil: Black Journalists, White Media* (New York: New York University Press, 2000), 67.

48. González and Torres, *News for All the People*, 288.

49. Ibid., 289–290.

50. Ibid., 290.

51. Davis, *Never in My Wildest Dreams*, 119.

Chapter 2

1. Mellinger, "The ASNE and Desegregation," 135–144.

2. Collins, *When Everything Changed*, 196.

3. Ibid., 197.

4. ASNE website: http://asne.org/content.asp?pl=15&sl=28&contentid=28

5. Mercedes Lynn de Uriarte, Cristina Bodinger-de Uriarte, and Jose Luis Benavides, *Diversity Disconnects: From Classroom to Newsroom* (Ford Foundation, 2003), Executive Summary, vii.

6. Ibid.

7. Ibid.

8. ASNE website: http://files.asne.org/kiosk/diversity/DIVERSITYFAQ.html

9. Alice Bonner, "Diversity: Employment," in *Encyclopedia of Journalism*, ed. Christopher H. Sterling (Thousand Oaks, CA: Sage Reference, 2009), 440.

10. Mark Trahant, *Pictures of Our Nobler Selves: A History of Native American Contributions to News Media* (Nashville, TN: The Freedom Forum First Amendment Center, 1995), 2, 24.

11. Newkirk, *Within the Veil*, 59.

12. Ibid.

13. Davis, *Never in My Wildest Dreams*, 96.

14. Ibid., 93–94.

15. Newkirk, *Within the Veil*, 73.

16. Robert C. Maynard Institute for Journalism Education. http://mije.org/black_journalists_movement/melba_tolliver

17. Uriarte, Bodinger-de Uriarte, and Benavides, "Diversity Disconnects," 78.

18. Ibid.

19. Uriarte, Bodinger-de Uriarte, and Benavides, "Diversity Disconnects," 81.

20. Steven Gray, "The Washington Post's Metro Seven: Thirty Years Ago, They Fought for a Fair Chance. Today, There's Still Work to Be Done." *NABJ Journal*, September 2002, Edited Version as it appeared on the Maynard Institute for Journalism Education website, Sunday, April 22, 2012. Accessed January 23, 2014. http://mije.org/richardprince/romney-wins-race-favorable-coverage#StevenGray

21. Lehrman, "Race and Ethnicity, Coverage of," 1182.

22. Gray, "The Washington Post's Metro Seven."

23. Newkirk, *Within the Veil*, 97.

24. Ibid., 115.

Chapter 3

1. Trahant, *Pictures of Our Nobler Selves*, 26.

2. Jill Nelson, *Volunteer Slavery* (New York: Penguin Books, 1993).

3. Newkirk, *Within the Veil*, 10.

4. Howell Raines, "My Times." *Atlantic Monthly*, May 2004, p. 63.

5. Newkirk, *Within the Veil*, 49.

6. Ibid., 137.

7. *The Clarion-Ledger*. "Jerry Mitchell's Entry and Biography," http://www.clarionledger.com/article/99999999/SPECIAL17/60416008/Jerry-Mitchell-s-entry-biography

8. Gutiérrez, "More Than 200 Years of Latino Media in the U.S.," page 106.

9. Allers, "Hollywood to Black Mothers: Stay Home."

10. Joshunda Sanders, "Media Depictions of Asian Americans Lack Important Depth," Accessed June 13, 2012, http://mije.org/mmcsi/general/media-depictions-asian-americans-lack-important-depth

11. Ibid.

12. Frank Wu, *Yellow: Race in America beyond Black and White* (New York: Basic Books, 2002), 281.

13. Jason McIntyre, "ESPN's Fired 'Chink in the Armor Editor Says It Was an Honest Mistake." *The Big Lead*, February 20, 2012. Accessed December 21, 2014, http://thebiglead.com/2012/02/20/espns-fired-chink-in-the-armor-editor-says-it-was-an-honest-mistake/

14. Michael McCarthy, "Asian Stereotypes Appearing in Coverage of Knicks' Jeremy Lin." *USA Today*, Last modified February 16, 2012, Accessed December 21, 2014, http://usatoday30.usatoday.com/sports/basketball/nba/story/2012-02-16/Asian-stereotypes-appearing-in-coverage-of-Knicks-Jeremy-Lin/53120426/1

15. Wu, *Yellow*, 41

16. Farai Chideya, "Fair Share?" *Columbia Journalism Review*, March 1, 2013. Accessed March 2013, http://www.cjr.org/cover_story/fair_share.php?page=all

17. Richard Prince, "Biggest Audience for an Entertainment Show since '04." *Richard Prince's Journal-isms*. Accessed March 4, http://mije.org/richardprince/blacks-latinos-find-much-oscar#Shorttakes

18. Newkirk, *Within the Veil*, 11

19. Chideya, "Fair Share?"

20. Sanders, "Mainstream Media Tend to Ignore Blacks' Mental Health Problems."

21. Kim Barker and Al Baker, "New York Officers' Killer, Adrift and Ill, Had a Plan." *New York Times*, December 21, 2014. Accessed December 22, 2014, http://www.nytimes.com/2014/12/22/nyregion/new-york-police-officers-killer-was-adrift-ill-and-vengeful.html?_r=0

Chapter 4

1. Patricia Hill Collins, *Black Sexual Politics: African Americans, Gender and the New Racism* (New York: Routledge, 2004), 57.

2. Simon Maloy, "CBS' 60 Minutes Offered No Rebuttal to Clarence Thomas' Claims about Anita Hill." *Media Matters for America*, Last modified October 2, 2007, http://mediamatters.org/research/2007/10/02/cbs-60-minutes-offered-no-rebuttal-to-clarence/140003http://mediamatters.org/research/2007/10/02/cbs-60-minutes-offered-no-rebuttal-to-clarence/140003

3. Lili Anolik, "It All Began with O.J." *Vanity Fair*, June 2014, http://www.vanityfair.com/society/2014/06/oj-simpson-trial-reality-tv-pop-culture

4. "Frontline: The O.J. Verdict. Rating the Media's Performance." Last modified October 2005,http://www.pbs.org/wgbh/pages/frontline/oj/themes/media.html

5. Ibid.

6. Deirdre Carmody, "Time Responds to Criticism Over Simpson Cover." The *New York Times*, June 25, 1994, http://www.nytimes.com/1994/06/25/us/time-responds-to-criticism-over-simpson-cover.html

7. "Frontline: The O.J. Verdict. Rating the Media's Performance."

8. Kent Babb, "How the O.J. Simpson Murder Trial 20 Years Ago Changed the Media Landscape." *The Washington Post*, June 9, 2014, http://www.washing tonpost.com/sports/redskins/how-the-oj-simpson-murder-trial-20-years-ago-changed-the-media-landscape/2014/06/09/a6e21df8-eccf-11e3-93d2-edd4be 1f5d9e_story.html

9. Ralph Blumenthal, "Black Youth Is Killed by Whites; Brooklyn Attack Is Called Racial." *New York Times*, August 25, 1989, http://www.nytimes.com/1989/08/25 /nyregion/black-youth-is-killed-by-whites-brooklyn-attack-is-called-racial.html

10. Sewell Chan, "The Death of Yusuf Hawkins, 20 Years Later." *New York Times*, Last modified August 21, 2009, http://cityroom.blogs.nytimes.com/2009/08/21 /the-death-of-yusuf-hawkins-20-years-later/

11. Alexis Okeowo, "Crown Heights, Twenty Years after the Riots." *The New Yorker*, August 19, 2011, http://www.newyorker.com/news/news-desk/crown-heights-twenty-years-after-the-riots

12. Joseph Berger, "In Crown Heights, Once Torn by Race Riots, A Friendly Game of Soccer," *New York Times*, June 8,2014, http://www.nytimes.com/2014 /06/09/nyregion/once-torn-by-riots-crown-heights-finds-harmony-in-soccer .html?_r=0

13. CNN Library, Los Angeles Riots Fast Facts, Last modified May 3, 2014, http://www.cnn.com/2013/09/18/us/los-angeles-riots-fast-facts/

14. Erna Smith, "Transmitting Race: The Los Angeles Riot in Television News." Joan Shorenstein Center on the Press, Politics and Public Policy. Discussion Paper Series, #R- May 11, 1994, Harvard University John F. Kennedy School of Government, http://shorensteincenter.org/wp-content/uploads/2012/03/r11_smith.pdf

15. Hemant Shah, "Press Coverage of Interethnic Conflict: Examples from the Los Angeles Riots of 1992." *Journal of Dispute Resolution* (2007), http://scholarship .law.missouri.edu/cgi/viewcontent.cgi?article=1528&context=jdr

16. Julia Dahl, "We Were the Wolf Pack: How New York City Tabloid Media Misjudged the Central Park Jogger Case, The Poynter Institute, July 15, 2011, http:// www.poynter.org/mediawire/top-stories/135971/we-were-the-wolf-pack-how-new-york-city-tabloid-media-mangled-the-central-park-jogger-case/

17. Natalie Byfield, *Savage Portrayals: Race, Media & the Central Park Jogger Story* (Philadelphia: Temple University Press, 2014), Online Excerpt, http://www .temple.edu/tempress/titles/2140_reg.html

18. Ibid.

19. Lynette Holloway, "Cosby Breaks Silence, Only Expects Black Media to Remain 'Neutral,'" *The Root*, December 14, 2014, http://www.theroot.com

/articles/culture/2014/12/bill_cosby_breaks_silence_only_expects_black_media_
to_remain_neutral.html?wpisrc=newsletter_jcr%3Acontent%26

20. Michael L. Dolfman, Solidelle Fortier Wasser, and Bruce Bergman, "The Effects of Hurricane Katrina on the New Orleans Economy," U.S. Bureau of Labor Statistics, *Monthly Labor Review*, June 2007, http://www.bls.gov/opub/mlr /2007/06/art1full.pdf

21. Steve Classen, "'Reporters Gone Wild': Reporters and Their Critics on Hurricane Katrina, Gender, Race and Place." *E-Media Studies* 2, no. 1(2009), https://journals.dartmouth.edu/cgi-bin/WebObjects/Journals.woa/xmlpage/4 /article/336#edn7

22. Jack Shafer, "Lost in the Flood." *Slate*, Last modified August 31, 2005, http://www.slate.com/articles/news_and_politics/press_box/2005/08/lost_in_ the_flood.2.html

.23. Samuel R. Sommers, Evan P. Apfelbaum, Kristin N. Dukes, Negin Toosi, and Elsie J. Wang, "Race and Media Coverage of Hurricane Katrina: Analysis, Implications, and Future Research Questions." *Analyses of Social Issues and Public Policy* 6, no. 1 (2006), http://library.chemeketa.edu/instruction/handouts/hurri canekatrinalooting.pdf

24. Tania Ralli, "Who's a Looter? In Storm's Aftermath, Pictures Pick Up a Different Kind of Tempest." *New York Times*, September 5, 2005, http://www.nytimes .com/2005/09/05/business/05caption.html?_r=0

25. Classen, "Reporters Gone Wild."

26. Shanto Iyengar and Richard Morin, "Natural Disasters in Black and White." *Washington Post*, June 8, 2006, http://www.washingtonpost.com/wp-dyn/content /article/2006/06/07/AR2006060701177.html

27. Chauncey DeVega, "Racial Framing and Superstorm Sandy: A Black Mother Begs for Help While Her Children Drown." *Daily Kos*, Last modified November 4, 2012, http://www.dailykos.com/story/2012/11/04/1155462/-Racial-Framing-and-Superstorm-Sandy-A-Black-Mother-Begs-for-Help-While-Her-Children-Drown

28. Chideya, "Fair Share?"

29. David Kaufman, "No Scrubs? The Dilemma of Modern African-American Women." *New York Post*, Last modified November 2, 2014, Accessed December 26, 2014, http://nypost.com/2014/11/02/no-scrubs-the-dilemma-of-modern-african-american-women/

30. Jeff Bercovici, "Steve Harvey Launches a Site to Help Women 'Become More Dateable.'" *Forbes*, Last modified October 9, 2014, Accessed December 26, 2014. http://www.forbes.com/sites/jeffbercovici/2014/10/09/steve-harvey-launches-delightful-help-women/

31. Ibid.

32. Sherry Ricchiardi, "Offensive Interference." *American Journalism Review*, December/January 2005.

33. Ibid.

34. Women's Media Center, *The Status of Women in U.S. Media, 2014*. Page 22. http://www.womensmediacenter.com/pages/2014-statistics

35. Ariel Levy, "Either/Or." *NewYorker*, November 30, 2009, http://www.new yorker.com/magazine/2009/11/30/eitheror

36. Laurie Abraham, "She's All That." *Elle* magazine, November 4, 2013, http:// www.elle.com/life-love/society-career/brittney-griner-on-her-sexuality

37. Ryan Chiachiere, "Imus Called Women's Basketball Team 'Nappy-Headed Hoes.'" *Media Matters*, Last modified, April 4,2007, http://mediamatters.org/rese arch/2007/04/04/imus-called-womens-basketball-team-nappy-headed/138497

38. Sherry Ricchiardi, "Offensive Interference." *American Journalism Review*, December/January 2005.

39. Women's Media Center, *The Status of Women in U.S. Media, 2014*, page 22.

40. Helena Andrews, "Shirley Sherrod Says She'll Never Work for the Government Again." *Washington Post*, January 14, 2014, http://www.washingtonpost.com /blogs/reliable-source/wp/2014/01/14/shirley-sherrod-says-shell-never-work-for-the-government-again/

41. Deggans, *Race-Baiter*, 66.

42. Ibid, 67–68.

43. Media Matters Staff, "UPDATED: Fox News' Long History of Race-Baiting." *Media Matters*, Last modified June 13, 2011, http://mediamatters.org /research/2011/06/13/updated-fox-news-long-history-of-race-baiting/180529

44. Tanzina Vega, "Magazine Cover Draws Claims of Racism." *New York Times*, Last modified February 28, 2013. http://mediadecoder.blogs.nytimes .com/2013/02/28/magazine-cover-draws-claims-of-racism/?_r=0

45. Ibid.

46. *Clutch* magazine, "T Magazine Editor Deborah Needleman Apologizes for All-White Issue," Last modified February 19, 2013, http://www.clutchmagonline.com /2013/02/t-magazine-editor-deborah-needleman-apologizes-for-all-white-issue/

47. Robert Huber, "Being White in Philly." *Philadelphia* magazine, March 1, 2013, http://www.phillymag.com/articles/white-philly/2/

48. Sewell Chan, "The Death of Yusuf Hawkins, 20 Years Later." *New York Times*, Last modified August 21, 2009, http://cityroom.blogs.nytimes.com/2009/08/21 /the-death-of-yusuf-hawkins-20-years-later/

49. Matt Hansen and Kurtis Lee, "Michael Brown's Raps: Money, Sex, Drugs—and a Vulnerable Side." *Los Angeles Times*, Last modified August 17, 2014, http://graphics.latimes.com/towergraphic-michael-browns-raps/

50. John Eligon, "Michael Brown Spent Last Weeks Grappling with Problems and Promise." *New York Times*, Last modified August 24, 2014, http://www.nytimes .com/2014/08/25/us/michael-brown-spent-last-weeks-grappling-with-lifes-mys-teries.html

51. Larry Buchanan, Ford Fessenden, K.K. Rebecca Lai, Haeyoun Park, Alicia Parlapiano, Archie Tse, Tim Wallace, Derek Watkins, and Karen Yourish,

"What Happened in Ferguson?" *New York Times*, Last modified November 25, 2014, http://www.nytimes.com/interactive/2014/08/13/us/ferguson-missouri-town-under-siege-after-police-shooting.html?_r=0

52. Joshunda Sanders, "Media Portrayals of Black Youths Contribute to Tension." Maynard Media Center on Structural Inequity, May 23, 2012, http://mije.org/mmcsi/general/media%E2%80%99s-portrayal-black-youths-contributes-racial-tension

53. Marc Fisher and Wesley Lowery, "Ferguson Violence Broke the Mold in Three Ways—One of Which Is Just Unfolding Now." *Washington Post*, November 25, 2014, http://www.washingtonpost.com/politics/ferguson-decision-and-its-aftermath-more-a-media-event-than-organic-moment/2014/11/25/b506ff72-7256-11e4-ad12-3734c461eab6_story.html?tid=HP_lede?tid=HP_lede

54. Moni Basu, "It's Her Ferguson—And It's Not All Black and White." *CNN Online*, Last modified November 17, 2014, http://www.cnn.com/2014/11/17/us/ferguson-biracial-couple/index.html?sr=sharebar_twitter

55. Blumenthal, "Black Youth Is Killed by Whites; Brooklyn Attack Is Called Racial."

Chapter 5

1. Stonewall 1969 by Mike Funk (Published in 2013), https://www.flickr.com/photos/mkfunk/8221605585/in/album-72157634381061896/; *http://www.buzzfeed.com/lilyhiottmillis/this-comic-explains-how-the-stonewall-riots-went-down#4ij4c8m*

2. Anita Chan, Yello Kitty, no. 2, 1999, "The Asian Invasion Is Coming. . ." Y2K for Kiddies of Color. "Mediated Disillusionment: Stories about Nanking and Beyond," *http://www.ricegirls.com/nonfiction/nanking.html*

3. Christopher Daly, "The Decline of Big Media, 1980s–2000s Key Lessons and Trends." *Journalist's Resource*, Last modified August 28, 2013, http://journalistsresource.org/studies/society/news-media/covering-america-journalism-professor-christopher-daly#sthash.2CFcnGCt.dpuf

4. Jeff Chang, *Who We Be: The Colorization of America* (New York: St. Martin's Press, 2014), 198.

5. Ibid.,110.

6. George Sylvie, "African American News Media," in *Encyclopedia of Journalism*, Vol. 1., ed. Christopher H. Sterling (Thousand Oaks: Sage Publications, 2009), 51.

7. Deggans, *Race-Baiter*, 124.

8. Ibid., 124–125.

9. Teresa Ridley, "Whatever Happened to Black Magazines from the 1990s?" *The Root*, Last modified August 23, 2010, http://www.theroot.com/photos/2010/08/whatever_happened_to_black_magazines_from_the_1990s.html

10. Daly, "The Decline of Big Media, 1980s–2000s Key Lessons and Trends."

11. Mercedes Lynn de Uriarte, Cristina Bodinger-de Uriarte, and Jose Luis Benavides, *Diversity Disconnects: From Classroom to Newsroom* (Ford Foundation, 2003), Executive Summary, viii.

12. Ibid., 4.

13. Ibid.

14. Ibid., 5.

15. Touré, *Who's Afraid of Post Blackness?*, 98.

16. Jeff Cohen, "Racism in Mainstream Media. Fairness and Accuracy in Reporting." Last modified October 1, 1999, Accessed December 28, 2014, http://fair.org/article/racism-and-mainstream-media/

17. John C. Watson, "Diversity: Policy," in *Encyclopedia of Journalism*, Vol. 1, ed. Christopher H. Sterling (Thousand Oaks: Sage Reference, 2009), 443.

18. Ibid., 444.

19. Author interview with Minal Hajratwala.

20. Ken Auletta, *Backstory: Inside the Business of News* (New York: Penguin Books, 2003), 254.

21. Uriarte, Bodinger-de Uriarte, and Benavides, *Diversity Disconnects*, viii.

22. Joshunda Sanders, "Jayson Blair Proves It's Not Easy Being Green." *San Francisco Chronicle*, May 18, 2003.

23. Uriarte, Bodinger-de Uriarte, and Benavides, *Diversity Disconnects*, 6–7.

24. Ibid., ix.

25. Daly, "A Narrative History of a Nation's Journalism." Library of Congress talk. September 19, 2012, http://www.loc.gov/today/cyberlc/feature_wdesc.php?rec=5632

Chapter 6

1. Ben Bagdikian, *The New Media Monopoly* (Boston: Beacon Press, 2004), 3, 9.

2. David Weinberger, *Everything Is Miscellaneous: The Power of the New Digital Disorder* (New York: Times Books/Henry Holt and Company, 2007), 130, 131.

3. Tammy Oler, "Pinned Down." *Bitch* magazine, 2012, http://bitchmagazine.org/article/pinned-down

4. Aaron Smith, "African Americans and Technology Use: A Demographic Portrait." *Pew Research Internet Project*, http://www.pewinternet.org/2014/01/06/african-americans-and-technology-use/

5. Amanda Hess, "Why Women Aren't Welcome on the Internet." *Pacific Standard*, January 6, 2014, Accessed December 29, 2014, http://www.psmag.com/navigation/health-and-behavior/women-arent-welcome-internet-72170/

6. Joshunda Sanders, "Up to Here with trolls? Tips for Navigating Online Drama." April 2, 2014. http://joshunda.com/2014/04/02/up-to-here-with-trolls-tips-for-navigating-online-drama/

7. Ibid.

8. Joanna Brenner and Aaron Smith, "72% of Online Adults Are Social Networking Site Users." *Pew Internet Research Project*, August 5, 2013, http://www.pew internet.org/2013/08/05/72-of-online-adults-are-social-networking-site-users/

9. Luke O'Brien, "How to Lose $100 Million: The Undoing of Tina Brown." *Politico*, May/June 2014, http://www.politico.com/magazine/story/2014/05/tina-brown-how-to-lose-100-million-105907.html#.VEKauOc_EXc

10. Dylan Byers, "Turbulence at the Times." *Politico*, April 23, 2013, http://www.politico.com/story/2013/04/new-york-times-turbulence-90544.html

11. Aaron Couch, "CNN Mocked for Lack of Texas Filibuster Coverage." *Hollywood Reporter*, Last modified June 25, 2013, http://www.hollywoodreporter.com/news/cnn-mocked-lack-texas-filibuster-574716

12. Ann Friedman, "Making Politics and Policy News Sexy." *Columbia Journalism Review*, June 27, 2013, http://www.cjr.org/realtalk/texas_tribune_ftw.php

13. Adam Liptak, "Supreme Court Invalidates Key Part of Voting Rights Act," http://www.nytimes.com/2013/06/26/us/supreme-court-ruling.html?pagewanted=all&_r=0

14. C. Daniel Baker, "African-American's Buying Power Projected to Be $1.1 Trillion by 2015." *Black Enterprise*, Last modified November 28, 2013, http://www.blackenterprise.com/small-business/african-american-buying-power-projected-trillions/#.UeRCEu8Yr38.twitter

15. "BET Awards Again Ranks Top in Cable with Adults 18–49 and 7.6 Million Total Viewers." *Target Market News*. Accessed January 10, 2014, http://targetmar ketnews.com/storyid07081301.htm

16. Smith, "Technology Trends among People of Color."

17. Ezra Klein, "Racism Isn't Over. But Policymakers from Both Sides Like to Pretend It Is." *Washington Post Wonkblog*, December 1, 2013, http://www.wash ingtonpost.com/blogs/wonkblog/wp/2013/12/01/racism-isnt-over-but-policy makers-from-both-parties-like-to-pretend-it-is/

18. Deggans, *Race-Baiter*, 78–79.

19. Astra Taylor, *The People's Platform: Taking Back Power and Culture in the Digital Age* (New York: Metropolitan Books, 2014), 7.

20. Julie Posetti, "Jay Rosen to Journalists and Editors: Facebook Has All the Power. You Have Almost None." *World News Publishing Focus*, Last modified July 10, 2014, http://blog.wan-ifra.org/2014/07/10/jay-rosen-to-journalists-and-editors-facebook-has-all-the-power-you-have-almost-none

21. Nikki Usher, "Citizen Journalism as Civic Responsibility," in *Will the Last Reporter Please Turn Out the Lights? The Collapse of Journalism and What Can Be Done to Fix It*, ed. Robert McChesney and Victor Pickard (New York: The New Press, 2011), 276.

22. Allison Stadd, "59% of Journalists Worldwide Use Twitter, Up from 47% in 2012." *AllTwitter*, June 26, 2013, http://www.mediabistro.com/alltwitter/journalists-twitter_b45416

Chapter 7

1. Emily Badger, "Americans Vastly Overestimate How Diverse the Country Really Is." *Atlantic CityLab*, October 22, 2013, http://www.theatlanticcities.com/arts-and-lifestyle/2013/10/americans-vastly-overestimate-how-diverse-country-really/7320/#.UmgKItudjOQ.email

2. Mark Jurkowitz, "ASNE: Two-Thirds of U.S. Newspapers Employ Women in Top Editing Jobs." *Pew Research Center*, Last modified, July 30, 2014, http://www.pewresearch.org/fact-tank/2014/07/30/asne-two-thirds-of-u-s-newspapers-employ-women-in-top-editing-jobs/

3. Denise Oliver-Velez, "NPR Might as Well Be Called No People of Color Radio." *Daily Kos*, July 1, 2014, http://kalamu.com/neogriot/2014/07/05/media-npr-might-as-well-be-called-no-people-of-color-radio/

4. Monica Anderson, "As News Business Takes a Hit, the Number of Black Journalists Declines." *Pew Research Center*, Fact Tank, August 1, 2014, http://www.pewresearch.org/fact-tank/2014/08/01/as-news-business-takes-a-hit-the-number-of-black-journalists-declines/

5. Kristen Hare, "Survey: Women and Minorities on TV and Radio Reach a High That's Still Pretty Low." *The Poynter Institute*, July 28, 2014, http://www.poynter.org/latest-news/mediawire/260584/survey-women-and-minorities-on-tv-and-radio-reach-a-high-thats-still-pretty-low/

6. Riva Gold, "Newsroom Diversity: A Casualty of Journalism's Financial Crisis." *The Atlantic.* July 9, 2013, http://www.theatlantic.com/national/archive/2013/07/newsroom-diversity-a-casualty-of-journalisms-financial-crisis/277622/

7. Deggans, *Race-Baiter*, 136.

8. Raines, "My Times," 62.

9. Craig Silverman, "Wrong, Wrong, Wrong, Wrong, Wrong, Wrong." *Columbia Journalism Review*, Last modified July 24, 2009, Accessed September 2014, http://www.cjr.org/behind_the_news/wrong_wrong_wrong_wrong_wrong.php?page=all

10. Steve Myers and Andrew Beaujon, "New York Times Removes Section from Alessandra Stanley 'Today' Show Review." *The Poynter Institute*, Last modified July 2, 2012, Accessed September 2014, http://www.poynter.org/news/mediawire/179490/where-did-alessandra-stanley-get-her-facts-about-thursdays-today-show/

11. Margaret Sullivan, "An Article on Shonda Rhimes Rightly Causes a Furor." *New York Times*, Last modified September 22, 2014, Accessed September 2014, http://publiceditor.blogs.nytimes.com/2014/09/22/an-article-on-shonda-rhimes-rightly-causes-a-furor/?smid=tw-share&_r=1

12. Ibid.

13. Rebecca Traister, "I Sort of Hope We Find Out That Jill Abramson Was Robbing the Cash Register." *The New Republic*, Last modified May 14, 2014, Accessed

May 2014, http://www.newrepublic.com/article/117767/jill-abramsons-firing-was-singularly-humiliating

14. Meg Heckman, "Women Were Digital Media Pioneers but There's Still a Gender Gap There." *Columbia Journalism Review*, Last modified March 24, 2014, http://www.cjr.org/minority_reports/early_digital_women.php

15. Michael A. Deas, "New Media, Old Problem: Where's the Diversity?" *Al-Jazeera*, April 14, 2014, http://www.aljazeera.com/indepth/opinion/2014/04 /new-media-old-problem-where-diver-2014414635267559.html

16. Nan Robertson, *The Girls in the Balcony: Women, Men, and the New York Times* (New York: Random House, 1992), 82.

17. Richard Prince, "Diversity's Greatest Hits, 2014." The Maynard Institute for Journalism Education, Last modified December 31, 2014, http://mije.org /richardprince/diversitys-greatest-hits-2014

18. González and Torres, *News for All the People*, 351.

19. Andrew Beaujon, "Minority Employment in Newsrooms Held Steady in 2012." *The Poynter Institute*, Last modified June 26, 2013, http://www.poynter.org/latest-news/mediawire/216787/minority-employment-in-newsrooms-held-steady-in-2012/

20. Rick Edmonds, "ASNE Census Finds 2,600 Newsroom Jobs Were Lost in 2012." *The Poynter Institute*, Last modified June 26, 2013, http://www.poynter.org/latest-news/business-news/the-biz-blog/216617/asne-census-finds-2600-newsroom-jobs-were-lost-in-2012/

21. George Sylvie, "African American News Media," in *Encyclopedia of Journalism*, Vol. 1., ed. Christopher H. Sterling (Thousand Oaks: Sage Publications, 2009), 50.

22. González and Torres, *News for All the People*, 320.

23. Puneet Pal Singh, "Newsweek Magazine Relaunches Print Edition." *BBC News*, Last modified March 7, 2014, Accessed January 1, 2015, http://www.bbc .com/news/business-26460261

24. Hadas Gold, "CNN Layoffs Continue." *Politico*, October 15, 2014, http:// www.politico.com/blogs/media/2014/10/cnn-layoffs-continue-197144.html

25. González and Torres, *News for All the People* (New York: Verso, 2011), 349.

26. Max Fisher, "The New Republic and the Beltway Media's Race Problem." *Vox*, Last modified December 5, 2014, Accessed December 31, 2014, http://www .vox.com/2014/12/5/7339473/new-republic-race

27. Ta-Nehisi Coates, "The New Republic: An Appreciation." *The Atlantic*, December 2014, Accessed December 31, 2014, http://www.theatlantic.com /politics/print/2014/12/the-new-republic-an-appreciation/383561

28. González and Torres, *News for All the People* (New York: Verso, 2011), 348.

29. Anderson, "As News Business Takes a Hit, the Number of Black Journalists Declines."

30. Jorge Rivas, "Infographic: How White Is the New Fall 2012 TV Season?" *Colorlines*, November 14, 2012, http://colorlines.com/archives/2012/11/infographic_how_white_is_the_new_fall_2012_tv_season.html

31. Chideya, "Fair Share."

32. Astra Taylor, *The People's Platform: Taking Back Power and Culture in the Digital Age* (New York: HarperCollins Publishers, 2014), 113–114.

33. Deggans, *Race-Baiter*, 5.

34. Andrew Beaujon, "Emilio Garcia-Ruiz Named Managing Editor of the Washington Post." Last modified May 24, 2013, http://www.poynter.org/latest-news/media wire/214436/emilio-garcia-ruiz-named-managing-editor-of-the-washington-post/

35. "Gwen Ifill and Judy Woodruff Named Co-Anchors, Managing Editors of PBS Newshour." *PBS Newshour*, Last modified, August 6, 2013, http://www .pbs.org/newshour/rundown/2013/08/gwen-ifill-and-judy-woodruff-named-co-anchors-managing-editors-of-pbs-newshour.html

36. Janelle Harris, "So What Do You Do, Roland Martin, Host of TV One's 'NewsOne Now'?" *TVNewser*, Last modified December 31, 2014. http:// www.adweek.com/tvnewser/so-what-do-you-do-roland-martin-host-of-tv-ones-newsone-now/251088

37. Chris Ariens, "Away from Daily News Grind, Soledad O'Brien Continues to Chart New News Path." *TV Newser*, Last modified August 28, 2013, http://www .mediabistro.com/tvnewser/removed-from-daily-news-grind-soleded-obrien-continues-to-chart-new-anchor-path_b193540

38. Emily Yahr, " 'Selma' Director Ava DuVernay Responds to Critics: 'Notion That Selma Was LBJ's Idea Is Jaw-Dropping.' " *Washington Post*, Last modified December 29, 2014, http://www.washingtonpost.com/blogs/style-blog/wp /2014/12/29/selma-director-ava-duvernay-responds-to-critics-notion-that-selma-was-lbjs-idea-is-jaw-dropping/

39. Barbara Friedman and John Richardson, " 'A National Disgrace:' Newspaper Coverage of the 1963 Birmingham Campaign in the South and Beyond." *Journalism History* 33, no. 4 (2008).

40. Ibid.

41. Author interview with Pamela Newkirk.

42. Aboubacar Ndiaye, "Diversity Hiring and the Concept of 'Fit.' " *The Billfold*, March 26, 2014, Accessed March 27, 2014, http://thebillfold.com/2014/03 /diversity-hiring-and-the-concept-of-fit/

43. Julianne Hing, "UCLA Study Finds Link between TV Diversity and Higher Ratings." *Colorlines*, Last modified October 16, 2013, http://colorlines.com/archives/2013 /10/ucla_study_finds_link_between_tv_diversity_and_higher_ratings.html

44. Logan Hill, "Mara Brock Akil and the Audience TV Forgot." *Business Week*, April 24, 2014, http://www.businessweek.com/articles/2014-04-24/bet-showrun ner-mara-brock-akil-and-the-audience-tv-forgot#rshare=email_article

45. Bill Carter, "Diversity in Action, as Well in Words." *New York Times*, September 3, 2014, http://www.nytimes.com/2014/09/07/arts/television/abc-aims-for-diversity-with-shows-like-black-ish-and-fresh-off-the-boat.html

46. Anne Johnston, and Dolores Flamiano, "Bridging the Border between Communities of Color and Mainstream Newspapers: Journalists Discuss Diversity Programs." Conference Papers—International Communication Association, *Communication & Mass Media Complete*, EBSCO*host* (May 23, 2003): 1–33.

47. Andrew Beaujon, "Chart Shows How Minority Employment at Newspapers Has Stalled." *The Poynter Institute*, Last modified May 28, 2014, http://www.poynter.org/latest-news/mediawire/253743/chart-shows-how-minority-employment-at-newspapers-has-stalled/#.U4dW1HaXD9M.email

48. Richard Prince, "Stories about Latinos Mostly about Crime, Undocumented." *Richard Prince's Journal-isms*, June 18, 2014, http://mije.org/richardprince/black-research-bastion-falls-hard-times#latino

49. González and Torres, *News for All the People*, 368.

50. Ibid.

51. Taylor, *The People's Platform*, 31.

52. Amy Mitchell, "State of the News Media 2014." *Pew Research Journalism Project*, March 26, 2014, http://www.journalism.org/2014/03/26/state-of-the-news-media-2014-overview/

53. Mandalit Del Barco, "In the Summer, Univision Is Numero Uno." *National Public Radio*, Code Switch blog, July 23, 2013, http://www.npr.org/blogs/codeswitch/2013/07/23/204604220/In-The-Summer-Univision-Is-Numero-Uno?ft=1&f=1048&utm_medium=email&utm_source=html&utm_campaign=post_link&utm_term=post_56254630544

54. Laurel Wentz, "Ad Age's 2013 Hispanic Fact Pack Is Out Now." *Advertising Age*, July 22, 2013, http://adage.com/article/hispanic-marketing/ad-age-s-2013-hispanic-fact-pack/243205/?sf15278861=1

55. "The Growing Buying Power of Women." *Time* magazine. Interactive, http://content.time.com/time/interactive/0,31813,2031700,00.html

56. Belinda Luscombe, "Woman Power: The Rise of the Sheconomy." *Time* magazine, Last modified Monday, November 22, 2010, Accessed January 4, 2015, http://content.time.com/time/magazine/article/0,9171,2030913,00.html

57. Kirsten Fleming, "Meet the Women of TV's First All-Female Sports Talk Show." *New York Post*, Last modified December 26, 2014, Accessed January 2, 2015, http://nypost.com/2014/12/26/meet-the-women-of-tvs-first-all-female-sports-talk-show/?utm_campaign=SocialFlow&utm_source=NYPTwitter&utm_medium=SocialFlow

58. Ann Friedman, "16 Women Whose Digital Startups Deserve Vox-Level Plaudits." *Columbia Journalism Review*, Last modified April 14, 2014, www.cjr.org/realtalk/women_digital_startups.php?page=all

59. Heckman, "Women Were Digital Media Pioneers but There's Still a Gender Gap There."

60. Angelo Carusone, "Rush Limbaugh Still Toxic for Advertisers One Year Later." *Media Matters*, Last modified March 1, 2013, http://mediamatters.org/blog/2013/03/01/rush-limbaugh-still-toxic-for-advertisers-one-y/192865

61. Jessica Grose, "Can Women's Magazines Do Serious Journalism?" *New Republic*, June 17, 2013, http://www.newrepublic.com/article/113511/can-womens-magazines-do-serious-journalism

62. Farai Chideya, "Media Money and Power in a Post-Post Racial Age." *Huffington Post*, Last modified October 1,2014, http://www.huffingtonpost.com/farai-chideya/media-money-and-power-in-_b_5639975.html?utm_hp_ref=tw

63. American Press Institute, "The Personal News Cycle: A Focus on African American and Hispanic News Consumers." September 16, 2014, http://www.americanpressinstitute.org/publications/reports/survey-research/african-american-hispanic-news-consumers/

64. Wu, *Yellow*, 248.

65. Gold, "Newsroom Diversity."

66. Justin McCarthy, "As a Major U.S. Problem, Race Relations Sharply Rises." *Gallup.* Last modified December 19, 2014, http://www.gallup.com/poll/180257/major-problem-race-relations-sharply-rises.aspx

Bibliography

Abraham, Laurie. "She's All That." *Elle* magazine, November 4, 2013, http://www
.elle.com/life-love/society-career/brittney-griner-on-her-sexuality

Alexander, Amy. *Notes from Uncovering Race: A Black Journalist's Story of Reporting and Reinvention*. Boston: Beacon Press, 2011.

American National Biography entry. "Payne, Ethel Lois." Accessed December 17,
2014. www.anb.org/articles/16/16-03900.html

American Press Institute. "The Personal News Cycle: A Focus on African American and Hispanic News Consumers," September 16, 2014, http://www.amer
icanpressinstitute.org/publications/reports/survey-research/african-american-
hispanic-news-consumers/

Anderson, Monica. "As News Business Takes a Hit, the Number of Black Journalists Declines." *Pew Research Center*, Fact Tank, August 1, 2014, http://www
.pewresearch.org/fact-tank/2014/08/01/as-news-business-takes-a-hit-the-
number-of-black-journalists-declines/

Andrews, Helena. "Shirley Sherrod Says She'll Never Work for the Government
Again." *The Washington Post*, January 14, 2014, http://www.washington
post.com/blogs/reliable-source/wp/2014/01/14/shirley-sherrod-says-shell-
never-work-for-the-government-again/

Anolik, Lili. "It All Began with O.J." *Vanity Fair*, June 2014, http://www.vanityfair
.com/society/2014/06/oj-simpson-trial-reality-tv-pop-culture

Auletta, Ken. *Backstory: Inside the Business of News*. New York: Penguin Books, 2003.

Babb, Kent. "How the O.J. Simpson Murder Trial 20 Years Ago Changed the Media
Landscape." *The Washington Post*, June 9, 2014, http://www.washingtonpost.com
/sports/redskins/how-the-oj-simpson-murder-trial-20-years-ago-changed-
the-media-landscape/2014/06/09/a6e21df8-eccf-11e3-93d2-edd4be1f5d9e_
story.html

Badger, Emily. "Americans Vastly Overestimate How Diverse the Country
Really Is." *The Atlantic CityLab*, October 22, 2013, http://www.theatlantic
cities.com/arts-and-lifestyle/2013/10/americans-vastly-overestimate-how-
diverse-country-really/7320/#.UmgKItudjOQ.ema

Bagdikian, Ben. *The New Media Monopoly*. Boston: Beacon Press, 2004.

Baker, C. Daniel. "African-American's Buying Power Projected to be $1.1 Trillion by 2015." *Black Enterprise*. Last modified November 28, 2013, http://www.blackenterprise.com/small-business/african-american-buying-power-projected-trillions/#.UeRCEu8Yr38.twitter

Barbassa, Juliana. "Summer Program for Journalists." *Hispanic* 11, no. ½ (1998): 106. *MasterFILE Premier*, EBSCO*host* (accessed November 8, 2013).

Barker, Kim, and Al Baker. "New York Officers' Killer, Adrift and Ill, Had a Plan." *New York Times*, December 21, 2014. Accessed December 22, 2014. http://www.nytimes.com/2014/12/22/nyregion/new-york-police-officers-killer-was-adrift-ill-and-vengeful.html?_r=0

Basu, Moni. "It's Her Ferguson—and It's Not All Black and White." *CNN Online*. Last modified November 17, 2014, http://www.cnn.com/2014/11/17/us/ferguson-biracial-couple/index.html?sr=sharebar_twitter

Beaujon, Andrew. "Emilio Garcia-Ruiz Named Managing Editor of The Washington Post." Last modified May 24, 2013, http://www.poynter.org/latest-news/mediawire/214436/emilio-garcia-ruiz-named-managing-editor-of-the-washington-post/

Beaujon, Andrew. "Minority Employment in Newsrooms Held Steady in 2012." *The Poynter Institute*, Last modified June 26, 2013, http://www.poynter.org/latest-news/mediawire/216787/minority-employment-in-newsrooms-held-steady-in-2012/

Berger, Joseph. "In Crown Heights, Once Torn by Race Riots, A Friendly Game of Soccer." *The New York Times*, June 8,2014, http://www.nytimes.com/2014/06/09/nyregion/once-torn-by-riots-crown-heights-finds-harmony-in-soccer.html?_r=0

"BET Awards Again Ranks Top in Cable with Adults 18–49 and 7.6 Million Total Viewers." Accessed January 10, 2014. http://targetmarketnews.com/storyid07081301.htm

Blumenthal, Ralph. "Black Youth Is Killed by Whites; Brooklyn Attack Is Called Racial." *New York Times*, August 25, 1989, http://www.nytimes.com/1989/08/25/nyregion/black-youth-is-killed-by-whites-brooklyn-attack-is-called-racial.html

Bonner, Alice. "Diversity: Employment." In *Encyclopedia of Journalism*, edited by Christopher H. Sterling. Thousand Oaks: Sage Reference, 2009.

Brenner, Joanna, and Aaron Smith. "72% of Online Adults Are Social Networking Site Users." *Pew Internet Research Project*, August 5, 2013, http://www.pewinternet.org/2013/08/05/72-of-online-adults-are-social-networking-site-users/

Buchanan, Larry, Ford Fessenden, K.K. Rebecca Lai, Haeyoun Park, Alicia Parlapiano, Archie Tse, Tim Wallace, Derek Watkins, and Karen Yourish. "What Happened in Ferguson?" *The New York Times*, Last modified November 25, 2014, http://www.nytimes.com/interactive/2014/08/13/us/ferguson-missouri-town-under-siege-after-police-shooting.html?_r=0

Byers, Dylan. "Turbulence at the Times," *Politico*, April 23, 2013, http://www.polit ico.com/story/2013/04/new-york-times-turbulence-90544.html

Byfield, Natalie. *Savage Portrayals: Race, Media & the Central Park Jogger Story*. Philadelphia: Temple University Press, 2014.

Carmody, Deirdre. "Time Responds to Criticism Over Simpson Cover." *The New York Times*, June 25, 1994, http://www.nytimes.com/1994/06/25/us/time-responds-to-criticism-over-simpson-cover.html

Carter, Bill. "Diversity in Action, as Well in Words." *The New York Times*, September 3, 2014, http://www.nytimes.com/2014/09/07/arts/television/abc-aims-for-diversity-with-shows-like-black-ish-and-fresh-off-the-boat.html

Carusone, Angelo. "Rush Limbaugh Still Toxic for Advertisers One Year Later." *Media Matters*, Last modified March 1, 2013, http://mediamatters.org/blog /2013/03/01/rush-limbaugh-still-toxic-for-advertisers-one-y/192865

Chan, Sewell. "The Death of Yusuf Hawkins, 20 Years Later." *New York Times*, Last modified August 21, 2009, http://cityroom.blogs.nytimes.com/2009/08/21 /the-death-of-yusuf-hawkins-20-years-later/

Chang, Jeff. *Who We Be: The Colorization of America*. New York: St. Martin's Press, 2014.

Chiachiere, Ryan. "Imus Called Women's Basketball Team 'Nappy-Headed Hoes.'" *Media Matters*, Last modified, April 4, 2007, http://mediamatters .org/research/2007/04/04/imus-called-womens-basketball-team-nappy-headed/138497

Chideya, Farai. "Fair Share?" *Columbia Journalism Review*, March 1, 2013, http:// www.cjr.org/cover_story/fair_share.php?page=all

Chideya, Farai. "Media Money and Power in a Post-Post Racial Age." *The Huffington Post*, Last modified October 1, 2014, http://www.huffington post.com/farai-chideya/media-money-and-power-in-_b_5639975.html? utm_hp_ref=tw

The Clarion-Ledger. "Jerry Mitchell's Entry and Biography," http://www.clarion ledger.com/article/99999999/SPECIAL17/60416008/Jerry-Mitchell-s-entry-biography

Clarke, Rachel, and Christopher Lett. "What Happened When Michael Brown Met Officer Darren Wilson." *CNN*, Last modified November 11, 2014, http://www .cnn.com/interactive/2014/08/us/ferguson-brown-timeline/

Classen, Steve. "'Reporters Gone Wild': Reporters and Their Critics on Hurricane Katrina, Gender, Race and Place." *E-Media Studies* 2, no. 1(2009), https:// journals.dartmouth.edu/cgi-bin/WebObjects/Journals.woa/xmlpage/4 /article/336#edn7

CNN Library. "Los Angeles Riots Fast Facts," Last modified May 3, 2014, http:// www.cnn.com/2013/09/18/us/los-angeles-riots-fast-facts/

Collins, Gail. *When Everything Changed: The Amazing Journey of American Women from 1960 to the Present*. New York: Little, Brown and Company, 2009.

Couch, Aaron. "CNN Mocked for Lack of Texas Filibuster Coverage." *The Holly-wood Reporter*, Last modified June 25, 2013, http://www.hollywoodreporter .com/news/cnn-mocked-lack-texas-filibuster-574716

Dahl, Julia. "We Were the Wolf Pack: How New York City Tabloid Media Mis-judged the Central Park Jogger Case." *The Poynter Institute*, July 15, 2011: http://www.poynter.org/mediawire/top-stories/135971/we-were-the-wolf-pack-how-new-york-city-tabloid-media-mangled-the-central-par

Daly, Christopher. "The Decline of Big Media, 1980s–2000s: Key Lessons and Trends." *Journalist's Resource*, Last modified August 28, 2013, http://journalists resource.org/studies/society/news-media/covering-america-journalism-pro fessor-christopher-daly#sthash.2CFcnGCt.dpuf

Daly, Christopher. "A Narrative History of a Nation's Journalism." Library of Con-gress talk, September 19, 2012, http://www.loc.gov/today/cyberlc/feature_ wdesc.php?rec=5632

Davis, Belva. *Never in My Wildest Dreams: A Black Woman's Life in Journalism*. San Francisco: Berrett-Koehler, 2010.

Deas, Michael A. "New Media, Old Problem: Where's the Diversity?" *Al-Jazeera*, April 14, 2014, http://www.aljazeera.com/indepth/opinion/2014/04/new-media-old-problem-where-diver-2014414635267559.html

Deggans, Eric. *Race-Baiter: How The Media Wields Dangerous Words to Divide a Nation*. New York: Palgrave Macmillan, 2012.

Del Barco, Mandali. "In the Summer, Univision Is Numero Uno." *National Public Radio*, Code Switch blog, July 23, 2013, http://www.npr.org/blogs /codeswitch/2013/07/23/204604220/In-The-Summer-Univision-Is-Num ero-Uno?ft=1&f=1048&utm_medium=email&utm_source=html&utm_cam paign=post_link&utm_term=post_56254630544

DeVega, Chauncey. "Racial Framing and Superstorm Sandy: A Black Mother Begs for Help While Her Children Drown." *The Daily Kos*, Last modified November 4, 2012, http://www.dailykos.com/story/2012/11/04/1155462/-Racial-Framing-and-Superstorm-Sandy-A-Black-Mother-Begs-for-Help-While-Her-Children-Drown

Dolfman, Michael L., Solidelle Fortier Wasser, and Bruce Bergman. "The Effects of Hurricane Katrina on the New Orleans Economy." *U.S. Bureau of Labor Statis-tics, Monthly Labor Review*, June 2007, http://www.bls.gov/opub/mlr/2007/06 /art1full.pdf

Edmonds, Rick. "ASNE Census Finds 2,600 Newsroom Jobs Were Lost in 2012." *The Poynter Institute*, Last modified June 26, 2013, http://www.poynter.org /latest-news/business-news/the-biz-blog/216617/asne-census-finds-2600-newsroom-jobs-were-lost-in-2012/

Eligon, John. "Michael Brown Spent Last Weeks Grappling with Problems and Promise." *New York Times*, Last modified August 24, 2014, http://www.nytimes .com/2014/08/25/us/michael-brown-spent-last-weeks-grappling-with-lifes-mysteries.html

Fisher, Marc, and Wesley Lowery. "Ferguson Violence Broke the Mold in Three Ways—One of Which Is Just Unfolding Now." *The Washington Post*, November 25, 2014, http://www.washingtonpost.com/politics/ferguson-decision-and-its-aftermath-more-a-media-event-than-organic-moment/2014/11/25/b506ff72-7256-11e4-ad12-3734c461eab6_story.html?tid=HP_lede?tid=HP_lede

Friedman, Ann. "Making Politics and Policy News Sexy." *Columbia Journalism Review*, June 27, 2013, http://www.cjr.org/realtalk/texas_tribune_ftw.php

Friedman, Ann. "16 Women Whose Digital Startups Deserve Vox-Level Plaudits." *Columbia Journalism Review*, Last modified April 14, 2014, www.cjr.org/realtalk/women_digital_startups.php?page=all

Friedman, Barbara, and John Richardson. "'A National Disgrace:' Newspaper Coverage of the 1963 Birmingham Campaign in the South and Beyond." *Journalism History* 33, no. 4 (2008).

"Frontline: The O.J. Verdict. Rating the Media's Performance." Last modified October 2005, http://www.pbs.org/wgbh/pages/frontline/oj/themes/media.html

Gold, Riva. "Newsroom Diversity: A Casualty of Journalism's Financial Crisis." *The Atlantic*. July 9, 2013, http://www.theatlantic.com/national/archive/2013/07/newsroom-diversity-a-casualty-of-journalisms-financial-crisis/277622/

González, Juan, and Joseph Torres. *News for All The People*. New York: Verso, 2011.

Gray, Steven. "The Washington Post's Metro Seven: Thirty Years Ago, They Fought for a Fair Chance. Today, There's Still Work to Be Done." *NABJ Journal*, September 2002, edited version as it appeared on the Maynard Institute for Journalism Education website, Sunday, April 22, 2012, http://mije.org/richardprince/romney-wins-race-favorable-coverage#StevenGray Accessed January 23, 2014.

Grose, Jessica. "Can Women's Magazines Do Serious Journalism?" *New Republic*, June 17, 2013, http://www.newrepublic.com/article/113511/can-womens-magazines-do-serious-journalism

Gutiérrez, Félix F. "More Than 200 Years of Latino Media in the U.S.: American Latinos and the Making of the United States: A Theme Study." The National Park Service. Accessed December 19, 2014. http://www.nps.gov/latino/latinothemestudy/media.htm#_edn8

Hansen, Matt, and Kurtis Lee. "Michael Brown's Raps: Money, Sex, Drugs—and a Vulnerable Side." *Los Angeles Times*, Last modified August 17, 2014, http://graphics.latimes.com/towergraphic-michael-browns-raps/

Hare, Kristen. "Survey: Women and Minorities on TV and Radio Reach a High That's Still Pretty Low." *The Poynter Institute*, July 28, 2014, http://www.poynter.org/latest-news/mediawire/260584/survey-women-and-minorities-on-tv-and-radio-reach-a-high-thats-still-pretty-low/

Herman, Edward S., and Noam Chomsky. *Manufacturing Consent: The Political Economy of Mass Media*. New York: Pantheon Books, 1988, 2002.

Hill, Logan. "Mara Brock Akil and the Audience TV Forgot." *Business Week*, April 24, 2014, http://www.businessweek.com/articles/2014-04-24/bet-showrunner-mara-brock-akil-and-the-audience-tv-forgot#rshare=email_article

Hing, Julianne. "UCLA Study Finds Link between TV Diversity and Higher Ratings." *Colorlines*, Last modified October 16, 2013, http://colorlines.com /archives/2013/10/ucla_study_finds_link_between_tv_diversity_and_higher_ ratings.html

Huber, Robert. "Being White in Philly." *Philadelphia* magazine, March 1, 2013, http://www.phillymag.com/articles/white-philly/2/

Ifill, Gwen. "Trash Talk Radio." *The New York Times*, April 10, 2007, http://www .nytimes.com/2007/04/10/opinion/10ifill.html?_r=0

Iyengar, Shanto, and Richard Morin. "Natural Disasters in Black and White." *The Washington Post*, June 8, 2006, http://www.washingtonpost.com/wp-dyn/con tent/article/2006/06/07/AR2006060701177.html

"Jerry Mitchell's Entry and Biography." *The Clarion-Ledger*. http://www.clarion ledger.com/article/99999999/SPECIAL17/60416008/Jerry-Mitchell-s-entry-biography

Johnston, Anne, and Dolores Flamiano. "Bridging the Border between Commu-nities of Color and Mainstream Newspapers: Journalists Discuss Diversity Programs." Conference Papers—International Communication Association, *Communication & Mass Media Complete*, EBSCOhost (May 23, 2003): 1–33.

Klein, Ezra. "Racism Isn't Over. But Policymakers from Both Sides Like to Pretend It Is." *The Washington Post Wonkblog*, December 1, 2013, http://www.washing tonpost.com/blogs/wonkblog/wp/2013/12/01/racism-isnt-over-but-policy makers-from-both-parties-like-to-pretend-it-is/

Lehrman, Sally. "Race and Ethnicity, Coverage Of." In *Encyclopedia of Journalism*, edited by Christopher H. Sterling. Thousand Oaks: Sage Reference, 2009.

Levy, Ariel. "Either/Or." *The New Yorker*, November 30, 2009, http://www.new yorker.com/magazine/2009/11/30/eitheror

Maloy, Simon. "CBS' 60 Minutes Offered No Rebuttal to Clarence Thomas' Claims about Anita Hill." *Media Matters for America*, Last modified October 2, 2007, http://mediamatters.org/research/2007/10/02/cbs-60-minutes-offered-no-rebuttal-to-clarence/140003http://mediamatters.org/research/2007/10/02 /cbs-60-minutes-offered-no-rebuttal-to-clarence/140003

McCarthy, Michael. "Asian Stereotypes Appearing in Coverage of Knicks' Jeremy Lin." *USA Today*, Last modified February 16, 2012, Accessed December 21, 2014, http://usatoday30.usatoday.com/sports/basketball/nba/story/2012-02-16 /Asian-stereotypes-appearing-in-coverage-of-Knicks-Jeremy-Lin/53120426/1

McIntyre, Jason. "ESPN's Fired 'Chink in the Armor' Editor Says It Was an Hon-est Mistake." *The Big Lead*, February 20, 2012, Accessed December 21, 2014 http://thebiglead.com/2012/02/20/espns-fired-chink-in-the-armor-editor-says-it-was-an-honest-mistake/

Media Matters Staff, "UPDATED: Fox News' Long History of Race-Baiting," *Media Matters*, Last modified June 13, 2011, http://mediamatters. org/research/2011/06/13/updated-fox-news-long-history-of-race-baiting /180529

Mellinger, Gwyneth. "The ASNE and Desegregation." *Journalism History* 34, no. 3 (Fall, 2008).

Mills, Kay. "Measuring Progress: Women as Journalists." *Nieman Reports*, January 10, 2011, http://www.nieman.harvard.edu/reports/article/102534/Measuring-Progress-Women-as-Journalists.aspx

Mitchell, Amy. "State of the News Media 2014." *Pew Research Journalism Project*, March 26, 2014, http://www.journalism.org/2014/03/26/state-of-the-news-media-2014-overview/

Neblett, Touré, *Who's Afraid of Post Blackness? What It Means to Be Black Now.* New York: Free Press, 2011.

Nelson, Jill. *Volunteer Slavery.* New York: Penguin Books, 1993.

Newkirk, Pamela. *Within the Veil: Black Journalists, White Media.* New York: New York University Press, 2000.

O'Brien, Luke. "How to Lose $100 Million: The Undoing of Tina Brown." *Politico*, May/June 2014, http://www.politico.com/magazine/story/2014/05/tina-brown-how-to-lose-100-million-105907.html#.VEKauOc_EXc

Okeowo, Alexis. "Crown Heights, Twenty Years after the Riots." *The New Yorker*, August 19, 2011, http://www.newyorker.com/news/news-desk/crown-heights-twenty-years-after-the-riots

Oler, Tammy. "Pinned Down." *Bitch* magazine. 2012, http://bitchmagazine.org/article/pinned-down

Oliver-Velez, Denise. "NPR Might as well Be Called No People of Color Radio." *The Daily Kos*, July 1, 2014, http://kalamu.com/neogriot/2014/07/05/media-npr-might-as-well-be-called-no-people-of-color-radio/

"The Personal News Cycle: A Focus on African American and Hispanic News Consumers." *American Press Institute.* September 16, 2014, http://www.americanpressinstitute.org/publications/reports/survey-research/african-american-hispanic-news-consumers/

Posetti, Julie. "Jay Rosen to Journalists and Editors: Facebook Has All the Power. You Have Almost None." *World News Publishing Focus*, Last modified July 10, 2014, http://blog.wan-ifra.org/2014/07/10/jay-rosen-to-journalists-and-editors-facebook-has-all-the-power-you-have-almost-none

Postrel, Virginia. "The Consequences of the 1960s Race Riots Come into View." *The New York Times*, December 30, 2004, http://www.nytimes.com/2004/12/30/business/30scene.html?pagewanted=1&_r=0

Povich, Lynn. *The Good Girls Revolt: How the Women of Newsweek Sued Their Bosses and Changed the Workplace.* New York: PublicAffairs, 2012.

Prince, Richard. "Biggest Audience for an Entertainment Show since '04." *Richard Prince's Journal-isms*, Accessed March 4, 2014. http://mije.org/richardprince/blacks-latinos-find-much-oscar#Shorttakes

Prince, Richard. "Stories about Latinos Mostly about Crime, Undocumented," *Richard Prince's Journal-isms*, June 18, 2014, http://mije.org/richardprince/black-research-bastion-falls-hard-times#latino

Prince, Richard. "Writing Beyond 'A Bunch of Immigrants Dancing on Stage." in *Richard Prince Journal-isms*, March 5, 2014, http://mije.org/richardprince/abu-jamal-case-roars-back-headlines#Kalita

Raines, Howell. "My Times." *Atlantic Monthly*, May 2004, http://www.theatlantic.com/magazine/archive/2004/05/my-times/302952/

Ralli, Tania. "Who's a Looter? In Storm's Aftermath, Pictures Pick Up a Different Kind of Tempest." *The New York Times*, September 5, 2005, http://www.nytimes.com/2005/09/05/business/05caption.html?_r=0

Ridley, Teresa. "Whatever Happened to Black Magazines from the 1990s?" *The Root*, Last modified August 23, 2010, http://www.theroot.com/photos/2010/08/whatever_happened_to_black_magazines_from_the_1990s.html

Rivas, Jorge. "Infographic: How White Is the New Fall 2012 TV Season?" *Colorlines*, November 14, 2012, http://colorlines.com/archives/2012/11/infographic_how_white_is_the_new_fall_2012_tv_season.html

Roberts, Gene, and Hank Klibanoff. *The Race Beat: The Press, The Civil Rights Struggle, and the Awakening of a Nation.* New York: Vintage, 2006.

Robertson, Nan. *The Girls in the Balcony.* New York: Random House, 1992.

Sanders, Joshunda. "Jayson Blair Proves It's Not Easy Being Green." *San Francisco Chronicle*, May 18, 2003.

Sanders, Joshunda, "Mainstream Media Tend to Ignore Blacks' Mental Health Problems," July 11, 2012, http://mije.org/mmcsi/health/mainstream-media-tend-ignore-blacks%E2%80%99-mental-health-problems

Sanders, Joshunda. "Media Depictions of Asian Americans Lack Important Depth," June 13, 2012, http://mije.org/mmcsi/general/media-depictions-asian-americans-lack-important-depth

Sanders, Joshunda. "Media Portrayals of Black Youths Contribute to Tension." Maynard Media Center on Structural Inequity, May 23, 2012, http://mije.org/mmcsi/general/media%E2%80%99s-portrayal-black-youths-contributes-racial-tension

Shafer, Jack. "Lost in the Flood." *Slate* magazine, Last modified August 31, 2005, http://www.slate.com/articles/news_and_politics/press_box/2005/08/lost_in_the_flood.2.html

Shah, Shah. "Press Coverage of Interethnic Conflict: Examples from the Los Angeles Riots of 1992." *2007 Journal of Dispute Resolution* (2007). http://scholarship.law.missouri.edu/cgi/viewcontent.cgi?article=1528&context=jdr

Smith, Aaron. "African Americans and Technology Use: A Demographic Portrait." *Pew Research Internet Project*, http://www.pewinternet.org/2014/01/06/african-americans-and-technology-use/

Smith, Aaron. "Technology Trends among People of Color." *Pew Research Internet Project*, September 17, 2010, Accessed February 2013, http://www.pewinternet.org/Commentary/2010/September/Technology-Trends-Among-People-of-Color.aspx

Smith, Elmer. "OPINION: Kerner Report Saw Racial Divides, and They're Still There." *Philadelphia Daily News, The (PA)*, March 4. *Newspaper Source* (2008), EBSCOhost (accessed November 8, 2013).

Smith, Erna. "Transmitting Race: The Los Angeles Riot in Television News." Joan Shorenstein Center on the Press, Politics and Public Policy. Discussion Paper Series, #R-11 May 1994, Harvard University John F. Kennedy School of Government, http://shorensteincenter.org/wp-content/uploads/2012/03/r11_smith.pdf

Sommers, Samuel R., Evan P. Apfelbaum, Kristin N. Dukes, Negin Toosi, and Elsie J. Wang. "Race and Media Coverage of Hurricane Katrina: Analysis, Implications, and Future Research Questions." *Analyses of Social Issues and Public Policy* 6, no. 1 (2006), http://library.chemeketa.edu/instruction/handouts/hurricanekatrinalooting.pdf

Stadd, Allison. "59% of Journalists Worldwide Use Twitter, Up from 47% in 2012." *AllTwitter*, June 26, 2013, http://www.mediabistro.com/alltwitter/journalists-twitter_b45416

Sylvie, George. "African American News Media." In *Encyclopedia of Journalism*, edited by Christopher H. Sterling (Vol. 1). Thousand Oaks: Sage Publications, 2009.

Taylor, Astra. *The People's Platform: Taking Back Power and Culture in the Digital Age*. New York: HarperCollins Publishers, 2014.

"T Magazine Editor Deborah Needleman Apologizes for All-White Issue." *Clutch magazine*, Last modified February 19, 2013, http://www.clutchmagonline.com/2013/02/t-magazine-editor-deborah-needleman-apologizes-for-all-white-issue/

Trahant, Mark. *Pictures of Our Nobler Selves: A History of Native American Contributions to News Media*. Nashville: The Freedom Forum First Amendment Center, 1995.

Uriarte, Mercedes Lynn de, Cristina Bodinger-de Uriarte, and Jose Luis Benavides. *Diversity Disconnects: From Classroom to Newsroom*. New York: Ford Foundation, 2003.

Usher, Nikki. "Citizen Journalism as Civic Responsibility." In *Will The Last Reporter Please Turn Out the Lights? The Collapse of Journalism and What Can Be Done to Fix It*, edited by Robert McChesney and Victor Pickard. New York: The New Press, 2011.

Vega, Tanzina. "Magazine Cover Draws Claims of Racism," *The New York Times*, Last modified February 28, 2013, http://mediadecoder.blogs.nytimes.com/2013/02/28/magazine-cover-draws-claims-of-racism/?_r=0

Wagner, Venise. "'Activities among Negroes': Race Pride and a Call for Interracial Dialogue in California's East Bay Region, 1920–31." *Journalism History* 35, no. 2 (2009): 82–90.

Waldman, Steve, and the Working Group on Information Needs of Communities. "The Information Needs of Communities: The Changing Media Landscape in a Broadband Age." Federal Communications Commission, July 2011. Accessed December 17, 2014.

Watson, John C. "Diversity: Policy." In *Encyclopedia of Journalism*, Edited by Christopher H. Sterling (Vol. 1). Thousand Oaks: Sage Reference, 2009.

Weinberger, David. *Everything Is Miscellaneous: The Power of the New Digital Disorder*. New York: Times Books/Henry Holt and Company, 2007.

Weiner, Joann. "Diversity Is Good. Why Doesn't Everyone Agree?" *She the People, Washington Post blog*, Last modified November 26, 2014, http://www.washingtonpost.com/blogs/she-the-people/wp/2014/11/26/diversity-is-good-why-doesnt-everyone-agree/

Wentz, Laurel. "Ad Age's 2013 Hispanic Fact Pack Is Out Now." *Advertising Age*, July 22, 2013, http://adage.com/article/hispanic-marketing/ad-age-s-2013-hispanic-fact-pack/243205/?sf15278861=1

Williams, Joan C., and Rachel Dempsey. *What Works for Women at Work: Four Patterns Working Women Need to Know*. New York: New York University Press, 2014.

Williams, Julian. "The Truth Shall Make You Free." *Journalism History* 32, no. 2 (Summer 2006): 106–113.

Wu, Frank, *Yellow: Race in America Beyond Black and White*. New York: Basic Books, 2002.

Index

About the Author

Joshunda Sanders is a writer based in Washington, D.C. Her work is widely anthologized, and she has lectured at the University of Texas at Austin and Bard College. Her work has appeared in *Salon*, the *San Francisco Chronicle*, *Bitch* magazine, the *Washington Post*, *The Root*, the *Seattle Post-Intelligencer*, *Vibe*, the *Houston Chronicle*, *The Week*, *BuzzFeed*, and the *Austin American-Statesman*, among many other publications.